Praise for *The First Americans*

"Throughout, Adovasio's pull-no-punches approach peppers the narrative with vigor. . . . In this lively telling, the journey to learn all the things we *don't* know has seldom been more fascinatingly rendered." —*Los Angeles Times*

"In the summer of 1973, University of Pittsburgh archaeologist James Adovasio began to excavate a nearby rock shelter. By the next summer, he had dug a hole ten feet deep exposing at least twenty separate layers of human occupation that included identifiable artifacts. He later encountered layers with decidedly human artifacts that were unknown to scholars. . . . [T]he radiocarbon dates . . . were about 13,000 years old, 1,500 years before the earliest accepted date for the peopling of the Americas. Eventually, Adovasio would get even older dates—16,000 years ago—from the Meadowcroft Rock Shelter. *The First Americans* tells the story of one of the most exciting and controversial research projects in the history of American archaeology." —*American Archaeology*

"In recent years many books have been written about the archaeology of the first Americans, but if there is an untold story, this is it. Adovasio's (and Page's) scholarly perspective is expert and sophisticated; Adovasio's arguments are boldly presented in clear, elegant prose."

—TOM D. DILLEHAY, author of
The Settlement of the Americas: A New Prehistory

"*The First Americans* is a lively look at a contentious debate by a man in the middle of it." —*Science News*

"James Adovasio is the perfect guide to the science, the infighting, and the passion surrounding a deceptively simple question: 'When was the Western Hemisphere first peopled?' Read to find where the bodies are buried. Read for enjoyment. But above all, read for honest answers."

—CLIVE GAMBLE, Centre for the Archaeology of Human Origins,
University of Southampton

"Adovasio . . . proved well-suited for the combat his work thrust upon him. . . . [H]e was taught the strictest standards of meticulous field research by legendary archaeologist Jesse D. Jennings at the University of Utah. As a result, his work at Meadowcroft is above technical criticism. . . . Adovasio offers a lengthy, lucid natural history of North America—glaciation, megafauna, extinction theories, climate changes—that is sheer pleasure to read. He also shows how politics, religion, racism and other preconceptions have hindered scientific observation of American Indians since the time of Columbus. And he presents frequent, dismissive criticisms of the way science is taught and done. . . . All in all, *The First Americans* is about as good as popular science writing gets." —*Sun-Sentinel* (Fort Lauderdale)

"This book offers us a frank exploration of the often nasty debates that swirl around the earliest archaeological sites that the Americas have to offer and the archaeologists who study them. A book like this could be written only by a bold insider—someone who has long worked in the area, has participated in all the debates, knows all the players, and is fearless. Adovasio is all these things."

—DONALD K. GRAYSON, professor of anthropology, University of Washington

"In all, readers get a lively, close-up view of how archaeologists study America's original discoverers."   —*Booklist*

"This is a story only Jim Adovasio could tell—he is simultaneously the most meticulous fieldworker and entertaining storyteller I have met in my thirty-five years as an archaeologist. It is archaeology from the inside."

—DAVE MADSEN, senior scientist,
Environmental Science Program, Utah Geological Survey

"The professor's discovery not only shook the very foundations of modern archaeology, it set Adovasio himself on a mission to uncover one of the greatest mysteries of all time: uncovering the origins of the first Americans and explaining how they got here. . . . [*The First Americans*] is well written and thoroughly researched, not surprising given Adovasio's impressive credentials, which include teaching at or performing research for the Smithsonian Institution, Youngstown State University, the University of Pittsburgh, the Carnegie Institute and Mercyhurst College (Pa.). What is surprising is Adovasio's—along with coauthor Jake Page's—lively prose and downright funny anecdotes. It's an enjoyable read."

—*The Post and Courier* (Charleston, S.C.)

"This book, written with Jake Page, is vintage Adovasio: incisive, funny, self-deprecating in his own imperial manner, and sure to trigger howls from the brethren at the receiving end of his barbs. But this is no hit-and-run book: it's a detailed and wide-ranging exploration of the history and current state of views on the archaeology, geology, and environment of late Pleistocene North America. It provides an important perspective on the fierce storm over the peopling of the Americas, from one who's been at its churning center for well on three decades."

—DAVID J. MELTZER, professor of anthropology,
Southern Methodist University

"[*The First Americans*] admirably lays out how new digs and new theories have further pushed back the ETA of the New World's first occupants some 30,000 years."
—*The Week*

THE FIRST AMERICANS

THE MODERN LIBRARY

NEW YORK

THE FIRST AMERICANS

IN PURSUIT OF ARCHAEOLOGY'S
GREATEST MYSTERY

J. M. ADOVASIO *with Jake Page*

2003 Modern Library Paperback Edition

This work was originally published in hardcover
by Random House, an imprint of The Random
House Publishing Group, a division of
Random House, Inc., in 2002.

Owing to limitations of space, acknowledgments of
permission to use illustrative material will be found
on page 329.

Library of Congress Cataloging-in-Publication Data
Adovasio, James.
The first Americans : in pursuit of archaeology's greatest
mystery / James Adovasio with Jake Page.
p.   cm.
Includes bibliographical references and index.
ISBN 0-375-75704-X (pbk.)
1. Indians—Origin.   2. Paleo-Indians.   3. America—
Antiquities.   I. Page, Jake.   II. Title.
E61 .A36   2002
970.01—dc21   2002069766

Modern Library website address: www.modernlibrary.com

Printed in the United States of America

4689753

Book design by Barbara M. Bachman

I've wanted to be an archaeologist since I was four or five years old. My early interest in the field was fashioned by my mother, Lena Adovasio, a quadruple major (ancient history, French, Latin, and German) at Marietta College. She provided my initial entrée into history, prehistory, and pale-ontology by teaching me to read books on those subjects and by continu-ally encouraging me in the direction to which she first steered me. My "choice" of careers was fostered by my sixth-grade teacher, Samuel A. Loree, who thought (and I hope still thinks) that archaeology was a wor-thy field of endeavor, and shortly thereafter I decided I wanted to go to the University of Arizona "when I grew up."

As most will attest, I never did grow up, but I did attend the University of Arizona, where my career trajectory was molded, wittingly or otherwise, by Malcolm McFee, William A. Longacre, and especially by the example of the late Emil Haury, the prototypical gentleman and scholar. I was also in-fluenced, at least indirectly, by C. Vance Haynes, who was already well on the road that would ultimately lead him to the National Academy of Sci-ences.

While I would like to think I became a passable anthropologist at Ari-zona, my transformation into an anthropological archaeologist would occur under the ominous shadow of The Dark Lord, Jesse D. Jennings, at the University of Utah, where I would also be profoundly influenced by C. Melvin Aikens and my colleagues Gary F. Fry, John "Jack" P. Marwitt, and D. "Dave" Brigham Madsen.

Through the intervening years, Madsen and Aikens have continued to represent the archetypes for anthropological scholars, as have David B. Meltzer and Thomas Dillehay, who appear frequently in this book and whose opinions I have valued for a very long time. The same can be said for the "sister" I never had, Olga Soffer, with whom I have collaborated for more than a decade and whose insights into prehistoric behavior as well as personal support during times of great personal stress have been profound. All of the aforecited individuals as well as my longtime fellow traveler in Pennsylvania, Kurt Carr, have helped shape the prism through which I look at the past and have contributed in a very real way to the formation or refinement of some of the ideas contained in this book. A special debt of gratitude is also owed to Dave Pedler (the longtime Mercyhurst Archaeological Institute editor and a close collaborator with me on many forays into Paleo-Indian commentary), who never ceases to remind me of the need to avoid convoluted Victorian prose when pontificating about the past.

Dave Meltzer, Tom Dillehay, Dave Madsen, Don Grayson, and Mike Collins also assisted in a very direct way in this production by reading and rereading various drafts of the manuscript and providing suggestions and corrections that, no doubt to their surprise, I took to heart. Many others also contributed directly to this volume, including Alan Bryan, Jim Chatters, Ruth Gruhn, Jim Richardson, Jerry McDonald, Mike Johnson, Tony Boldurian, Al Goodyear, Paul Goldberg, and Trina Arpin, who graciously provided illustrations.

Obviously, this volume would not exist without the primary encouragement of Jake Page, who not only broached the idea for a "different look" at the initial colonization of the Americas but shouldered the laborious but not thankless task of rendering the archaeological experience accessible to the general reader in ways no one with whom I have ever associated could ever approach. Once begun, our work was immeasurably furthered by the efforts of our agent, Joe Regal, who thought there might be a market for such a tome and quickly found a venue for it in Random House. Once suitably housed, the ultimate configuration of the book was hammered out by our editor, Scott Moyers, while the nuts and bolts of production, design, and copyediting were squired with great skill by Elena Schneider. Assistance in preparing the bibliography was provided by Mia Bruno and Whitney Swan.

Finally, Jake and I owe special debts of gratitude to Susanne Page and Judith Thomas for actually aiding and abetting our collaboration, reading, rereading, and constructively criticizing our efforts, and pointedly reminding us not to sink into Swiftian misanthropy, tempted as we might be in certain parts of the book. We also owe and gratefully acknowledge an immense debt to Jeff Illingworth, who produced the various drafts of this book, entered the countless changes, corrections, and emendations, criticized our individual and collective failings, solicited and collated the illustrations, and generally acted as the primary interface between ourselves and Random House. In a very real way, this book is as much his as ours.

CONTENTS

_____

NOT FOR THE TIMID OF HEART

D amn!" I said.

The dates hadn't come as a real surprise. We had suspected we were getting into a nasty realm where traction was poor and plenty of archaeologists before me had spun out. But here they were, two apparently firm dates that would completely change my life. Maybe these two "facts" in front of me—so neatly typewritten, so crisp, so cool—were wrong. I had little reason to think so. Whatever the extent to which I had been steering my career as an archaeologist, it was now about to veer and yaw off into the archaeological badlands. So my first reaction, standing in a ten-foot-deep excavation about thirty-five miles southwest of Pittsburgh, Pennsylvania, was to say, out loud, "Damn."

It was July 13, 1974, and I held in my hand a report from an impeccable source, the radiocarbon-dating lab at the Smithsonian Institution. Most Americans rightly considered the Smithsonian the very essence of the Authentic, and archaeologists all knew it as one of the very best dating facilities then in existence. Even so, I knew perfectly well that once my colleagues got wind of these two dates, they would start throwing verbal rocks at me and my crew.

On the piece of paper in my hand were eleven dates, all of them ordinary, unsurprising, nothing to really catch anyone's attention, except for the two that challenged one of American archaeology's most cherished dogmas.

J. M. Adovasio during the 1975
excavations at Meadowcroft Rockshelter.

The two dates were based on charcoal taken from two firepits, or hearths, near the very bottom layer of soil and rock that lay on top of the bedrock floor of a large shallow "rockshelter" or "rock overhang" called Meadowcroft Rockshelter. They said that humans had been there using these two hearths in about 13,000 B.C. (The actual dates were 12,975 ± 650 B.C. and 13,170 ± 165 B.C.) That meant that people had been here in western Pennsylvania some four thousand years before any human being was supposed to have set foot anywhere in this hemisphere. That no one had been here as early as these dates suggested was a tenet of archaeology that had come about in the 1930s, when a distinct kind of stone spear point had been discovered near Clovis, New Mexico, associated with the bones of a mammoth. Clovis Man, a mighty hunter, the dogma went, was the first here, and the dogma had survived hundreds of challenges in the intervening forty years.

In 1975, just a year later, we obtained more dates that confirmed the first ones. These were announced in an archaeological journal and picked up by *The Washington Post,* which published the news a couple of days before President Nixon resigned his office. With the future of the Republic in some jeopardy, nobody much cared about my dates or what most normal

*General view of Meadowcroft Rockshelter from the south bank
of Cross Creek, facing north.*

people would consider a relatively minor flap in a fairly arcane subject of little contemporary import: When did the first humans reach North America?

But it seems that when the future of the Republic is secure, the World Series is decided, and other major preoccupations are satisfied, the American public does like to get caught up in a good controversy, even on so remote a subject as the populating of the New World at some time long before memory. That subject has never been more controversial than in the past few years, and not just in academic circles. It has recently erupted onto the covers of newsmagazines and even into federal courts. It has been said that academic disputes are so bitterly waged because the outcomes are of so little lasting importance. This one, however, has stirred up not only scholars but also many of today's Native American peoples by casting doubt on the legitimacy of their claim to be the descendants of the first Americans. It even brought a momentary epiphany to a band of Scandinavian-American loonies who, in their fifteen minutes of fame, laid fleeting claim to the title (and lands) of the first Americans. In the field of North American archaeology— almost never a realm of courteous and collegial discussions over a bit of brandy before a toasty fire—it would be putting it mildly to say that hackles have been raised. The work of lifetimes has been put at risk, reputations have been damaged, an astounding amount of silliness and even profound stupidity has been taken as serious thought, and always lurking in the background of all the argumentation and gnashing of tenets has been the question of whether the field of archaeology can ever be pursued as a science.

My intention, back in the early 1970s, was to involve myself in nothing of this sort. Up to 1974, I was looking forward to a career teaching the most rigorous techniques of field archaeology and a lifetime as an expert in a tiny pond in the mostly stone-filled archaeological landscape. I studied the artifacts that tend to turn up the least often in the archaeological record: baskets, cloth, cordage, nets, sandals, and the like. These are called perishable artifacts for the obvious reason that they tend to rot away over time, vanishing from the record, unlike a stone arrowhead, which can lie in the ground dormant but intact for eons.

But now I was going to turn out to be the latest of many to tilt at what has been called the Clovis Bar.

The Clovis Bar went up soon after the first Clovis spear points were found. They were exquisitely made, the result of very fine, very controlled chipping, or flaking, and were also "fluted," meaning that a long vertical

Schematic of a Clovis point
from Blackwater Draw, New
Mexico, drawn by S. Patricia.

flake was chipped off both sides of the point's base in order to produce grooves. This so-called fluting was unique in the archaeological record anywhere on the planet: only in America. Clovis points then began to turn up here and there around the West and then elsewhere, all the way to the Atlantic Ocean and even on down into Mexico and points south.

Having been found with mammoth remains, Clovis points clearly were the work of people who lived in North America during the last Ice Age, which scholars at the time were sure had ended around 10,000 years ago. As the decades went by, an accurate dating technique—radiocarbon dating—permitted many Clovis finds to be dated with some precision. It turned out that these people lived between 11,250 and 10,550 years ago (or from 9250 years B.C. to 8550 B.C.). Then, suddenly, humans didn't make Clovis points anymore. More important, no one could find any evidence that people had lived in North America earlier than Clovis Man. This, then, was the Clovis Bar, and while some archaeologists over the years announced new evidence that humans had been here at an earlier date, most North American archaeologists were not merely content with the bar but built their scholarly career on its foundation.

Frankly, in the early 1970s, I didn't give much of a hoot about Clovis Man. Most of my research with perishable artifacts had been done in the Great Basin area of the West on what is called Archaic material, artifacts that were more recent than Clovis. To the extent that I had ever bothered to think about it, I believed the idea that Clovis Man had leapt fully armed (out of the head of some Siberian Zeus) into midcontinent and proceeded to overrun the hemisphere in less than a millennium to be, at best, an oversimplified notion and, at worst, hopelessly naive if not simply dumb. To my mind, the Clovis First hypothesis did not allow enough time for the diversity of lifeways that had come into being shortly after the last Clovis point was chipped 10,500 years ago—not to mention the diversity that appeared to exist even during Clovis Man's tenure.

I also knew, from studying the remains of perishable artifacts of early societies—that is to say, the efforts mainly of women—that most of my Clovis-loving colleagues had a phallocentric, lithic hang-up: as noted, stone is far more likely to be preserved in the ground for long periods, and people associate stone artifacts such as projectile points with males. For some seventy years, Clovis Woman was conspicuous by her absence.

In any event, I knew there would be trouble when I went up against the Clovis Bar with my pre-Clovis dates. The annals of North American archaeology are peppered with reports that this or that site showed clear and unimpeachable evidence of human habitation in North America before 11,500 years ago. Many of the hundred-odd claims were advanced with great vigor, often with promotional campaigns worthy of Madison Avenue. And virtually all of them were soon consigned to a well-deserved oblivion. Though my own interests lay elsewhere, when I began work at Meadowcroft, I was aware, like anyone in the field, of some of these archaeological train wrecks. Indeed, I knew that the cavalcade of loser localities was taken by many archaeologists as proof that no one was or could have been in the New World before the fluted-point makers. Such a belief is, of course, not science. And it is not logical. It is, in fact, more like a religious dogma.

One of my colleagues once said that a great deal of American archaeology has been "a pissing match to see who can come up with the oldest spear point." Just why so many people—archaeologists and all manner of laymen—want the Americas to have been inhabited anciently as opposed to only recently is a question not often asked and with few straightforward answers. After all, Americans pride themselves as a nation on having accomplished a great deal in a very short period of time—going from a ragtag collection of rebels to the world's only superpower in little more than two hundred years. Why, then, do they want America's prehistory to be such a long-running show?

Of course, some Native Americans feel that they themselves were the first humans and originated here on this continent—some of them call it Turtle Island—later migrating to become the people found in all other parts of the world. Linguists, confronting the existence of some nine hundred Indian languages in the New World at the time of European colonization, want more than twelve thousand years for all those languages to have come about. Back in the nineteenth century, once Europeans had discovered Neanderthal Man and early stone tools, many Americans simply wanted their own ancient and primitive people.

Whatever the reasons, many laypeople and science journalists will grab hold of any piece of news, any assertion, however flimsy, that the first Americans arrived longer ago than previously thought, even as far back as hundreds of thousands of years, and hug it to their bosoms so tightly it is very difficult to root out. Some professional archaeologists are driven by the same urge, creating a situation in which expectations override a calm, cool assessment of the facts. This isn't science either.

So we have two extremes here. Many scholars of such matters refuse to entertain any evidence whatsoever of an earlier arrival—in spite of what appear to be facts. Indeed, archaeological history can appear to be full of hidebound, grumpy naysayers throwing cold water on the hopes and dreams of both Indiana Jones types and some serious archaeologists as well.

The subject of the first Americans has always been, and may always be, a mare's nest. Certainly, it is now a nearly open field again. A few years back, Dave Meltzer, an archaeologist at Southern Methodist University and an assiduous historian of the search for the first Americans, inscribed a copy of one of his books to me with a bit of doggerel that recounted some of the flak I had, by then, received for the Meadowcroft dig. It ended:

> *The tattered flag still flies, on the banks of old Cross Creek,*
> *Adovasio is wiser now, more gray hairs, but still standing*
>   *on his feet.*
> *What lessons learned? Many true ones to last,*
> *and even one about archaeology, the science of the past.*
> *The lesson is one that all should know from the start,*
> *When it comes to the first Americans:*
> *Archaeology ain't for the timid at heart.*

The quest to discover who the first Americans were and when they got here began long before there was such an enterprise as archaeology. We like to think that today archaeologists practice a craft free of preconceived notions, but such notions are still to be found and not all that far below the surface. One that is much with us, for example, is embodied in the phrase still much in use: Clovis *Man.*

The best way to understand all this is to start at the beginning—with the early notions about who the American Indians could have been and how they could have gotten here. Without knowing this tale, with its heart-felt philosophical certainties and astounding leaps of imagination, one can't fully understand the situation into which I was thrust by the receipt of those fateful pre-Clovis dates. Ever since three barely seaworthy ships fetched up on a Caribbean isle, manned by Europeans with their preconceptions, the native peoples of the Americas and their deep history have baffled most non–Native Americans.

The First Americans

GLIMPSES THROUGH

THE LOOKING GLASS

When Christopher Columbus first slogged ashore on October 12, 1492, on either the Caribbean island of San Salvador or Samana Cay, he was met by Arawak-speaking people who called themselves Taino and who apparently made an excellent first impression. "They are affectionate people," Columbus reported, "and without covetousness and apt for anything, which I certify." He went on to write, "I believe there is no better people or land in the world. They love their neighbors as themselves and have the sweetest speech in the world and gentle, and are always smiling." Not knowing who these seemingly happy-go-lucky folk were, Columbus imagined them to be Asians—perhaps Hindus or Spice Islanders. Yet, despite his boosterism, he was disappointed to find these natives less advanced than he expected of Asians. In fact, the Tainos were fairly sophisticated agriculturalists living in villages of a thousand or more, each with up to fifty round, conical-roofed houses of wood and thatch ringed around a plaza and presided over by a chieftain. The villages were organized into district chiefdoms; two social strata, nobles and commoners, existed; and local artisans worked in wood, ceramics, weaving, and other crafts, including gold imported from mainland South America. Even so, they were hardly what might be expected by someone who had read about Marco Polo's travels to the Orient.

Soon the neighbor-loving Tainos made it plain that their particular neighbors, known as Caribs and located to the south in what we call the Virgin Islands, were cannibals bent on wiping out the Tainos. Here we have an early version of two of the longest-running stereotypes about the native peoples of America—the noble savage and the bloodthirsty barbarian. Before many more years passed, both the Tainos and the Caribs (who were probably innocent of cannibalism) were largely extinct, victims of European diseases, the vicissitudes of Spanish enslavement, and outright murder. But untold millions of other native peoples awaited the Europeans in the New World, and once it became clear that this was not Asia, the questions soon arose: Who the hell are these people, where did they come from, and when did they get here? Even after the passage of more than five hundred years, the answers to these simple questions remain somewhat imprecise.

Early on, some Europeans wondered if the native populations of the New World were actually people—humans, as Europeans defined the word. This was in spite of the fact that by 1510 Cortés had encountered the Aztec empire and entered its capital, Tenochtitlán, a vast city grander and more beautiful, by accounts, than anything in contemporary Europe. The Spanish thus had an early realization of the breadth of cultural diversity to be found in the New World, but even the Aztecs, with their own version of high society, did not fit well into the pigeonholes of European preconceptions. And it was only a few years after the Spanish arrival that even the Aztecs and Incas were reduced to peonage, their civilizations effectively razed.

At the time, maps of much of the world outside Europe still reported that "there be monsters here," and stories abounded of creatures on distant shores who were part human, part animal. Unicorns could still appear to those whose lives had been perfectly meritorious, and as late as the next century an English adventurer, Martin Frobisher, would return from an Arctic voyage with tales of gold and with the single horn of what he believed to be a sea unicorn (an object we know as a narwhal tusk), which he presented to Queen Elizabeth. Coming upon the shores of America, one might imagine, then, that creatures with so little by way of the trappings of civilization were people, yes, but people without souls, just as animals were without souls.

Paracelsus, the brilliant sixteenth-century Swiss physician who is often thought of as the father of chemical medicine, believed that the aboriginal

Americans were not "of the posterity of Adam and Eve" but had been created separately and were without souls. The matter would continue to be debated for the remainder of the century by Spanish philosophers and papal theologians. Generally speaking, the men of the Church took the most benign view of the Indians, believing that the pope's benevolent sway should be extended over the natives' lives in order to save their souls. (At the outset, Columbus commented that the Arawaks' easygoing nature made them excellent candidates for enslavement, and the Spanish colonists saw them all as little more than useful chattels.) Some theologians cited Aristotle's *Politics* to the effect that many people were born to be ruled over, and the Native Americans, having no "written laws, but barbaric institutions and customs," were among them—meaning that they could be enslaved or killed in order to bring them to Christ (in the afterlife). People on the ground, however, typically took an even less benign view. Amerigo Vespucci, sailing for the Portuguese, found the natives of South America to be hardly more than brutes, as well as worshipers of the Devil, given to cannibalism and other amoralities. Later, a Dominican missionary, Tomás Ortiz, perhaps by way of explaining the difficulty of his holy task, wrote the following description:

> On the mainland they eat human flesh. They are more given to sodomy than any other nation. There is no justice among them. They go naked. They have no respect either for love or for virginity. They are stupid and silly. They have no respect for truth, save when it is to their advantage. . . . Most hostile to religion, dishonest, abject, and vile, in their judgements they keep no faith or law. . . . I may therefore affirm that God has never created a race more full of vice and composed without the least mixture of kindness or culture. . . . We here speak of those whom we know by experience. Especially the father, Pedro de Córdoba, who has sent me these facts in writing . . . the Indians are more stupid than asses and refuse to improve in anything.

Depressingly enough, sentiments very much like these were heard throughout the ensuing centuries, even to the present. On the other hand, the Native Americans had their early champions as well, none more vigorous and devoted than the Spanish Fray Bartolomé de Las Casas, who argued eloquently for the rights of the natives. He claimed that the pope had no temporal or coercive power over the native populations, that the gospel should be preached to them but only peacefully, and that the conquistadors' claims on the Indians' land and persons were illegal. He saw all people, including the Native Americans, as humans in various stages of cultural development and thought the natives of the New World were probably quite ancient. Las Casas had a good deal of influence on the powers back home, as did another cleric, the Dominican Bernardino de Minaya. Minaya deserted Pizarro in disgust and went to Rome to persuade Pope Paul III to issue a papal bull in 1537 that rejected the idea of Indians as mere brutes and declared them capable and desirous of embracing the Catholic faith. Not only that, the bull proclaimed, even those Native Americans who chose not to follow Christ were not to be enslaved or have their property taken. This was too much. Bristling with secular outrage, Emperor Charles ordered all copies of the bull confiscated and prevailed on the pope to rescind the bull altogether. For his efforts Minaya was thrown into jail by the head of his order.

Even as late as 1590, one sympathetic Spanish Jesuit missionary in Peru, José de Acosta, felt the need to denounce the "common opinion" that the natives of the New World were mere brutes without reason. They were barbarians—meaning non-Christian—to be sure, and de Acosta attempted to put all barbarians into one of three categories. First were peoples such as the Japanese and Chinese, who had permanent governments, cities, commerce, and writing. This class of barbarians was to be proselytized to and converted to Christianity *without force*. Second were those such as the Aztecs and Incas, who were without writing but enjoyed permanent governments and recognizably religious ceremonies. If such peoples—so far from what he called "right reason"—were not put under Christian rule and *ordered* to become Christian, they probably could not be converted and thus would remain barbarians. The third class of barbarians was free-roaming savages, without government, laws, or fixed settlements. They were the people of whom Aristotle had spoken—who deserved to be enslaved—and, like the Caribs, they needed to be forced to accept Christianity or suffer the consequences. Of course, this all led to a philosophical conundrum: If an illiterate barbarian—a savage, say—were converted to the Cross, was he still a barbarian? Could there be such a thing as a Christian barbarian?

Interestingly, many of the early European explorers and adventurers noticed the similarity in appearance between the Indians and Asians. De Acosta took this a step further, suggesting that the Americas had been populated by a slow overland migration from Asia, perhaps as early as two thousand years before the arrival of the Spaniards. This was an astonishing insight, considering that no European had even come close to the Bering Sea or had any notion of the configuration of the lands to the north. Indeed, on maps of the time, the whole area from northeast Asia to the Urals was called simply Tartary. By 1648, the Englishman Thomas Gage had posited the Bering Strait area as the region crossed by Mongolian-type people—a path that would become a certainty only in the next century, when Vitus Bering, a Dane sailing in behalf of the Russian czar, discovered the strait that bears his name.

As for the early Spanish soldiers and settlers, if they intended to enslave the native people of the New World whenever they were needed (and that was indeed their intent), and if they sought justification (which they rarely did), Aristotle's pronouncement about people born to be subjugated was moral balm. Even more convenient was the word of Saint Augustine, who, in the fifth century, had first enunciated the Christian notion of a just war: one waged to right an injustice or wrong by another nation, one such wrong being (by implication) not being Christian. Any refusal by the barbarians of the New World to let a missionary preach or to let a Spaniard "sojourn" among them could now be construed as sufficient cause to launch a just attack.

To sojourn meant to trade, in fact, and the right of men to do commerce anywhere in the world was soon added to the mandate to promulgate the Cross as a justification for war shared by all the European nations in the New World. When Native Americans stood in the way of what we now think of as free trade, they became mere impediments to be shoved aside or eliminated. This was especially true of the British colonists, who had little interest in converting the natives to their own versions of Christianity. With a few notable exceptions, such as William Penn and, to an extent, the clergyman Roger Williams, the British were mainly intent on taking over as much land as they could and removing the aboriginal inhabitants from it as quickly as possible.

Even the French—many of whom were (like the Spanish) given to intermarrying with the natives and (unlike the Spanish) adapting to their ways—initially had trouble even seeing them accurately. One of the earliest representations of American natives appeared among the decorations on a French map of 1613, an engraving based on drawings by Samuel de Champlain himself. Along with such identifiable local fruits as hickory

figure des sauvages almouchicois

*An early French rendering of Native Americans from a
drawing prepared by Samuel de Champlain.*

nuts, plums, and summer squash is a "savage" couple evidently from Nova Scotia, then called Acadia. They both have feathers in their hair and earrings; the man holds a knife and an arrow in his hands, while the woman holds an ear of corn and a squash (neither was grown aboriginally in Nova Scotia). She wears only a loincloth and he what looks for all the world like a Speedo bathing suit. Both have wavy blond hair, European facial features, and the muscular calves and delicate feet of Renaissance art.

Most Europeans, whether botanists, artists, or philosophers, tried to fit all the astounding new finds from the New World into the classical schemes that informed the Renaissance—which, as art historian Hugh Honour has pointed out, were largely "wish-fulfillment dreams" of an Arcadian past that had never existed. For reasons not hard to imagine, early reports about the so-called Indians dwelled on the widespread nudity and what Europeans believed to be free love. (It was not uncommon for Europeans to be offered the use of women when they first arrived, as part of the gift giving typical of many American native cultures.) Those practices, plus the apparent absence of property and laws among the natives, reminded Europeans of their own imagined Golden Age. Even in the nineteenth century, European artists would still represent the New World allegorically as a naked woman wearing little but feathers.

Of course, there was the other side of all this: to begin with, the widespread reports of cannibalism, always a disruptive note in your classic Golden Age fantasy. Indeed, early on, Europeans developed a schizoid sense of America, most of them seeing its wonders only through the eyes of naturalists and other travelers (and in some cases through observing a few savages brought back to European courts as exotic talking booty).

Of all the continents coming under European scrutiny, North and South America were seen as probably the last to be inhabited and the last created—as the poet John Donne put it, "that unripe side of earth." There the mammal population had degenerated, as did Europeans who stayed too long. Some compared the natives to the fabled European wild men of the woods; in reports from the New World, Shakespeare found an inspiration for Caliban. The philosopher Thomas Hobbes was speaking about Native Americans when he wrote his famous dictum about the uncivilized, savage life being "solitary, poor, nasty, brutish and short."

Given even an artist's incapacity to *see* these people, it is no wonder that philosophers back home happily spun a bundle of assumptions and what today we would call stereotypes into grand theories about the aboriginal Americans, such overarching schemes as "the noble savage" and the "treacherous and murdering savage," both of which still haunt Native

Americans, although the terms are a bit different today. We no longer have Rousseau's innocent, Edenic noble savage, given to purity of feeling as opposed to the degraded world of reason (which was a wondrous bit of condescension, no matter that it helped power the French Revolution). Instead, we have today's ecosaints, a race of people instinctually attuned to abiding on the land without leaving even the trace of a moccasin print, a race so spiritual that virtually every New Ager has linked up with a native shaman from one past life or another. On the other hand, gone are the no-good, bloodthirsty "redskins" who once marauded innocent sodbusters and did battle with John Wayne's blue-coated cavalry; we now have the no-good Indian incapable of a full day's work in his tribe's Mafia-controlled casino and instead typically found in a sodden stupor in the gutter of some squalid off-reservation town like Gallup, New Mexico. One of the greatest difficulties throughout the centuries and still today has been to look upon the Native Americans not as ciphers or metaphors for one or another fantasy but, first and finally, as human beings.

It is little wonder, then, that when white Americans came across the most monumental works of the original inhabitants of North America, they assumed them to be the product of some other, master race long since vanished: the mound builders. For by then, whatever gossamer notions about Native Americans (or libels) the Europeans back home were spinning, most settlers on the frontiers of the New World took a dim view of the native peoples they encountered. Everyone from the lost tribes of Israel to escapees from Atlantis would be invoked to explain the mysterious monuments the colonists (and later U.S. citizens) found all over the landscape once they pushed their way across the Appalachians. There is nothing like lost civilizations and vanished races to stir the imagination.

THE MOUND BUILDERS

From western New York State to Nebraska, from the Great Lakes to the Gulf of Mexico, the land was once littered with mounds, many of them enormous in height and extent. The largest were flat-topped like the pyramids of Central America, and they all would have necessitated huge crowds of workers. They were built of vast tonnages of dirt, many with as-

Reconstruction of Cahokia at its apogee, ca. A.D. 1150,
by William R. Iseminger.

tonishingly precise angles, some in the form of a perfect circle. In what would become East Saint Louis, a huge metropolis seemed once to have existed along the Mississippi, in a place called Cahokia. It was some five square miles in area, with a hundred mounds grouped around central plazas. Most spectacular of the Cahokia mounds was what came to be called Monk's Mound: covering sixteen acres, it was the largest single earthwork ever built by prehistoric people in North America. A temple evidently once sat atop this mound, one hundred feet above the surrounding area and visible to the entire population. It has been estimated that this one mound called for the quarrying and piling up of more than 21 million square feet of dirt. Estimates of the resident population ran in the tens of thousands, though current estimates suggest something far less—perhaps five thousand in Cahokia's heyday, which is still a big place if one is accustomed only to the stereotype of the Native American as living in small bands of hunter-gatherers wandering around in the woods or riding over the plains. (In fact, at the time of European discovery, most natives, by far, were village or town-dwelling agriculturalists who also hunted and gathered resources from the surrounding countryside.)

The greatest concentration of mounds was in America's continental heart—Ohio, Illinois, Indiana, and Missouri. *Ten thousand* had been built in the Ohio Valley alone. Some were in the form of animals and one, the Great Serpent Mound in Adams County, Ohio, is a snake nearly a quarter

An aerial view of the Great Serpent Mound, Adams County, Ohio.

of a mile long, its five-foot-high body writhing southward from a coiled tail, its gaping mouth in midgulp of an oval burial mound. It is the largest representation of a snake anywhere in the world.

Effigy mounds, such as the Great Serpent, typically had no mortuary purpose, but virtually all others were found to be the sites of burials, some astonishingly elaborate, the graves of what were clearly great leaders, filled with all manner of valuables from copper neckpieces and stone carvings to freshwater pearls in the thousands, and in some cases, especially in the southern mounds, the corpses of family members and retainers sacrificed to accompany the leader on his journey—or hers; some of the prominent people of these societies were apparently women. In sheer quantity, and in

the size of many of them, the earthen mounds nearly equaled the monumental structures of Mexico. Eighteenth- and nineteenth-century antiquarians and patriot boosters of North America could rejoice. Here were
achievements to rival the antiquities of Europe and the grandeur of the ancient worlds of Egypt and the Middle East.

Well, almost.

At the very least, ancient North America was not an embarrassingly
depauperate place with nothing to suggest its own glorious and mysterious
past. For here certainly—and well to the north of the Aztec and Mayan
ruins—was the work of a populous, highly civilized race, people with a
means of making accurate measurements, people with elaborate religious
ceremonials . . . and people who definitely could not have been the ancestors of the relatively few pathetic, seminomadic, unambitious, ignorant,
often drunk savages who now—as the newcomers saw it—lived in this region. Once the French were run out of the area in the so-called French and
Indian War that ended in 1763, the British view of native peoples predom-
inated: contemporary natives were clearly incapable of the sheer sustained
labor of hauling so much dirt, much less some of the complex architectural
detailing of the mounds. Nor did they have any current traditions about
mound construction. When asked by British colonists, the Cherokees in
western North Carolina whose villages were built on mounds had essentially shrugged and said the mounds had already been present when the
Cherokees had arrived.

A fourth kind of mound appeared to be defensive in nature, and it was
soon assumed that the race of master builders, whoever they were, had
eventually succumbed to attacks by hordes of savages (probably coming
from the north and ancestral to the American Indians), just as Rome had
fallen to the swarming barbarian Huns and Visigoths. Noting a particular
geographic progression (or regression)—relatively small effigy mounds in
the north, conical burial mounds in the middle, and large flat burial
mounds and temple platforms in the south—some would wonder if the
original mound builders had moved from north to south with ever-
increasing sophistication, eventually reaching Mexico, where they had
discovered the use of stone for construction. Others would see Mexican
master builders moving north, losing sophistication along the way. And

still others would choose the builders from an astounding array of candidates from all over the world. The ancient human art of conjuring up astonishing tales from the sparsest of information was happily under way.

By the time of the American Revolution, plenty of opinions existed about the mounds and their builders. The naturalist William Bartram (son of the naturalist John Bartram) made a long trek through the South and concluded, rightly, that some mounds were contemporary while others were older, even relatively ancient. Some, he thought, were temple mounds like those he saw still in use. In 1787, an Ohio traveler, Benjamin Smith Barton, suggested that the mounds had been built by Danes who had moved on to Mexico, but a decade later he changed his mind, saying that most of the mounds had probably been the work of ancestral Indians, who, he said, might well have arrived about 6,000 years ago, a time that fit well enough with most generally accepted notions of the age of the earth in the late eighteenth century.

It should be pointed out that at the end of the eighteenth century in Europe and America, there was no such thing as the field we call archaeology. No formal method of investigating ancient sites was known, and no way of judging findings accurately existed. People who were interested in "antiquities" were what we would today call amateurs or hobbyists. At the time, the Bible, for most people, represented a true and precise history—and chronology—of humanity and the world. There was no intellectual concept by which those whom we think of as early humans could be understood. There was no sense of the extreme age of the world and very little notion of the nature of life besides the immutability of species as they had been created by God, all at once, in the manner described in the Book of Genesis. With the publication of Lyell's book between 1830 and 1833 came the distinct (and heretical) possibility that the Bible did *not* represent the actual chronology of the world, that the Book of Genesis should be seen more as poetry than as fact. But the European world was also on the edge of industrialization, and by the end of the 1850s it was presented with the ideas of Thomas Malthus, the first look at a human of the ice age (a gent called Neanderthal), and the astonishing revelations of Charles Darwin. With the earth's age extended radically far into the past and Darwin's theory of natural selection (published in 1859) to explain the mechanism of what some naturalists, including Darwin's grandfather, had earlier begun to see as evolutionary processes in nature, the entire world was new. Until such concepts were in place, there was really no hypothetical framework in which such (to us) commonplace occurrences as cultural change over time could be perceived, much less analyzed. And certainly there was no methodology by which an antiquarian could examine the archaeological record and test one hypothesis or another. In short, no means of scientific reasoning existed for examining the ancient, prehistoric past. That is why Thomas Jefferson appears in this context, as in so many others, as an astoundingly astute and, in this case, precocious observer.

Jefferson had heard most of the available theories about who had built the mounds, and in his systematic way, in 1784, he dug out a small, twelve-foot-high mound on his property near the Rivanna River in his native Virginia. He uncovered successive layers of burials, each separated by layers of gravel and stone. From this, he concluded rightly that they had been the work of the present Indians' ancestors. When the burials had occurred, however, "was a matter of doubt." Historians of science have said that this was "the first scientific excavation in the history of archaeology" and that it anticipated the methods of modern archaeology by more than a century. In other words, Jefferson was, however distantly, one of the fathers of modern archaeology (a field that benefited, like most others, from multiple sirings), just as it has been said that for his careful reporting of native lifestyles Fray Bartolomé de Las Casas was a "father" of ethnography.

In any event, Jefferson's pioneering methodology—the first excavation designed not to recover artifacts but to solve an archaeological question—was sufficiently ahead of his time that it had virtually no real impact on subsequent work for at least another century. Nor, it seems, did his circular written ten or so years later to the other members of the American Philosophical Society, newly formed in the young nation's intellectual capital, Philadelphia. In it he called for accurate surveys of the mounds and their contents by way of cross-section trenching, tree-ring counts, the measuring of the length, breadth, and height of walls, and the recording of the nature of any stonework. (It could be argued that it was not Philadelphia but Jefferson's estate that was the nation's intellectual capital.)

In particular, Jefferson's levelheaded approach to the mound builders did not resonate in the mind of the American public. Other notables of his time entertained more far-out possibilities: Ben Franklin, for example, thought that the mounds might be the work of de Soto and his expedition through the South in the 1540s. Others, including DeWitt Clinton, governor of New York, picked the Vikings, holding that a band had arrived at some point and made their mound-building way south and west, eventually reaching Mexico, where they turned into the Toltecs. Others, hearing a Delaware Indian epic from myth time, concluded that the mounds had to have been the work of the Cherokees, whether they remembered building the mounds or not.

Many of the notables of the new nation formed the American Antiquarian Society in Boston in 1812, modeled on European versions, and in 1820 it published its first *Transaction,* which included a long piece entitled "Description of the Antiquities Discovered in the State of Ohio and Other Western States." The author was Caleb Atwater, postmaster of Circleville, a village in Ohio. Atwater had grown up among the Ohio mounds, and Circleville, founded in 1806, was laid out around two large mounds. Seeing such structures beginning to disappear under the increasing onslaught of settlers bent on clearing land for farms, he trekked throughout the state, mapping and describing many of its mounds. Here and there he found bits and scraps of metal, copper items, and while he reported these finds soberly and scoffed at other reporters who took off on great flights of fancy based on looking at one or two mounds, he inadvertently gave comfort to those who wished to exaggerate or spin romantic yarns. Some later writers would take his reports of a few metal objects and turn them into proof of a high civilization capable of significant metallurgical feats. (In fact, in a few places in the upper Midwest, native copper occurred in large natural globs that were cold-worked into decorative pieces and traded widely.)

Atwater was an assiduous amateur. He carefully described the mounds he encountered and attempted to sort American antiquities into three kinds: materials made by the natives, those of European origin that had been traded to the aboriginals, and those of the lost race of mound builders, who, he postulated, had to have been far more sophisticated than the ancestors of the living Native Americans. Who had they been?

Like all deeply religious Westerners, Atwater believed that all humanity had originated from Noah's landing at Mount Ararat, spreading from there. He believed as well that savage Asian hunters had come across the

Bering Strait and became the American Indians but that, prior to their arrival, gentle shepherds and farmers had emigrated to North America by the same route, after trekking through eastern Asia and Siberia from India. Atwater found a three-headed ceramic pot in a Tennessee mound that he took to represent the three main Hindu gods—"Brahma, Vishnoo, and Siva." Probably, he guessed, the mound builders had migrated here via Alaska as early as "the days of Abraham and Lot" and worked their way slowly south, increasing in sophistication and winding up in Mexico.

While his explanation of the mounds was wide of the mark, his survey was methodical and sober and is still of value, and for this work he was called by some the first American archaeologist. But of course, the area of interest that would one day become archaeology was still a long way from casting off the attractions of myth and grappling with fact. Indeed, it would not be until well after the Civil War that anything approaching a scientific archaeology would begin to come into being. Several other sciences—in particular, geology—would have to reach a certain maturity first.

Making up the dates, routes, and identities of the mound builders soon became a minor industry; poets and novelists leapt in, playing on the popular fantasies of the time. The first fictional account of the mound builders' downfall saw the light of day as early as 1795. Later, Sarah Hale, a New Hampshire poet, portrayed the master builders as the descendants of two peripatetic, star-crossed Phoenician lovers. In 1832, in a poem titled "The Plains," the dreary New England poet William Cullen Bryant wrote of the "race, that long has passed away" who had built the mounds, heaping up dirt on their dead till . . .

> The red man came—
> The roaming hunter tribes, warlike and fierce,
> And the mound-builders vanished from the earth.
> The solitude of centuries untold
> Has settled where they dwelt . . .

And so on.

Oddly prescient, though not for any reasoning we would today think of as scientific, an 1839 novel by Cornelius Mathews, *Behemoth: A Legend of the Mound-Builders,* had woolly mammoths alive at the same time as the mound people. (Their coexistence would be a much-gnawed bone of contention in scientific circles in the decades to come.) In what seems for all the world like the forerunner of the Godzilla movies, Mathews pictured an ancient North America full of cities that were almost destroyed by a particularly enormous woolly mammoth called Behemoth, civilization being saved at the eleventh hour by a hero who figured out how to kill the monster.

In the 1830s, Josiah Priest, a forerunner of Immanuel Velikovsky, created a wondrous tale of utter nonsense, calling it by the learned-sounding title *American Antiquities and Discoveries in the West*. It sold a huge number of copies for its time, some 22,000. Priest had the continent from the Rockies to the Alleghenies populated by many millions, with large clashing armies reminiscent of Alexander the Great's, battle horns sounding, banners aflutter—an epic predecessor of the Cecil B. De Mille approach to the past. Some of the mounds, Priest said, had been built prior to the biblical Deluge, and North America was where Noah's Ark had come to rest once the waters subsided. That the mounds were not the work of mere Indians was obvious to Priest, though he could not choose who the mound builders were from an extensive list of candidates he reviewed, including Egyptians, Greeks, Israelites, Scandinavians, Scots, Chinese, and Polynesians.

One contemporary of Priest's who was fascinated by such tales was Joseph Smith, who grew up near Palmyra, New York, and later, in a nearby cave, allegedly came upon the golden tablets that, once transcribed, became the Book of Mormon. The Book of Mormon describes several ancient diasporas of people from the Middle East to North America, including one in about 600 B.C.: just before Jerusalem was destroyed by the Babylonians, some Jews crossed the ocean to North America and began building great cities on top of mounds. Then a split occurred, creating the Nephites (the good guys) and the Lamanites (who became dirty and wild). God punished these godless savages, turning their skin a dark red. But then the Nephites themselves became corrupted, and, to punish them, God let the Lamanites overrun the Nephite mound cities. In the year A.D. 401, near Palmyra, the last of the Nephites bit the dust but one: a priest named Mormon lived long enough to write all this history down on golden tablets. Until well into the second half of the twentieth century, Mormon missionaries explained to Native Americans (and blacks) that if they joined the Church of Latter-Day Saints, their skin would gradually lighten.

Even with perfervid American imaginations at their most creative, more systematic observations were beginning to be made. By 1845, the geologist and explorer Henry Rowe Schoolcraft had made himself expert in Native American languages and folklore and would later be considered a major figure in the earliest beginnings of American anthropology. Before his work on the mounds, he was already a man of many accomplishments, which included finding the source of the Mississippi River in Itasca Lake, Minnesota, and serving as the superintendent of Indian affairs in Michigan, where he married an Ojibway woman (and signed a treaty by which the Ojibways ceded most of northern Michigan to the United States).

Finding some stone tubes in mounds along the Ohio River, Schoolcraft concluded that the mound builders might have been early astronomers and were perhaps of a race different from the Indians of the time. But six years later, in 1851, when he began publishing his six-volume work, *Historical and Statistical Information Respecting the History, Condition, and Prospects of the Indian Tribes of the United States,* he wrote, "There is little to sustain the belief that these ancient works are due to tribes of more fixed and exalted traits of civilization, far less to a people of an expatriated type of civilization, of either an Asiatic or European origin, as several popular writers very vaguely, and with little severity of investigation, imagined." (Later, Schoolcraft produced *Algic Researches,* which became the basis of Longfellow's poem *The Song of Hiawatha,* which wrenched the historical character Hiawatha out of the Iroquois country and plopped him into the Great Lakes.)

Meanwhile, more than a decade before Schoolcraft's first volume appeared, a doctor (whom some suggest as being the father of American *physical* anthropology), Samuel G. Morton of Philadelphia, had amassed a substantial collection of skulls from around the world, including some from native Ohio tribes and some from the mounds. From a systematic analysis that consisted of making ten detailed measurements of each skull, he determined that the mound builders and modern Native Americans were all of the same race. Like Jefferson's and William Bartram's earlier observations, Morton's findings were easily ignored by believers in a separate, "higher" race. After all, Morton's opinion was based on a mere eight mound-builder skulls, an awfully small sample, and who (it was asked) was to say that they weren't in fact modern Indian skulls that had inadvertently been buried in old mounds?

No less a force than the Smithsonian Institution, in nearly its first public act, played into the hands of the "higher race" believers. Schoolcraft, along with former Treasury secretary and then linguist and ethnographer Albert Gallatin and others at the recently founded American Ethnological Society, decided in 1845 that a full-scale survey of the mounds was called for. Gallatin and later-to-be-U.S.-president William Henry Harrison disagreed with Schoolcraft on the identity of the mound builders, seeing them as a "lost race." By way of resolving the issue, as well as cataloguing and preserving the now fast-vanishing mounds, the society eventually hired a journalist and politician for the job, Ephraim George Squier of Chillicothe, Ohio. With a fellow townsman and physician, Edwin H. Davis, Squier proceeded to open some two hundred mounds and about a hundred earthwork enclosures between 1845 and 1847, surveying them and creating excellent contour maps of them as well.

Squier tried to put a date on the mounds; at Fort Hill in Highland County, Ohio, he counted the rings on a huge old chestnut tree that grew on top of the mound, counting some four hundred, and estimated the mound's age at perhaps a thousand years. (Squier was not the first to use tree-ring dating. In 1788, the minister Manasseh Cutler used the growth rings of trees to arrive at the conclusion that a mound under study in Marietta, Ohio, dated at least as far back as the fourteenth century and maybe earlier, evidently becoming the first student of prehistory ever to use this dating technique, now called dendrochronology—another of archaeology's countless sires.)

Squier prepared a three-hundred-page manuscript, the publication of which was well beyond the funds of the fledgling American Ethnological Society. So he applied to the newly founded Smithsonian Institution, brought into existence in August 1846 thanks to a $500,000 bequest from James Smithson, an obscure British mineralogist and the bastard son of the Duke of Northumberland, to the United States to create "an establishment for the increase & diffusion of knowledge among men."

The Smithsonian's first leader, Secretary Joseph Henry, a renowned physicist, had planned a publication series but not necessarily on Indians.

In fact, even as the now-famous Smithsonian "castle," designed by Romantic architect James Renwick, was getting under way, it was not at all clear what such an institution should be—a museum, a library, an observatory, a university? Anyway, once Henry was presented with Squier's work, he agreed to make it the Smithsonian's first publication in the series known as *Smithsonian Contributions to Knowledge*. Called *Ancient Monuments of the Mississippi Valley*, the 1848 volume instantly became a keystone of American archaeology, still valuable as a record of the mounds as they appeared in 1847 (and no longer do, many having been lost to one or another depredation, mostly cleared away by farming).

Describing those mounds that had clearly served as fortifications, Squier said they showed a great deal of military sophistication, "a degree of knowledge much superior to that known to have been possessed by the hunter tribes of North America." Going on to discuss what he took to be sacred enclosures, he called attention to the engineering skills needed to build circular structures a mile in circumference, octagons, and other intricate forms.

As to who had built the vast flat-topped temple and burial mounds in the South, Squier had little to say, but of the burial mounds of the Ohio Valley, he asserted, noting the sophisticated pottery found in many of them, that it far exceeded "anything of which the existing tribes of Indians are known to be capable." The copper and other ornaments found in the mounds were, once again, superior to the "clumsy and ungraceful" work of the existing tribes, so the mound builders must have been a more civilized race than the American Indians. He concluded his report by stating that the mound builders had surely been very numerous, in the millions, and of necessity had been agriculturalists—a conclusion that Albert Gallatin had reached earlier. Who they had been and where they had gone, however, were admittedly beyond Squier's ability to answer.

Squier would go on to a diplomatic career in Honduras and Peru, where, in his spare time, he explored and wrote up numerous prehistoric sites and antiquities. In 1856, less than a decade after Squier's work on the North American mounds appeared, Samuel F. Haven, the librarian of the American Antiquarian Society, wrote the eighth of the *Smithsonian Contributions* (since Squier's, three others had been devoted at least in part to the mounds). This bulletin, based on a review of the relevant literature about the mounds rather than on-site inspection, expressed the view that the North American mounds were really not all that advanced compared to the magnificent structures of Mexico and farther south. They were un-accompanied by roads, bridges, stone structures, signs of metallurgy or as-tronomy—in short, no signs of an extraordinary civilization, nothing that the natives wouldn't have been perfectly equal to. By denigrating the mounds themselves (however accurately), Haven could damn the Native Americans with faint praise. Yes, he was saying, the Indians' ancestors had built the mounds, but what of it?

Even with its change of heart, the Smithsonian's impact on the public view of the mound builders remained slight. A self-proclaimed trader with Indians, William Pidgeon, soon published a long and allegedly historical account of the mound builders, based on information he received from an elderly native named De-coo-dah, who explained that he was descended from an ancient race known as the Elk People (who were perhaps of Dan-ish extraction). It was the Elk People who had built the northern mounds, De-coo-dah said, while Mexicans had built the southern ones. The two groups had met midway, fought, and exhausted each other to the point that they had been easy prey to the hordes of red Indians swarming out of Asia. Not until 1886 were Pidgeon and his Elk People fully discredited, by a surveyor named T. H. Lewis, who, among other things, proved that Pid-geon had failed to visit most of the sites he had written about. Lewis re-ferred to De-coo-dah and all the rest as "modern myths, which have never had any objective existence; and that, consequently, the ancient history of the volume is of no more account than that of the Lost Tribes in the Book of Mormon."

Never mind. Popular accounts still held the American fancy after the years of the American Civil War and would continue to do so well into the twentieth century, while scientific archaeology was in the process of being born. Then as now, Americans felt free to make of science whatever they wished, picking and choosing which findings they liked and rejecting oth-ers. In the same vein, modern-day Creationists reject evolution and, with it, most of physics and chemistry but have their biological myopia healed using surgical lasers, which could not have come into being without the science they so righteously reject. From accepted science combined with what we call pseudoscience, people felt free, then as now, to come up with whatever explanations they desired. In any event, the eons of geological time that had been postulated by Lyell and made popular in the work of Charles Darwin came as good news to many of those who wanted to believe in a higher race of mound builders: it provided a conveniently long period of time that could have elapsed between the end of the lost race and the arrival of the red man. At the same time, skeletons were turning up from places such as Egypt that were clearly at least 2,500 years old—and they were almost perfectly preserved. The fact that the skeletons found in the North American mounds were typically in a state of considerable decay also suggested that they were very ancient indeed—older than the pharaohs!—particularly to people unmindful of the effects of moisture on corpses.

A prominent scientist of the time added fuel to the fires in the hearts of the proponents of separate races. In 1873, J. W. Foster, president of the Chicago Academy of Sciences, published *Prehistoric Races of the United States of America,* in which he took note of the discovery in Germany of the remains of Neanderthals—those heavy-browed prehumans (so it was thought)—and the long periods he believed would have been necessary for human evolution to have taken place. He wrote, "The Indian possesses a conformation of skull which clearly separates him from the prehistoric Mound Builder." This was the opposite conclusion from that of Dr. Morton of Philadelphia three decades or so earlier. On the other hand, while Morton believed that the ancestors of the contemporary Indians were the mound builders, the Indians were, in Morton's view, nonetheless of a lesser race of men. In this period many people of a scientific bent believed that humanity had originated once—as in the biblical tale—and may well have subsequently degenerated into several races. This was called monogenism. Others—and Morton was among them—believed in polygenism, meaning that the several races had originated independently and were separate and, by implication, some were lesser species. Polygenism made it all the easier to justify slavery and other racial practices (just as making one's national adversaries seem less than human makes it easier on the mind to kill them: in World War II, for example, the Japanese were widely represented in the

United States as vicious little bucktoothed killer monkeys). In a condemnation that echoes that of Father Ortiz three *centuries* earlier and was in keeping with the polygenist view of humanity, the Chicago scientist Foster wrote rather gratuitously of the Indian:

> His character, since first known to the white man, has been signaled by treachery and cruelty. He repels all efforts to raise him from his degraded position: and whilst he has not the moral nature to adopt the virtues of civilization, his brutal instincts lead him to welcome its vices. He was never known voluntarily to engage in an enterprise requiring methodical labor. . . . To suppose that such a race threw up the strong lines of circumvallation and the symmetrical mounds which crown so many of our river-terraces, is as preposterous, almost, as to suppose they built the pyramids of Egypt.

Then, in a peculiar leap, Foster went on to assert that the mound builders had had skulls similar to those called Neanderthal, meaning that they had been of "a low intellectual organization, little removed from that of the idiot." Most of the mound builders, he explained, had been "mild, inoffensive" people who had placidly and unquestioningly built the mounds under the direction of a postulated handful of Svengalis (whose superior skulls had not been preserved—or found—and so were not available for inspection). So dim-witted were these people that they would have easily fallen prey to "treacherous" and "degraded" Indians once they appeared on the scene.

It is, of course, easy and amusing to look back on the suggestions, theories, and certainties of earlier times and to ridicule them from the convenient advantage of simply having come along later, when more information and better techniques are available. Anyone who does so, however, deserves to be treated similarly by people who are yet to follow and who, in turn, will benefit from even greater information and even more sophisticated techniques for obtaining and analyzing it. Even so, Foster's "idiot savant" theory of the mound builders does seem to have been stretching that day's scientific reasoning to the point of bursting—and soon enough an especially tough-minded contemporary man of science would say so.

It is worth remembering as well that during the time white Americans were looking for answers about the mounds and the mound builders, they were also busily shoving Native Americans out of their way—by treaty, purchase, deception, and, whenever needed, brute force—in order to achieve America's Manifest Destiny, which was to see white settlers on the land from sea to shining sea. Demonizing the native populations made it all the easier to displace them or eliminate them. By the time (1880) that the notion of an ancient race of mound builders came under serious and sustained attack by the slowly advancing practice of archaeology, the only real resistance to white Manifest Destiny that remained came from a few hundred Chiricahua Apaches who were busily raiding white settlers (and Mexicans) in Arizona while holding off about one-quarter of the U.S. Army. All the other tribes were either extinct or living uneasily on reservations of one sort or another. But in 1886, when Geronimo and his band of about fifty men, women, and children surrendered to the cavalry and were packed off to prison camp, it was still necessary for most Americans who thought about them at all to make out Indians as lesser beings—certainly not "us."

One American who didn't hold that view was John Wesley Powell, the one-armed Civil War veteran who led the first successful expedition down the Colorado River through the Grand Canyon in 1869, and who became late-nineteenth-century America's most important scientist. He was in effect the creator and director of both the U.S. Geological Survey and the Bureau of American Ethnology (the latter being part of the Smithsonian Institution). Among other things, these two agencies put the U.S. government solidly into the business of science, from which position it became the world's most generous scientific patron.

Powell was a largely self-taught naturalist who became especially expert in geology and Indian linguistics during his several expeditions into the American Southwest. As a boy he had spent a good deal of time poking around the mounds in the Midwest, where he had been raised the son of a farmer and itinerant Methodist preacher. By 1881, though, when he had grown to be the government's leading science administrator, he was not very interested in prehistory. Instead he recognized that the cultures of the present-day Native Americans were rapidly disappearing, and he wanted to document them before they were completely gone. (This was a

John Wesley Powell (right) with an unidentified Native American woman.

perception widely shared at the time—even, sadly, by most of the tribes themselves.)

In the first publication of the Bureau of Ethnology, Powell devoted only 8 of 638 pages to the mounds, saying—correctly, we now know—that they had clearly been the work of the ancestors of modern tribes, and that most likely they had come from several different stocks and worked at several different times. The next year Congress demanded that Powell devote one-fifth ($5,000) of his next appropriation to the mound builders. Powell grumbled but complied, appointing a botanist and geologist, Cyrus Thomas, to head a division of the bureau given over to the mounds. In the Bureau of Ethnography's second annual report in 1882, Powell returned to the topic, attacking "false statements" and "absurdities" in the accounts of so-called mound experts, along with the "garbling and perversion of the lower class of writers." Earlier researchers, he wrote, "were swept by blind zeal into serious errors even when they were not imposed upon by frauds and forgeries."

Some of those "earlier researchers" were still at work, among them the members of the Davenport, Iowa, Academy of Sciences, who prided themselves on their archaeological expertise. A squabble soon broke out when the Bureau of Ethnography's second annual report suggested that the academicians of Davenport had fallen prey to a hoax when they had held up some effigies as elephantine, thus "proving" that the mound builders had coexisted with the mammoths. (Among the artifacts turning up from the mounds from time to time were also "tablets" inscribed with one or another form of ancient script, such as one found in Newark, Ohio, by a man who had already convinced himself that the mound builders were Hebrews. On this tablet, found in 1860, appeared what was billed as a likeness of Moses along with his name and, on the flip side, the ten commandments. The town of Newark was something of a center for the manufacture of fake artifacts for the tourist trade.) In Davenport, the locals accused the Smithsonian, with its overwhelming influence, of intellectual tyranny in the field of archaeology, an accusation that wasn't yet true but would prove so in a few more decades.

Then, in 1882, a book appeared that had been written by a lieutenant governor of Minnesota and eight-year member of Congress who had also run for the office of vice president of the United States. The book reached a great deal more people than any report from the Smithsonian before or since. Its author was Ignatius T. Donnelly and its title *Atlantis: The Antediluvian World*. It asserted that Plato's report of the existence of the mid-Atlantic continent of Atlantis was not fable but historical fact. Atlantis, Donnelly wrote, had been the site of the Garden of Eden and then the first civilization, a mighty nation some of whose people had gone on to become

the royal lineages of all the other nations through history. And when Atlantis had sunk, disappearing forever under the waves thanks to a titanic
earthquake, some Atlanteans had escaped and made their way to Central
America, where they had become Toltecs and Aztecs (the linguistic connection between the words Aztlán and Atlantis was too obvious, he suggested, to be a coincidence). They had then moved north, becoming the
mound builders of North America, building mounds as they had always
done all over the world. They had withdrawn to Mexico, Donnelly asserted, before 231 A.D., having been attacked by hostile people from the
north. In fact, Donnelly threw everything into his account but Jung's racial
memory: virtually every minor myth, legend, tall tale, and hoax ever mentioned about the mounds was added to this astonishing stew.

The book was wildly successful. It remains in print to this day, available in both hardcover and paperback from dot-com bookstores, one of
the revered reference works of the Age of Aquarius. And of course there
are plenty of such people who prefer to believe that the pyramids of Egypt,
the Nazca lines of Peru, and other monumental creations were the work
not of ancient humans but of aliens arriving in spaceships—a bizarre per-
mutation of racism, to be sure. And even among the nonloonies today,
some people still believe that the mounds were the products of another
vanished aboriginal race—but not the Native Americans.

While Donnelly's book was becoming a publishing sensation, Cyrus
Thomas was directing a sizable staff of assistants who were extensively
surveying the existing mounds. In a photographic portrait of Thomas, we
see a handsome, prosperous-looking white-haired man with an aquiline
nose, a generous brow with an eyebrow raised in skeptical inquiry, and a
ferocious, doubting frown so intense as to wrinkle his broad and impressive jaw. (It is said that much portrait photography of this era showed
rather ferocious-looking people, mainly because they had to hold their ex-
pressions for several seconds. But even discounting that, Thomas was
clearly not a man to be trifled with.) Initially, he had been of the separate-
race school, but the data pouring in over nearly a decade convinced him
otherwise. Not only had the mounds been the work of ancestral Indians,
but, he believed, different tribal groups had built different mounds. His report, an enormous work of chiefly descriptive material published by the
bureau in 1894, once and for all put to rest—for professionals at least—the

lost-race theory. Also, it has been said to mark (you guessed it) "the birth of modern American archaeology."

THE STATE OF THE ART

Indeed by this time, near the turn of the century, there were such people as professional archaeologists—which is to say, people who, unlike amateurs and hobbyists, were paid to do archaeological work on at least a part-time basis. Their work was sponsored by scientific societies, museums, the government, and universities, and by the end of the nineteenth century, a few American universities were training people in a more systematic kind of archaeology. This had become possible thanks to many developments—in particular the development of geology as a science and the early understandings of the great depth of time during which the earth had existed and people had lived upon it. Darwin's insights into evolution arose in part as a result of geological developments and would soon open up great vistas in the studies of early humans. These were not, of course, merely academic matters, since they flew in the face of most theological views of the world. It was for many a shocking, wrenching time. These developments originated mostly in Europe and came to American shores later, but with no less force. These developments, to be described in the next chapters, had a profound influence on American notions of who the first Americans might have been and when they might have arrived.

At the turn of the twentieth century, archaeology per se was still in what one of its historians calls the "Classificatory-Descriptive Period," meaning mostly cataloguing and mapping such things as the works of the mound builders and sorting such things as pottery into geographical types. No one at this point had much of a handle on such factors as chronology or any way of probing such a question. In fact, many think that truly modern American archaeology emerged from the womb far to the south in Latin America, where archaeologists trained in Europe had begun to create methods that would permit an understanding of the sequences of prehistory. The leader—modern American archaeology's real sire—was Max Uhle, a German.

Uhle began his academic studies in philology but switched to archaeology and ethnography, then took a job as a curator in the Dresden Museum. There, in the early 1890s, the young Uhle developed a commanding knowledge of Inca and earlier Peruvian pottery as well as sculptural style— from artifacts and photographs that had been brought back by travelers and early antiquarian expeditions. I feel a certain distant kinship to Uhle, having also started out my archaeological career not in the field but in a host of museums.

When Uhle did get out into the field in Peru and elsewhere along the western coast of South America, he took note of small changes in the artifacts in differing strata and became one of the first archaeologists to make a case for gradual, cumulative cultural change over time. Well ahead of his contemporaries anywhere else in the Western Hemisphere, he developed in the early 1900s an areawide chronology of cultures in Peru that is still in use, albeit highly modified, almost a century later. Uhle wrote, "In Americanist studies, the first thing that had to be done was to introduce the idea of time, to get people to admit that the types [like pottery types and therefore cultures] could change over time."

In fact, one of his earliest efforts to chronicle this sort of microchange in culture came not in South America but when, in the first years of the twentieth century, he took some time to excavate the Emeryville shell mound in California's San Francisco Bay. There, excavating stratum by stratum, he noted not only the difference in artifacts from the top and bottom strata but also the continuity among the strata, which he took to represent about a thousand years of habitation and cultural development. At the time, however, one of the grand panjandrums of American anthropology, Alfred L. Kroeber of the University of California, did not approve of Uhle's notion of small, cumulative changes in a culture, preferring to find significance only in huge changes brought on by major technological innovations.

Kroeber was well meaning enough, but most of his archaeological notions have not held up very well. He believed that Indian cultures throughout North America had changed very little over prehistoric time, even changing little with the arrival of Europeans. From this idea of cultural stasis, Kroeber postulated that there had never been very many Native Americans, perhaps some 3 million all told from coast to coast. This meant, among other things, that the European diseases introduced upon contact had had relatively little effect either culturally or demographically.

We now know that diseases such as smallpox, to which the aboriginals had little or no resistance, were utterly devastating, killing off as much as 90 percent of many tribes, especially those that lived in close quarters such as large towns or even small villages. These diseases evidently raced ahead of European contact into the interior, scrambling many native cultures like so many eggs. It is medically possible that the widespread cause of such death was not the primary diseases, such as smallpox and measles, but secondary infections, such as pneumonia, lack of nourishment (both food and water), general terror, and, with large numbers of a given population infected simultaneously, lack of healthy individuals to care for the sick or work in the fields to bring in food.

Certainly, the Aztec empire fell to Cortés and his relative handful of troops in a matter of days not so much because of superior European arms but primarily because the population of Tenochtitlán was reduced to about *one-tenth* by smallpox before Cortés returned to conquer it. By 1650, the Mexican population had been reduced to one-tenth its precontact size. To the north, descendants of the great mound-building cultures of the American Southeast, which had been thriving before de Soto's excursion in the early 1540s, virtually disappeared before the onslaught of the European pathogens he had inadvertently brought—his only inadvertent violence. Today even conservative estimates of the pre-Columbian population of what is now the United States suggest that at least 11 million native people were here in about 1500, if not twice that many. By 1900, only some 500,000 Native North Americans remained, disease and its aftereffects having accounted for infinitely more deaths over that period than the U.S. Cavalry could ever claim.

The question here about the size of the pre-Columbian Indian population is not merely an academic matter, of course, but also a question of how great the devastation of native populations (in real numbers) by the arrival of Europeans was, as well as a matter of intent. The fewer killed off, the less blame, and this disputatious matter remains with us today. The broad field of anthropology, and even what would seem to be a somewhat less urgent arena, archaeology, has rarely avoided being hauled into the political realm.

In any event, not until North American archaeologists began to use Uhleian methods in the American Southwest would they begin to catch up with the sophistication of the European-trained archaeologists in Latin America and develop proper (and lasting) chronologies of past cultures. While all this was going on, North Americans continued to invent their own brand of archaeology with little reference to the techniques of the Europeans or those working in South America. This odd provincialism on the part of North Americans continues to this day in many quarters—and I would soon run afoul of it, as several of my colleagues have recently.

To summarize, it is fair to say, however, that if North American archaeology was "born" with Cyrus Thomas's myth-shattering report on the mound builders in 1894, it was still in an almost purely descriptive stage. It had neither the conceptual nor methodological tools to answer most questions one might reasonably ask of the deep American past and the hemisphere's first inhabitants. Perhaps the most intractable question of all at the turn of the century had to do with time. When did the mound builders do their work? When did the first Americans arrive here? Already before the end of the nineteenth century, American antiquarians and professional archaeologists alike—not to be outdone by their European counterparts—were scouring the countryside looking for "our" own Ice Age people. Years later, Clovis Man would prove to have lived at the end of the Ice Age, when the glaciers had been receding northward. When my crew and I came up with our pre-Clovis dates at Meadowcroft, it meant that someone had been in southwestern Pennsylvania when the glacier was only about a hundred miles away.

In the early 1970s, we prehistorians had collectively come a long way from the early guesses about the mound builders. It wasn't all that much earlier, after all, that the adolescent science of geology had determined that such a thing as an ice age had actually existed, much less Ice Age people.

_____

CHAPTER TWO

THE GLACIER'S EDGE

For a long time—no one knows how long—people in the Alps and probably in other mountainous areas in the northern part of the globe were aware of strange features of the land such as house-sized boulders made of nonlocal rock sitting on the ground like uninvited guests, huge natural amphitheaters carved out of rock, and polished rocks with grooves and striations all running in the same direction. To those who wondered about such features, Noah's biblical flood could be invoked as the cause—and, indeed, was so invoked well into the nineteenth century. The great waters had moved the boulders, scoured out the amphitheaters, and pushed angular rock over rock to create the grooves. The biblical version of history was a powerful vise on the minds of people in both Europe and America.

Generally, it was taken as a matter of certainty that the earth and everything including the life-forms on it had experienced Genesis all at once, about six thousand years earlier, the date having been established by James Ussher, Archbishop of Armagh, Primate of All Ireland, and vice-chancellor of Trinity College, Dublin, who determined the date of creation as October 23, 4004 B.C. (a Sunday), by counting all of the Bible's begats backward to the beginning of all things. Shortly after Ussher's date was announced, Dr. John Lightfoot (another vice-chancellor of Trinity College) further pinpointed the moment of Creation to nine o'clock in the morning. There was at the time practically no concept of the earth's antiquity and therefore no context in which anyone could have imagined the immense amount of time human beings, much less humanlike ancestors or various monsters such as dinosaurs, had been on the earth.

A few exceptions to this certainty existed. In the latter years of the eighteenth century, a Scot named James Hutton plunged into the realm of geology and, remarkably ahead of his time, concluded that the same processes visibly going on in the present—such as erosion, the silting up of lakes, and flows of lava from erupting volcanoes—could account for all the earth's landforms. He concluded that one did not need supernatural explanations for them, and since these visible processes went very slowly, as well as cyclically, the world had to be very, very old. This notion, that the geologic processes of the past and the present were the same, was called "uniformitarianism," as opposed to "catastrophism" (meaning a calamitous and sudden flood, for example, or, more recently, meteorite impact). Most people in Hutton's time, including those devoted to science of one sort or another, remained wedded to the biblical timescale and the catastrophic-flood notion. Hutton had been trained as a lawyer and then as a doctor, neither of which professions much interested him, and gave both up in order to pursue his scientific interests, particularly geology.

At this time in history a great many British naturalists were clergymen. They were educated men, to begin with, and many were located in parishes that called for many trips around the countryside. The best known was Oxford-educated Gilbert White, whose book, *The Natural History of Selborne,* published in 1798, remains a classic to this day largely because of his keen sense of observation. When these curious men of the cloth found such oddities as primitive human artifacts—stone points, for example—associated with the likes of elephant remains, they had to assume that the period in question lay somewhere this side of Ussher's moment of Genesis. And when it came to many of the features we now associate with the waxing and waning of glaciers, they could still, in the 1830s, be explained by the Flood or by a subsequent cold period when icebergs might have floated from the north over the floodwaters covering Europe, dropping boulders and scouring rock as they went. Not every reverend naturalist's eyes were clouded by dogma, however. A remarkable Catholic priest and antiquarian named Father Joseph MacEnery discovered associations of artifacts and Ice Age animals sealed under an unbroken floor in Kent's Cavern in the town of Torquay, in southwest England, during the years 1825 to 1829 and recognized them for what they were: evidence of very great human antiquity. But his kind was all too rare.

Picking up where James Hutton had left off, another Scot, Charles Lyell, scoured Europe for its ample evidence of uniformitarianism and, well armed, began in 1830 publishing *Principles of Geology,* a three-volume work that would go through twelve editions before his death in 1875. Lyell's work inaugurated the modern science of geology and, among other things, provided the time frame within which Charles Darwin and others would perceive the long evolution of life on earth. Lyell redefined the stage on which life itself had existed and humans had played out their roles: he made it possible to begin, however dimly, to perceive the length of time that had elapsed since the first human habitation of places such as England (and then later America). Darwin would later write of Lyell's work, "it altered the whole tone of one's mind, and therefore . . . when seeing a thing never seen by Lyell, one yet saw it partially through his eyes." But acceptance of all this was hardly immediate: Lyell's perception of the great antiquity of the earth was sufficiently sacrilegious and dangerous that women and children, those highly susceptible creatures, were barred from his public lectures.

Lyell's work literally made the ice ages conceivable. Generally, the realization that much of the lands of northern Europe, Asia, and North America had once, sometime long ago, been covered by ice is attributed to Louis Agassiz, a Swiss ichthyologist (a student of fish both live and fossil), who in 1836 began looking into the movements and effects of the glaciers of his home country. In 1840, he published *Études sur les glaciers,* for which he is much better remembered than for his piscine concerns. Agassiz later came to the United States and took a professorship at Harvard, where he not only explored the glacial history of North America and became one of the country's leading scientists but also became its most influential teacher of science. Study nature, he is reputed to have said, not books—which remains pretty good advice. (He was also a polygenist and, as such, an apologist for slavery, and, as we shall also see, an anti-Darwinist—which is a reminder that a scientist who is brilliant in one field can be way off base in others. Beware the Nobel Prize–winning physicist who invents a new diet.)

Louis Agassiz (left) and Benjamin Pierce.

The origin of glacial theory has its own historical "stratigraphy," and Agassiz lies near its earliest stratum, but there were others below him. He was the first to publish a major explication of the role glaciers might have played in creating the European landscape, but that is because he was a quick study rather than the first to put it all together. When he began to look into glacial features in 1836, he was bent on proving the then-prevalent notion that at some time in the past, icebergs had been bred in the far north, floated southward, and dropped the big boulders called "erratics" here and there (because they were thought to have been laid down by melting icebergs that drifted south, some glacial deposits are still called "drift"). A few field trips with other naturalists changed Agassiz's mind, and he began talking up the idea of glacial expansion and contraction.

But others had gotten to that point earlier than he. One was a less well known mining engineer named Johann von Charpentier of Saxony. Charpentier simply couldn't buy the idea that floods or icebergs had been the moving force behind the big boulders in the Rhône Valley and elsewhere in Europe. He began looking into the subject in 1834, two years ahead of Agassiz, but published his account, *Essai sur les glaciers,* only in 1841. In

Glacial erratic left by the retreat of the Ross Ice Shelf at Cape Crozier, Antarctica.

it he graciously gave credit to yet an earlier thinker on such matters, a peasant he had met while out on a mountain one day studying a large granite boulder. The peasant allowed as how there were plenty of boulders like that on the mountain but said they had come from elsewhere. When Charpentier asked how the boulder could have gotten there, the man replied that the glacier had brought them when long ago it had extended much farther. He went on to explain why water could not have been the vehicle. Charpentier wrote:

> This good man would never have dreamed that I was carrying in my pocket a manuscript in favor of his hypothesis. He was greatly astonished when he saw how pleased I was by his geological explanation, and when I gave him money to drink to the memory of the ancient glacier and to the preservation of the boulder.

In any event, Charpentier, who was bitter at being scooped by Agassiz, went on to slip below the radar of most histories of science, while Agassiz promoted glacial theory with exuberance and great accumulation of data against the still widely held diluvian theory of Noah's Flood. There were plenty of reasons, Agassiz thought, including the advance of glaciers across the landscape, to render species of plants and animals extinct, though he would nevertheless continue till death to believe in divine intervention in the *creation* of new species, as opposed to Darwinian natural selection.

But credit for the understanding that much of the world was once covered by ice goes back yet further than Charpentier or his rural sage! The great German poet, dramatist, and natural philosopher Johann von Goethe had earlier concluded that there must have been an "epoch of great cold," and peasants in the Alps had long figured that the glaciers above them had once been more extensive. One of these, J. P. Perraudin, communicated this notion to a Swiss civil engineer as early as 1815, and by 1824 a Norwegian scientist had reached the same conclusion. But all this concerned only local glaciers. It fell in 1832 to a German professor, A. Bernhardi, to infer that glacial ice from the far north had once extended as far south across Europe as Germany. (He also postulated a polar ice cap in the north that we now know doesn't exist, though the phrase continues in use.) Agassiz had the advantage of being a remarkably clear and forceful expositor of science, which is why he got the credit in his day and, in many accounts, still does.

FOSSILS, FLOODS, ICE
———

Glaciers were soon under suspicion as murderers. Until the glaciers were discovered, it had been the Flood that was taken as the force that had wiped out all the big fossil animals that had been turning up for more than a century, many of which naturalists recognized as creatures that no longer dwelled upon the earth. It had taken a bit of time for people to recognize that species of animals could indeed go extinct; such a thought was taken as something of a slur on the Deity's planning. Nevertheless, the bones of huge mammals did turn up in places where living versions were no longer seen—in either Europe or America—and they needed to be accounted for.

One of the first speculations about the nature of the oversized fauna of America was made by Thomas Jefferson, who, upon laying eyes on a huge claw of an unknown animal found in western Virginia, assumed it was that of an enormous catlike carnivore. He called it *Megalonix* ("giant claw") in a 1799 paper in the *Transactions of the American Philosophical Society*—the first and the last scientific paper ever delivered by a sitting American vice president. (It later turned out to be the claw of a giant ground sloth, named *Megalonyx* in Jefferson's honor in 1822.)

Earlier finds of the fossil bones of giant animals were treated more fancifully. In 1706, the governor of Massachusetts wrote to that fire-breathing preacher and scourge of the sinful, Cotton Mather, about a number of bones and a large tooth he had been given by a man who had discovered them near the Hudson River. The tooth, half a foot long and weighing two pounds, looked for all the world like a human eyetooth, and the governor opined in his letter that it was the remains of one or the other race of giants mentioned in the Bible. It could not, he said, be an elephant tooth. As the decades went by, the Russian czar Peter the Great took an interest in such remains, receiving a mammoth tusk from Siberia and encouraging others to find a whole skeleton of the animal. In fact, Peter the Great had an almost ghoulish interest in remains of all sorts: his storeroom contained stuffed humans (especially hairy ones), the remains of Siamese twins, and all sorts of specimens of which the mammoth tusk was hardly the most bizarre. In 1766, Benjamin Franklin received a collection of mastodon bones and guessed that the teeth belonged to a meat eater, but he later changed his mind: the teeth could just as easily have been useful for chewing branches. While this was a good guess, more insightful was Franklin's opinion that the bones (found in Ohio) came from a region too cold for modern elephants. This led him to suggest that the climate of North America must have been altered at some time, perhaps by a shift in the earth's axis.

By this time in Europe, many students of natural history had begun to realize that the earth had to be a much older place than a literal reading of the Bible permitted. The great French naturalist and writer Georges Buffon popularized the idea that the 6,000-odd years of history referred only to human history. Prior to the arrival of people and the modern form of the earth, much of a dynamic nature had taken place: theologians could see good sense in the notion that the hand of divine providence might well have spent a good deal of time preparing the earth for God's children. Still, however, the devout could not bring themselves to entertain the idea that God could have created animals that subsequently had not worked out and had gone extinct. They believed that the spaces for life had been filled once and remained filled, and this was Jefferson's belief too. He fully expected that somewhere live mastodons would be found, along with *Megalonyx*.

In this belief, Jefferson was simply remaining in tune with a basic idea about the nature of creation that was much in vogue at the time—the Great Chain of Being, which accounted in a thoroughly hierarchical manner for all creatures, with angels on top, then mankind, below which were, according to Alexander Pope's version in his *Essay on Man* of 1734, "Beast, bird, insect what no eye can see." It was a fragile chain, as Pope reported: "From Nature's chain whatever link you strike, Ten or ten thousandth, breaks the chain alike." In other words, the extinction of any type of creature would have led to the disintegration of the entire chain.

By 1812, however, another French natural historian, Georges Cuvier, showed that extinctions had indeed occurred, and quite frequently. He could assert that by this time, for example, there were no more woolly mammoths in the Old World and no more giant ground sloths in the New. The remains of these beasts were often, if not typically, found in gravels and clays of a distinct kind, and Cuvier reasoned that whatever had deposited the gravel and clay had also caused the extinctions—no doubt the great floods that had occurred six thousand years earlier. He went on to point out that no one had thus far found any human remains *below* the deposits that bore mammoth and sloth remains, so humans had therefore probably not coexisted with those animals. Thus it could not be, as some would soon suggest, that the big mammals had been wiped out by humans. Cuvier was what came to be called a "catastrophist," believing that catastrophic events—in this case, the Flood—from time to time brought about huge and rapid geological change. While the mammoths might have been killed off by a sudden refrigeration, all the others had perished in the Flood, their remains being found in such places as gravel beds that looked like the detritus of floods.

With the discovery of the glaciers, the catastrophists could make the same claim—a rapid dying out—but caused in this case by the ice. As Agassiz put it with characteristic drama, "To the movement of a powerful creation succeeded the silence of death. Springs dried up, streams ceased to flow, and the sun's rays, in rising over those frozen expanses (if they still reached there), were met only by the whistling of the northern winds and the thunder of the crevasses as they split the surface of this vast ocean of ice."

Meanwhile the geologist Lyell, a uniformitarian of the first order, pointed out that the remains of the large and now extinct animals were, in fact, found both below and above the so-called diluvium (such as gravel beds attributed to the Flood). Thus these extinctions too had occurred in a more gradual manner.

The questions of pace and cause soon grew more complex. At this time, for example, hippopotamuses were known to live in Africa, but now-extinct antediluvian hippos had existed in Europe. This had to suggest a gradual extinction process. But the catastrophism-uniformitarianism dichotomy continued nonetheless. Catastrophists were hard put to specify a direct cause of the extinctions they saw occurring over long periods of time—they thought they probably had something to do with changes in "station" (or what we would call habitat) caused by one or another event here and there.

But there was another answer that some preferred. It went back as far at least as the discovery in the eighteenth century in Big Bone Lick,

Kentucky, of some fossil bones that for reasons obscure were taken to be the remains of a meal of a carnivorous mastodon. One commentator of the time wrote that this huge animal must have been "at once the terror of the forest and man," and so it made sense to think that men had killed off the mastodons to render the world safer. This indictment of humans as the potential cause of extinctions depended on two separate questions: Could men indeed wipe out a whole species? And was there any evidence suggesting that humans and the big extinct mammals had coexisted? European scientists, such as the geologist Lyell, gradually concluded that humans were capable of such activity, but few went along with the contemporaneity issue, since no satisfactory proof had emerged—no association of human remains or tools with the remains of the great beasts. But the human angle continued to have its adherents.

One of these was the Reverend John Fleming, a Scot who, in addition to his priestly duties, was a naturalist of some note, especially a zoologist. In an early version of a technique that would plague archaeology even until the present, Fleming took two wholly unsubstantiated claims (one of them some elephantine remains found near a bronze battle-ax, the other some human bones below now-extinct mammals) and proclaimed that humans and these now-extinct beasts had lived at the same time. Therefore humans had been the guilty party. And the "extirpation operations" Fleming postulated would have taken place over a long period of time.

Though contemporaneity—the crucial issue—remained unproven until about 1860, the "human-as-extirpator" notion became more and more popular among scientists, with even Lyell admitting that in North America it might well have been Indian arrows that had finally exterminated the American giant fauna. What was the difference between North America and Europe? American geologists were quick to take up Agassiz's glacial theories and fanned out across various parts of the continent in search of glacial traces. By the 1850s, it had already been established that the presence of glaciers in North America had not extended all the way south across the continent but had stopped, for the most part, just south of the northern tier of the United States. Again, the notion of human agency in extinctions of old was based on little more than supposition; there still was no acceptable proof. But an objective measure of such things did by this time exist: stratigraphy.

If one could find human remains indisputably among or below those of extinct animals, it would be unarguable that people had existed prior to the divine preparation of the earth for its human inhabitants. That would be the sort of thing that would cause, among other upheavals, major seizures in the biblical view of the world and its history. It would mean that humans had not been the reason for the creation of the planet. But while Europeans did go on to find what they thought were such proofs, no one accepted their findings, and for what at the time seemed perfectly valid scientific reasons. Most discoveries of human remains associated with those of extinct animals were made in caves, and it was believed at the time that stratigraphic information in caves was not just difficult to obtain but almost impossible to get right. After all, in one case, searchers had found the bones of extinct Pleistocene creatures intimately associated with artifacts unquestionably made by the Romans. Not only were caves unreliable in themselves, but virtually all such finds were made by what the scientific sophisticates of Paris and London took not just as amateurs, but provincial ones to boot. Such people could not in fact be expected to have the theoretical or technical expertise to fulfill the criteria set down for such work. The criteria were perfectly reasonable; they called for (1) indisputable human artifacts or, better yet, human bone; (2) the remains of extinct Pleistocene animals; and (3) an undeniable relationship of the two. So no findings from caves were accepted as valid by those of a scientific bent, and for several decades more, this major theological buttress of what was taken as the core of Western civilization—the idea of a providential earth created for mankind—held firm.

This would remain the case until the years just before and after the American Civil War. The year 1859 would be the watershed year when the short world of familiar biblical time would cease to exist. In the meantime, however, scientists were engaged in an increasingly vigorous, widespread, and sophisticated study of glacial geology that would eventually shed light not only on the ice itself and the timing of ice ages but on the mechanisms of glacial growth (and death), glaciers' geography, and the interplay among glaciers, climate, and weather. All of this growing body of information would have a profound effect on our understanding of the story of how humans populated the world, including the life and times of the first Americans.

GLACIAL AMERICA

Before the turn of the twentieth century, it was clear that the North American ice had advanced southward and then receded several times over some long period of time and that the last advance had brought the glacial edge as far south as northern New Jersey, Cincinnati, and Saint Louis (see map). Ice had stretched along a wildly erratic line from the Atlantic westward

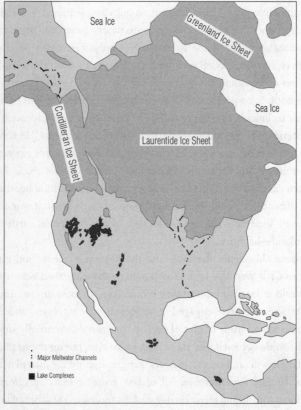

North America and adjacent Siberia during the glacial maximum,
ca. 20,000 B.P. (after Porter, 1988).

almost to the Rocky Mountains, north across Canada, and eastward to cover Greenland and even Iceland.

Today we know that for at least the last 1.89 million years, the world has been subject to the repeated advances of ice (periods called "glacials") and retreats (called "interglacials") during what is called the Pleistocene Epoch, a term Charles Lyell coined from the Greek words for "most" and "recent." The Pleistocene is said to have ended ten thousand years ago with the last glacial retreat (though that date's main claim is that it is a nice round number), and we currently live in the Holocene—a word later coined by a French scholar that also etymologically means "most recent," but never mind. Another way to look at it is to put aside the self-satisfied notion that we thoroughly modern humans are so marvelous that we must have our very own epoch, the Holocene, and admit that we simply live in the latest Pleistocene interglacial. The beginning of the Holocene is in fact pegged to the beginning of the latest interglacial, and it can be expected to be succeeded by another glacial period—whatever the near-term effects of the current state of global warming. Anatomically modern human beings came into being only within the last 120,000 years, which is to say, only in the last fifteenth of the Pleistocene. Clovis culture, so long thought to be the first in the Americas, existed for only a nanoblink of geological time (about a half millennium) at the Pleistocene's very end, when the great ice sheets that covered about a quarter of the planet's landmass had begun to recede.

This vast ice sheet, which at its height covered most of Canada and a good deal of the northern part of the United States, is called the Laurentide Glacier. Part of Alaska and the Yukon Territory, as well as the so-called bridge known as Beringia, had been spared, but ice had crept south from the rest of Alaska, turning the Aleutian Islands into an icebound thumb and covering the west coast of North America down to Seattle and east over the Rocky Mountains. This long, thin glacier is called the Cordilleran Glacier, and for much, if not most, of its career it was separated from the Laurentide.

Though the two great glaciers are often shown as conjoined during the height of the last glacial maximum, there is very contradictory evidence on precisely when and for how long such a confluence may have occurred. Exactly when the corridor was open or closed has been debated endlessly, especially by Clovis Firsters. According to their argument, any migrants into the New World were bottled up in the unglaciated Bering Refugium until the ice sheets parted like the Red Sea for some Clovis Moses to lead his intrepid band of spear-toting, mammoth-slaying wayfarers to the south. Which is very dramatic and probably very wrong. The bottom line on the corridor is that for most of the time between 75,000 and 10,000 years ago it was open. While it may not have been particularly welcoming—cold and windy, with icy lakes and tundralike conditions—animals could and did live there, and people obviously moved through it sometime after passing over the land bridge.

The phrase "land bridge" suggests some sort of a fragile isthmus across which the Asian pioneers teetered fearfully on their way to a new land, but it was nothing like that at all. The landmass we call Beringia, which periodically emerged between Siberia and Alaska throughout the Pleistocene down to the end of the last glacial period, was about a thousand miles across from north to south, mostly a relatively barren tundra- and steppelike place crossed by occasional rivers with their associated streams and swales, and probably sparsely populated by the same big-game animals the pioneers were familiar with from Siberia—notably woolly mammoths, bison, and horses. No people pioneering a path across this landmass, or along its southern coast, would have suspected they were crossing anything like a bridge or, indeed, that they were changing continents. They were just moving on, following the game, headed generally east toward the morning sun.

Beringia came about as a direct result of the glaciers, those vast storehouses of frozen moisture mined from the oceans. And the creation of the glaciers lowered the sea level, exposing a great deal of real estate that is now under water. At their most extensive, about 20,000 years ago, the Laurentide and Cordilleran glaciers (along with those covering northern Europe, parts of northern Asia, and South America) dropped the sea level as much as 440 feet below the present level, perhaps more. That was a hell of a lot of moisture locked up in the ice—an estimated 12 million cubic *miles* more ice than exists today. The Laurentide Glacier was two miles thick in places and almost a mile thick at its southerly edge. The Cordilleran, which reached a thickness of one and a half miles in places, was essentially the growing together of separate montane glaciers into one continuous if narrow blanket of ice that extended south well into Puget Sound. Here and there on its western edge, the Cordilleran spread across the exposed continental shelf, calving icebergs into the Pacific but leaving some ice-free coastal areas as well.

Glaciers form only under relatively special circumstances. Basically, they begin in elevated mountain basins where the rate of annual snowfall exceeds the rate of yearly melting for a considerable period of time. The presence of uplands is critical, and where there are no mountains, as in the so-called Bering Refugium, glaciers cannot and do not form.

Within the highland basins, snowfields form, and under the weight of subsequent snowfalls the pressure of gravity converts previously porous flakes to rounded particles called "firn" or "névé." Gradually, the porosity decreases further as the pressure from still more new snow accumulates, converting the firn deep in the snowfall, or recrystallizing it, into ice. This initial glacier is restricted to an amphitheater or half-bowl-like depression (called a "cirque"). Then eventually it grows larger, flows out of the bowl and down into adjacent valleys, and becomes a valley glacier. If the process continues, valley glaciers can conjoin in the foothills to form piedmont glaciers, which ultimately coalesce into great continental ice sheets spreading across the lowlands. The Cordilleran glacier was the consequence of the confluence of a great many mountain and valley glaciers, while the Laurentide was the result of the merging of three ice domes into one mighty ice sheet whose margins crept across the landscapes as long as the glacier was being fed with additional snow.

The edges of continental ice sheets move in spasmodic thrusts called stadials and often form distinct lobes whose margins may rest or actually retreat a little (interstadials) even during an overall advance cycle. If you could see the speeded-up process, the movement of a continental glacier would seem like that of a huge, undulating amoeba, its edges pulsing as it grows, devouring most of the northern half of the continent. Then, finally, the amoeba would stop growing, its lobes would retreat, its edges would thin, and it would begin to die. The last "death," the start of an interglacial period, occurred about 10,000 years ago and marks the beginning of the Holocene.

While we understand rather clearly the factors that influence the short-term health of a glacier, what causes ice ages themselves is a much more murky matter. Almost as soon as it was recognized that ice ages had existed in the past, various explanations were offered for their genesis. Of the early explanations, by far the most important and in some ways the most enduring was James Croll's *Climate and Time,* published in 1875.

Croll believed that the origin of the ice ages lay in changes in the orbital geometry of the earth. Using calculations derived by yet another scholar to describe the orbits of the planets, Croll hypothesized that there had been eight glacial-advance cycles, each followed by an interglacial, between 240,000 and 80,000 years ago. Unfortunately, Croll had the dates of the ice ages all wrong, and when it was shown that glacial interludes had existed up until much more recently, Croll's entire orbital change theory was thrown out.

Ultimately, Croll's cyclical change hypothesis was resurrected by Milutin Milankovitch, a Serbian mathematician. Between 1924 and 1941, Milankovitch reanalyzed Croll's data, supplemented it with new information, then asserted that there were not one but three cycles that affected the earth's climate. The longest cycle, of 100,000 years' duration, derives from changes in the shape of the earth's orbit. A shorter cycle, of 41,000 years, is due to rhythmic changes in the tilt (back-and-forth movement) of the earth's axis and determines the amount of sunlight that reaches the northern latitudes. The third and shortest cycle, of 19,000 to 23,000 years, reflects changes in the precession (wobble or side-to-side movement) of the earth on its axis. This last cycle influences equatorial latitudes and conditions, which in turn affect the lengths of the seasons. Like Croll, Milankovitch posited eight major and complete glacial cycles, but his were each about 100,000 years in duration.

Confirmation of Milankovitch's calculation would not come until the 1970s, when deep-sea cores revealed that there had indeed been systematic changes in the earth's climate that corresponded to Milankovitch's predictions. Changes in the ratios of two oxygen isotopes (O^{18}, which is common in the skeletons of tiny one-celled creatures called "foraminifera" when the oceans are cold, and O^{16}, which is more abundant when the waters are warm) confirmed that all three of Milankovitch's cycles had indeed occurred in the past. These cores also revealed that a cold climate with limited mountain glaciation extended back 2.5 million years ago into the Pliocene (the period before the Pleistocene) but that extensive climatic deterioration accompanied by large continental ice sheets did not occur until just after 1 million years ago.

The cores further showed that though the "signature" of the 100,000-, 41,000-, and 19,000-to-23,000-year cycles was readily detectable, only the shorter cycles were directly attributable to orbital changes. In order to have an effect on climate, the long cycle—which has also been documented well into preglacial times—would require an additional stimulus or trigger. In other words, some additional factor or factors would have to be at work to set major, long-term glacial cycles into motion. Some scholars suggest that when the drifting minicontinent of India slammed into Asia, creating the Himalayas and the Tibetan plateau in the collision, that great uplift of land, with its concomitant effect on the jet stream, air circulation, and rainfall patterns, could have provided the additional "push." Others have suggested changes in the temperatures of oceans and/or shifts in the amount of carbon dioxide in the earth's atmosphere as additional causes. Whatever triggered the recurrence of long-term glacial fluctuations, we do know that the severity and duration of these cycles have differed in the past. Between about 1.6 million and 900,000 years ago, a complete and rather modest glacial cycle occurred about every 40,000 years. Between 900,000 and 450,000 years ago, the cycles grew in length and severity to 70,000 years. Since then the cycles have been a full 100,000 years long, with extreme continental glaciation.

Whatever their duration, an often overlooked feature of these recurring glacial periods is that the Northern Hemisphere always experienced summers and winters. As my colleague Olga Soffer of the University of Illinois constantly reminds me, if the Pleistocene began 1.6 million years ago, there have been 1.6 million Januarys *and* 1.6 million Julys—an annual cycle of cold and warm (or at least less cold). The summer temperatures as far north as Alaska today get to be 70 to 80° F. Even at the greatest extent of the glaciers during all these periods, it has not been all bad, all cold, all unbearable, everywhere on earth. During the time of the last glacial maximum, about 20,000 years ago, hippos were frolicking in the Sahara, which was not a desert but a place of shallow lakes and often dense lakeside vegetation. Ice Age Florida, though a bit cooler and moister, would still have been a choice destination for your Pleistocene Christmas vacation.

Between 115,000 and 110,000 years ago, during the last interglacial, the planet enjoyed a period with climates that were actually warmer and drier than today's. Then the climate began to deteriorate, global cooling started again, and by 110,000 years ago what has been termed in North America the Wisconsinan glacial stage was under way. By 70,000 years ago, global temperatures had dropped by some six degrees Fahrenheit, and sea levels had fallen by about two hundred feet. The ramifications were, of course, worldwide—the snow line on Mount Kenya, for example, dropped about two thousand feet lower than it is today—but the cold and its effects were more pronounced in the north and in highland South America.

Let's stop for a moment and consider the matter of these lowering snow lines. They are among the most distinctive effects of a glacial advance. Their immediate impact is to force high-elevation plants to move down the mountains or go extinct. Typically, plants from the upper regions then find themselves among lower-elevation neighbors, creating what we think of as ecologically anomalous environments. As a result, animals are forced into what might previously have been unlikely—and for the animals probably uncomfortable—associations. This is widely common in glacial times; indeed, one finds the remains of woolly mammoths next door to those of whitetail deer or mastodons sharing territory with elk. One of the chief environmental effects of glaciers is to create what would strike us today as a highly unsettling patchwork of habitats for local plant and animal populations.

In any event, in the north, the ice pulsed and grew until about 50,000 years ago, when the climate warmed somewhat and the ice began to recede a few hundred miles. Then, 25,000 years ago, the glaciers began their last great advance. By 19,000 years ago, the Laurentide glacier had reached its maximum extent in the region from Illinois to Wisconsin and Iowa but continued to grow in the East, reaching its maximum, in most areas, between 18,000 and 20,000 years ago. Meadowcroft, by the way, lay but a scant fifty miles from the ice front at its greatest extent. Far to the northwest, the glacier continued creeping south until about 13,000 years ago. The effects on the land of this enormous blanket of ice were profound and still lie around us today.

As the glaciers snatched up moisture that normally would have returned to the sea, thus lowering the sea levels, the shape and size of North America were altered considerably. The west coast extended about another fifty miles farther seaward in some areas. On the east coast, where the continental shelf today is far wider, dry land extended some two hundred miles out into the Atlantic. To those who are aware that the notion of *terra firma* is a highly relative term, what with continents moving about over time, it should come as no surprise that the enormous weight of the ice caused the land below it to sink. This led to a postmelting phenomenon called "glacial rebound," wherein the earth rises back up. In certain areas around the Great Lakes, the land is still rising at the rate of approximately two-tenths of an inch a year. And as the glacier's lobes pulsed this way and that depending on local and global conditions, the land below was gouged out, planed, polished, bent, and torn. One result was the Great Lakes, excavated by the glacier as it advanced and retreated. One lobe of the Laurentide ice sheet came to rest just off the present coast of Massachusetts, having shoved great quantities of rocky detritus ahead of it into a great curved embankment called a glacial moraine; this is what we know today as the southern arm of Cape Cod. Such moraines, large and small, are one of the most noticeable features of glacial advance and retreat, and they were one of the main features besides erratic boulders that tipped off Agassiz and his predecessors to the idea of glaciers.

ICE AGE ECOSYSTEMS

During the maximum extent of the Wisconsinan glacial period, the overall global temperature was about 12°F lower than today's, and near the glacier's edge it was—on average—18° cooler. Anticyclonic winds spun clockwise above the glacier, and cold winds tended to sweep downslope from ice to the exposed land near the glacier, which would have tended *generally* to be tundra underlain by permafrost for perhaps some 125 miles south. All in all, it was a seemingly inhospitable place, but no more so than much of the Arctic today. On the other hand, local conditions at the glacier's edge varied considerably, depending on a host of factors: weather, topography, and so forth, but especially elevation.

The very presence of the huge blanket of ice had a modulating effect, in fact, on the seasonal weather south of the glaciers (and to their northwest in ice-free parts of Alaska), making summers generally less hot than today and winters less cold. One effect of the cyclonic winds was to render the eastern lands of the United States wetter and some western lands drier. At the same time, cooler, moist air was common in today's American Southwest and Great Basin area, with far more rainfall then than now. One result was the occurrence of huge so-called pluvial lakes, some reaching the proportions of inland seas, such as the Lake Michigan–sized Lake Bonneville in Utah, once more than 1,200 feet deep, the remains of which can now be seen in Great Salt Lake and the Bonneville Salt Flats, where maniacs set land-speed records on the dead-flat bottom of the old lake. The closest thing we have today to those pluvial lakes is Kenya's Lake Turkana, which, being so shallow, changes its size annually based on rainfall. North America's pluvial lakes occurred in the Southwest's many closed basins and achieved their maximum extent and depth at the very height of the glacial maximum. They seethed with life, serving among other things as seasonal homes for what were probably millions of migratory birds, their marshy shores attracting all kinds of life-forms, including, at some point, humans.

Even at the time of the glaciers' maximum extent, meltwater burst from beneath them, depositing sediments in valleys and on outwash plains—vast quantities of silt and sand sometimes a hundred feet deep. Strong winds blew the silt and sand elsewhere. Huge areas of active sand dunes formed downwind, and minute particles of silt, called loess, blew across much of the Midwest, mantling vast areas far beyond the narrow, tundralike region near the glacier's edge. Today we owe a great deal of the agricultural productivity of the American Midwest to this blanket of loess created between 29,000 and 12,000 years ago, when the glaciers were still advancing and the lands beyond were cold, dry, and windy.

At the end of the glacial period, virtually all paleoecological maps show a thin line of tundra vegetation next to the glaciers, with pockets of tundra leading southward along the tops of the Appalachian Mountains. In the east, in a wide belt south of the tundra, such coniferous trees as jack pine, fir, and spruce marked the landscape, and south of that, temperate forests of southern pine, oak, and hickory dominated. Florida, a much wider peninsula then, supported cypress, gum, and sand dune scrub. The southern plains were mostly grassland, while the western mountain region was dominated by mosaics of plant communities ranging from desert scrub to juniper and pine woodlands. All of these life zones were in relatively constant flux as the local conditions changed. As we will see later, this snapshot, with its strip of tundra between the glacier's edge and the lands to the south, is extremely soft-focus—that is, coarse-grained. I would find out soon enough that the world in those days at the end of the Pleistocene was not so simple. And it would only get more complicated.

THE HOLOCENE SCENE

In eastern Washington State one finds an astounding landscape called the Channeled Scablands. It is a place of huge labyrinthine channels cut into bedrock, enormous basins carved from basalt headlands, some up to eight miles wide and two hundred feet deep. Tremendous boulders and chunks of basalt have been moved around through the channels. Extinct waterfalls abound. Not far off, in the bottom of an extinct glacial lake in Montana called Lake Missoula, geologists have found ripple marks like those you see in beach sand and on river bottoms, but these Bunyanesque ripples are twenty feet high and spaced as much as three hundred feet apart. Here, obviously, there be monsters, or at least Paul Bunyan.

The first scientific exploration of the Channeled Scablands was by a geologist, J. Harlen Betz, who wrote about them in 1923, explaining that no normal erosional process would have had the energy to produce such gigantic features. Instead it had to have been . . . yes . . . a catastrophic *flood*. He reasoned that an ice dam holding back the waters of an enormous glacial lake filled with meltwater in western Montana had failed, and untold quantities of water had exploded onto the land to the west. His account was met with extensive derision on the part of his colleagues. After all, catastrophic floods were still a sensitive matter among geologists, who had only recently suffered being reviled by religionists for knocking Noah's Flood as the Big One. Just when all that dust had settled and catastrophism was out, here comes Betz challenging uniformitarianism with this talk of a fantastic flood of mythic proportion. But the later discovery of the ripples of Lake Missoula proved Betz right. Only the passage of water over some kind of ground, like sand on a flat beach, causes ripples.

This so-called Spokane flood was surely one of the most appalling floods in the continent's existence, but the many floodwaters pouring out of glacial lakes and the glacier itself from about 25,000 to 7,000 years ago had to have been one of the dominant terrors facing any sentient beings present. Woe surely betided any creature downstream of an ice dam when it gave way.

Given the chance, of course, water will make maximum haste downhill and back to the oceans from whence it came. What had begun as fairly gentle braided streams and rivers issuing out from beneath the advancing glacier would have turned into land-gouging torrents, roaring across the landscape to the sea. The huge Mississippi drainage that extends today from the Rockies to the Appalachians essentially came into being in this period as millions of cubic *miles* of water were freed from the ice. One source was a vast lake called Lake Agassiz, five times the size of Lake Superior today. Its waters flowed into the Mississippi system and at least once, when some dam of ice or debris gave way, sent a blast of water downstream strong enough to move the giant river into another valley altogether.

In addition, some excellent real estate on the eastern and western margins of the continent was being inundated by the rising sea levels, and wildlife and people were forced to migrate inland before the tide. As the salt water rose, it filled the mouths of some of the great, rushing rivers, slowing them down and forming marshes and bays large and small. Chesapeake Bay and San Francisco Bay, the two largest bays in the lower forty-eight states, came about at this time. Seawater created sounds, such as Puget Sound, and inland seas that, as the land rose, became landlocked and in due course turned into freshwater lakes. New York's Lake Champlain was one of these. By 10,000 years ago, Beringia was dry land no more, but it persisted for a while under shallow water that could be crossed by large mammals, humans included, when the water seasonally turned to ice. The rate of the oceans' encroachment on land was occasionally slowed by the rising of the earth's crust as it escaped from the weight of the glacier; some places, such as the coast of Maine, are still rising slightly. Elsewhere, the huge pluvial lakes of the Southwest were shrinking, evaporating, leaving increasingly salty waters behind, until most of them were nothing more than a monotonously flat, dead, white, and rapidly diminishing memory in the genes of migratory birds.

Estimates suggest that as the result of changes in the earth's orbital position as well as a rise in atmospheric carbon dioxide, solar radiation increased near the southern margin of the ice sheets by about 5 percent over the 5,000 years beginning 15,000 years ago. The increase in temperature not only doomed the glaciers' southern extremities but also led to the evaporation of the pluvial lakes, lower rainfall in the Southwest, greater rainfall over and near the ice, the decay of alpine glaciers, the rise of mountains' tree lines, and a host of other changes that altered the landscape at varying rates and in a patchwork of outcomes.

One such change took place in the Southwest, where mountains and small chains of mountains are often isolated in the middle of large flat areas in what is called basin and range topography. Here, as the lowlands heated up and approached the status of desert, plants and animals that had thrived in colder, damper times would have been outrun by the climate, unable to migrate northward toward suitably cooler areas fast enough, so they had no place to go but up. As a result, today you can drive up the mountains that loom over Tucson in southern Arizona, for example, where summer temperatures are typically above 100° F., and in the course of an hour pass through five distinct ecological zones ranging from dry Sonoran desert lands to the more humid summit with approximately the same climate and the same vegetation as the lands around Hudson Bay, 2,000 miles to the north. The marmots, Engelmann spruces, and other subarctic lifeforms isolated high up on these "sky islands" are direct and literal relics of the Ice Age.

During the Clovis era, which began about 11,500 years ago and continued for a few hundred years thereafter, the living things of North America were undergoing what was one of the more traumatic times in the history of the earth. For people living here at the time, the world may well have seemed an unstable place. Familiar animals might suddenly disappear, seeking their favored food, which had also gone somewhere else. What might have been a good place for your parents might change into something that would not support you. People would have been on the move.

The shifts in overall climate, regional weather, and some, but not all, local weather profoundly altered even those stately, semipermanent, and slow-to-react ecosystems called forests. We tend to think of forests as coherent communities consisting of several species of trees, some of which are dominant, even diagnostic. They change very slowly—after all, a maple tree can live for four hundred years, so something that suddenly makes it difficult for maple seeds to germinate may have little immediate effect on a maple forest. But 10,000 years ago, in parts of the Midwest, spruces that had reigned supreme for millennia gave up the ghost in a mere century and a half.

On the other hand, ponderosa pines, those grand sentinels of our high, parklike forests, spread like weeds from a few cool places in the South to cover the upper reaches of the Rocky Mountains. Deciduous trees—oaks, hickories, maples, beeches—moved north and all about, each species responding in its own time and with its own speed to the changing local conditions. Some trees moved north thanks to windborne seeds, but one of the more efficient tree movers was the jay, which developed the habit of running off with the acorns of oak trees and depositing them in little caches on the edge of the forest, where the sun might raise them into trees. At this time of the world, oak trees moved at the rate of about a thousand feet a year—or two hundred miles in a millennium. In many regions near to and far from the edge of the ice, what appear to have been patchwork quilts of differing plant communities (and, on the edges where two or more plant communities met and mixed, even more complex plant communities) became more uniform. This was, in fact, an unscrambling of plants and their communities back to a previous, preglacial state. The glacier's edge had brought about situations where plants and animals from separate ecosystems had been thrown together; now, in this newest warm period of the many that punctuated the million and a half years of the Pleistocene, they were dispersed again.

One result was a great many more species going extinct, not unlike what had happened in all the previous interstadials. These ecological changes were driven, of course, by the relatively rapid climate change that brought on the relatively rapid disintegration of the glacial ice: by 7,000 years ago, the ice was about what it is today in extent and location. The particularly important results of the overall climate change under way were the reestablishment of four-season continental climates and the increase in seasonal extremes—colder winters, hotter summers—which unquestionably stressed the creatures that had adapted to somewhat more consistent year-round conditions. There's only so much cold a southern white pine can take, for example, and only so much summer heat a blue spruce can live through. In this chaotic late Pleistocene–early Holocene period, the limits of everyone and everything were being tested. Creatures needed to readjust to new ranges. Among mammals, size transformation proved a more salutary strategy than the conservative one of simply sweating it out: the 350-pound beaver gave way to a successor more like today's, for example, smaller in size and behaviorally more clever. Changing patterns of precipitation (and evaporation) would have created similar challenges. New habitats were being created in virtually every part of North America, a shifting kaleidoscope of ecosystems that meant tremendous change for any creatures present, including humans.

In many regions, especially in the lands west of the hundredth meridian and east of the Sierras in California, the result of intensifying seasonal extremes was the creation of *far less diverse* communities—what are called monocultures. The vast plains in the nation's midsection began to sort themselves out into broad, vertically striped regions of long-grass, medium-grass, and short-grass prairies in response to different moisture regimes and seasonal differences. This was all to the good for bison, which proliferated along with many other grazers, though it favored smaller animals. The gigantic bison of the late Pleistocene—a huge creature with long horns—gave way to smaller and smaller species until, for a time at least, today's *Bison bison* became (along with the wildebeests of Africa) one of the most numerous grazing species the world has ever seen. Similarly, the condor that was ancestral to today's California condor, a bird with a ten-foot wingspan, was *Teratornis terribilis,* twice the size of today's version with a wingspan of *twenty feet,* one of the largest feathered flying birds ever. Such a bird, soaring overhead spying out a corpse, would have blanked out the sun for a noticeable moment and, for my money, could have been the creature that gave rise to the Thunderbird of American Indian legend.

All of the Europeans who saw the great herds of bison on the American plains and wrote about them were at a loss for words to describe their numbers, the thunder of their passing, their sheer multitude. One of the earliest European witnesses to the great bison herds was Fray Alonso de Benavides, custodian of missions in New Mexico in the late 1620s. In a *Mission* (report) to King Philip IV of Spain in which he described this now-thirty-year-old addition to the Spanish empire, he wrote of the bison, "I have dwelt on these cattle because they are so numerous and widespread that we have found no end to them. . . . There are so many of them that they blot out the plains. These cattle by themselves would be enough to make a prince very powerful, if he had or were given a means by which to convey them elsewhere." That is hardly poetry, but then NASA sent no poets to the moon either. In any event, until they became a market commodity for consumption and use by people other than the local Plains Indian tribes, the vast bison herds, paralleled only by the caribou in the Arctic and Subarctic, were the last truly astonishing wildlife spectacle in temperate America. Even those enormous herds were probably pretty thin soup compared with what the first Americans stumbled onto when they made their way south of the ice. This astonishing animal life of late Pleistocene–early Holocene America was part of the promise—and part of the terror—that the small bands of the first Americans faced. Whenever they got here, at whatever time they arrived, and by whatever route, they found themselves among not only myriad sources of meat on the hoof but also a spectacular array of large, swift predators with which they might have to compete—or from which they would need to escape. In those days, sharing the world with wildlife had a somewhat different connotation from what it might today.

CHAPTER THREE

CHARISMATIC MEGAFAUNA

The mammoth stands in its final agony, the oily black ground giving way under him, sucking at his legs, while a ferocious lion snarls, mouth agape, lethal fangs glistening. Enormous vultures, those handmaidens of death, await the end in solemn congregation, their huge wings folded over their backs. Scenes like this must have taken place often throughout much of the continent over the eons, as well as right here amid the sounds of the internal combustion engines roaring along Wilshire Boulevard between Fairfax and La Brea Avenues in Los Angeles. For this is the site of the La Brea Tar Pits, the single most productive source of the remains of the grand megafauna that roamed the North American continent in the late Pleistocene age. Judging from the museum's confident reconstruction of the mammoth's final hours, as well as numerous museum dioramas elsewhere and countless paintings and illustrations of this late Pleistocene/early Holocene bestiary that have appeared over the years in museum dioramas, books, magazines, and elsewhere, you would guess that there isn't much we don't know about those creatures and their world. But among the many unknowns are why they died out and exactly when. Another unknown is exactly how important a factor these large mammals were for the first Americans, whenever it was that they arrived here.

For example, it is hard to imagine that the first Americans could easily have avoided the attentions of the several species of lions that stalked the herds of huge bison and other grazers. Or the clutches of the short-faced bear, a predator that stood as high at the shoulder as a moose and could probably run, at least in spurts, as fast as the camels and horses that, among other prey, it ate. Known to science from minimal remains and called *Arctodus simus,* this graceful monster was almost certainly the most dangerous predator that roamed Ice Age America. Not long ago, a Russian paleontologist visited the Natural History Museum in Utah and was shown the largest short-faced bear femur known—it was longer than an entire human leg. The Russian erupted in exasperation, asking "Why does the United States have the biggest everything on the planet?"

It is hard to imagine that this gigantic bear, capable of rearing up to some fifteen feet or higher, does not still lurk somewhere in the cultural

Short-faced bear, Arctodus simus, *drawn by Bill Parsons.*

memory of the first Americans' descendants—in their worst nightmares and perhaps in their stories of myth time. Could they have become the giants that in Navajo histories of the beginning of things had to be killed by the monster-slaying hero twin sons of the sun so that the world could become safe for people? Some scholars of the ice ages, in an only somewhat more scientifically tenable suggestion, have opined that human beings (who have enough trouble killing a brown bear with so rudimentary a weapon as a spear) could not have settled and survived in North America until the short-faced bear went extinct.

And where are the elephants in American Indian stories? After all, their ancestors—those highly carnivorous people called Clovis—supposedly hunted these great beasts, maybe even to extinction, and made them a principal part of their diet, along with giant ground sloths and the other vast mammals that roamed the warming plains and plowed through the expanding forests and swamps. In fact, there is at least one vestigial tale that suggests a memory of an elephantine presence: the Beothuk people of Newfoundland (who probably were the *"skraelings"* who harassed Leif Eriksson and the other Vikings when they showed up there out of the northern mists, a millennium ago) had a story about a monstrous quadruped with a long, pendulous nose. But all such speculation about the origins of myths and dreams, though wonderful fun, is just that—speculation—and as lacking in any means of resolution one way or another as are the tenets of Jungian psychology or the disputes of postmodernist literary critics.

By as early as the 1920s, scientists knew a great deal about the kinds of animals that roamed Ice Age America. Charles Knight painted enormous murals in the American Museum of Natural History in New York, images that are basically fixed in the recesses of the public mind that dwell even briefly on this amazing era. Other images were not long in coming, and still today one sees in popular books, especially for kids, those wondrously crowded landscapes with herds of bison and other grazers, stalked by every kind of predator, and in the cramped, oblong foreground sloths and other bizarre specimens going about their business, mostly oblivious of one another. Probably they weren't really quite so crowded.

We learn more about such creatures all the time. As this chapter was being written, paleontologists from the Denver Museum of Natural History announced the discovery in Porcupine Cave in Colorado of a particularly rich cache of Pleistocene mammals that dated back more than a million years, including some of the earliest known remains of such animals as cheetahs in North America. Was the cheetah an African beast that spread to here, or vice versa? We don't know all the answers even today. But we do know that the woolly rhinoceros that patrolled Europe and parts of Asia never made it to the New World. To this day no one knows why. Perhaps it was simply a matter of timing, which, when it comes to migrations through glacial environments, was as important as it is in show business.

AN ICE AGE BESTIARY

Through the 1.6 million years of the Pleistocene, the glaciers came and went on a schedule of approximately every 100,000 years, with 10,000- to 20,000-year warm interglacials in between. And remember that even during the glacial periods, there were times when things warmed up some-

Ice Age camel, Camelops herternus.

what. A migration from Asia across the Bering Sea needed to take place during glacial times, when the ice lowered the sea level enough to create Beringia (which was open for migratory business during much of the Pleistocene). Even earlier, in a warmer epoch altogether called the Pliocene, local glaciers, though nothing like the huge ice sheets of the Pleistocene, came and went in the north as well as on Antarctica, and a land bridge sometimes emerged between the two continents.

At various pre-Pleistocene times, then, Old World animals made it across to the New World. Many of these, like ancestral hyenas, were long extinct in the Americas by the time of the last great ice advance. Although North America would become a major zoological melting pot, it did also produce its own originals. Horses originated in North America as small three-toed creatures of the woodlands, and by late Pleistocene times they were much like today's Grevey's zebra, perhaps even with similar markings. Meanwhile, other equine forms—asses, true horses, and the unfortunately named half-asses—had evolved and were passing back and forth between the New World and Old World like commuters, so much so that it is still not clear if true horses and asses arose first in the New World or the Old. Camellike animals had their beginnings in the New World as well, producing three strains—in the ice ages—that were giant forms: camels with one hump like today's dromedary, llamas, and llamalike camels with

Llama, Palaeolama mirifica; *tapir,*
Tapius veroensis; *and equus,* Equus scotti.

humps. Gigantic tortoises, larger than those seen in the Galápagos Islands, waddled about, and beavers reached the weight and size of brown bears, some 350 pounds, but acted more like muskrats than dam-building beavers. Sloths were New World creatures and remained so, failing to make it past the ice into Asia. In the meantime, Old World mammals migrated here in great and noticeable quantities.

By 4 million years ago, two strains of elephantine creatures (a.k.a. proboscideans)—the mammoths and the mastodons—had long since roamed the North American continent, both deriving originally from Africa and having made their way from there into Europe and Asia. Mastodons were originally four-tusked, with both upper and lower tusks, but they lost the bottom ones and the uppers became long and curved. Otherwise, being what biologists call conservative, they changed little over time. Unlike the sociable elephants we know today, these slope-backed animals appear to have been loners for the most part. Ten to twelve feet at the shoulder, they

Mastodon, Mammut americanum.

fed chiefly on branches and other brushy material, perhaps with a preference for evergreens. Indeed, in both their habitat and their tendency to be loners, they were not unlike the moose with whom they would later share forested areas and swamps for a time. In late Pleistocene times, they were accordingly more common in the eastern portion of North America than in the more open lands of the West. In addition to Ice Age moose (and stag-moose, a moose-elk combo that was among the world's largest natural hat-racks ever) were elk, caribou, and deer. It would, in fact, take a highly expert student of deer to tell the difference between today's white-tailed deer and its direct ancestors 3 million years ago, so conservative were *they.* Other beasts still familiar today were numerous small mammals: badgers, shrews, moles, weasels, and both spotted and striped skunks.

The other elephantine creatures here were mammoths, monsters with extravagantly long curved tusks spiraling to the point where, especially among males, the tips often crossed each other, making them no longer useful for spearing enemies, though they were most likely devastating as clubs. The first mammoths in the New World were a breed of southern

Columbian mammoth, Mammuthus columbi.

mammoths that had slowly adapted to the cold of northeastern Asia but then readapted to slightly warmer climes in the southwestern parts of the United States and continued on southward, eventually populating South America as well. Wandering about in small groups not unlike today's elephant herds, they were more social than the mastodons and, some like to speculate, perhaps matriarchal, as are today's elephants (which are in fact a different strain of proboscidian altogether). Mostly creatures of open areas such as plains, they were rarely in competition with the forest-dwelling mastodons.

In addition, there were the woolly mammoths—beasts of Siberia, the frozen north, and the edge of the glaciers in North America. The woolly mammoth typically was about fourteen feet tall, more than a foot taller than the largest elephant ever measured, the huge African one that has long stood guard in the rotunda of the Smithsonian's National Museum of Natural History. The woolly mammoth had a shorter trunk than the southern mammoth as well as smaller ears (the better to conserve heat), a subcutaneous fat layer, and a woolly undercoat covered by a coat of long black hair. Many woolly mammoth tusks have turned up with the bottom surfaces heavily worn, evidently a result of using them to shove snow and ice aside to find morsels of pasturage underneath. As the late paleontologist Björn Kurtén wrote, the woolly mammoth is "the embodiment of the ice age. Long may it live in our imagination, a black, top-heavy shape looming up in the swirling snow, great tusks gleaming: to our forefathers, perhaps, a demigod."

Bison, Bison antiquus.

Less demigodlike, surely, were the burro-sized mammoths that evolved on Santa Rosa Island off California, an example of the dwarfism often found in island populations where predators are few if not altogether absent. When all the mammoths (and the shorter, stockier mastodons) finally ran up against the forces unleashed at the end of the Pleistocene, they vanished—except for a population of woolly mammoths that survived in the frigid steppes of Wrangel Island off Siberia until Roman times.

Other notable Eurasian migrants to North America were gigantic bison—much larger, longer-horned, and probably less fleet than today's, but capable of hanging out in the frozen lands of Alaska until an ice-free corridor allowed them to move south, where they found something akin to bison nirvana in the open lands of the West, spreading eastward as well as southward from there. Present in North America as early as 30,000 years ago, they were replaced by slightly smaller, slightly shorter-horned bison called *Bison antiquus,* which survived well after the end of the Ice Age and upon which early Americans preyed with considerable skill and effectiveness. These imperceptibly graded into the still smaller bison of today. Meanwhile musk oxen (but not, strangely enough, the equally well adapted yak) came in from Siberia across Beringia, which itself may have served as something of a hotbed of evolution when it appeared above the waves for lengthy periods. The land bridge was a swinging door that swung both ways.

One other notable no-show, at least south of the ice, was the saiga antelope, which did make it into North America but never penetrated into the interior of the continent. Today's American "antelope," otherwise and more correctly called the pronghorn, is in fact not an antelope but a goat relative, itself the descendant of a far larger Ice Age version.

Sometime between 3 million and 4 million years ago, members of a wholly different fauna were added to what had begun in North America or found its way here from Asia. A land bridge (the current isthmus of Panama) appeared between South and North America, the result of islands being shoved upward on a rising piece of land as one gigantic tectonic plate rose up above another. This in turn gave rise to what has been called the Great Faunal Interchange—though it was but one of several intercontinental interchanges, as we have seen. For millions of years the two New World continents had been separated, not by much in the way of water but enough to prevent most mammals from crossing. Armadillos came about in South America and made it north, reaching seven feet in length. Armadillos and sloths are both of the mammalian group called edentates, meaning "toothless," and another edentate was the huge, armored creature called the glyptodont. This oddball mammal of riverbanks looked more like an enormous turtle with its vaulted carapace, but it had a long tail, it measured ten feet in length and five feet in height, and it moved around on short, pillarlike legs. Even its tail was armored with a tubelike arrangement of rings of armor.

South America had been isolated for millions and millions of years after it separated from Africa and moved west. It had its own special fauna, much of which consisted of marsupials. Among the other South American oddities was a variety of large flightless birds, at least one of which made its way to Florida once the land bridge came about. Known as *Titanis,* it was an immense, ostrich-sized predatory bird with thick legs and a curved beak like that of an eagle. Flightlessness often occurs among birds, but usually in places where there is little or nothing to worry about in terms of predators, in particular, on islands. *Titanis* and the other large flightless birds of South America flourished because the mammals (including the

Giant armadillo, Dasypus bellus, *and giant sloth,* Eremotherium rusconii.

marsupials) remained relatively small. Once it reached North America, *Titanis*'s career was doomed, for while it might have fended off those early hyenas, it would have been no match for the lions and other carnivores that were present.

Sloths evidently made their way north across the new land bridge, though some suggest that giant sloths, good swimmers, could have made it over before a dry-land passage existed by island-hopping. In the other direction, small mammals and large invaded the south, perhaps in part to escape the deteriorating climate of the north. Mastodons, horses, camelids, bears, and deer were followed by big predators such as lions, and this new fauna virtually overwhelmed the endemic one.

In the north, in addition to the short-faced bear, lions reigned supreme. These were not the small lionlike cats of today—pumas, jaguars, and so forth—but lions that reached as much as eight feet in length, huge animals with brains that were evidently larger than those of any other lions then or now, suggesting a high degree of sociality and effectiveness in the hunt. They may have been a bit slower than today's smaller, sleeker lions found in Africa (where lions originated some 2 million years ago), but they were also stronger. The brainy, brawny American strain made it south as far as Peru, making the lion at the end of the Pleistocene the most widely distributed wild animal in the world, present on five continents and missing from only Australia and Antarctica.

In North America, on the open lands south of the glacier, the lion was joined in predatory swagger by the American version of the cheetah, the fleetest land animal known today and doubtless just as fast in Pleistocene times, along with at least two forms of saber-toothed cats. One of these was the scimitar cat, a big animal with long fangs (but nothing like those of the saber-toothed "tiger") that were sharp-edged and serrated, the perfect tool for slicing meat. These cats, called *Homotherium,* had long front legs and short back legs and apparently preferred to hunt baby mammoths, perhaps attacking with a slicing bite to the neck and then retreating until the dangerous adult mammoths went away. But the signature Pleistocene predator was the misnamed, fantastic saber-toothed tiger, *Smilodon fatalis,* a Latinate name that even without translation sounds fit for a serial killer in a thriller novel. It was the size of today's African lion but heavier and shorter of leg, its upper canine teeth thrusting down below its lower jaw by several inches. It may have used these protruding sabers with its mouth closed to slice up its prey, which it would have overcome with sheer strength, not necessarily speed. It was a loner like a tiger and less brainy than the lions, with which it must have competed to some extent. It was a heavily armed supercarnivore, and its entire jaw (which opened to 95 degrees), skull, and neck were devoted to the moment when the huge, glistening, serrated saber teeth would stab into hot flesh. At the same time, it may not have been especially bright—it was the second most frequently trapped carnivore in the La Brea Tar Pits (more than 1,000 have been found). The most frequent was the dire wolf (about 1,600), larger and heavier but shorter of leg than the timber wolf, with a big head and hugely strong jaws. Dire wolves, which ranged throughout unglaciated North America and as far south as Peru, probably hunted in packs and most likely hunted the large bison, *Bison antiquus*. One can imagine a pack of them in a snarling frenzy over some prey, driving the slow-moving *Smilodon* away, but one can equally imagine them slinking away upon the approach of the big-toothed monster.

By the late Pleistocene, then, North America's population of large mammals included homegrown fauna, some of which were more than a million years old, joined by Eurasian and South American migrants, some of such long standing as to be practically natives—in all, an astonishing array of prey and predator unparalleled in diversity anywhere before or since. And it was into this unbelievably rich, partly familiar but mostly exotic, promising, terrifying menagerie that the first Americans must have come. These new, bipedal arrivals, the most charismatic megafauna ever to hit the hemisphere—whenever exactly they arrived—were just as much children of the ice as were the Pleistocene giants they encountered in their migrations.

CHILDREN OF THE COLD

The trail leading to the New World ultimately began thousands of miles from Beringia in the savannas of east Africa. There, sometime around 2.6 or 2.5 million years ago, in the late Pliocene era, a diminutive hominid began to make stone tools sufficiently standardized to be recognizable as the products of human agency rather than objects shaped by natural processes. The hominid in question was either a member of the genus *Australopithecus* or, more likely, the earliest representative of our own genus, *Homo*. These first recognizable stone tools are assigned to the Oldowan tradition (after Olduvai Gorge, the place where they were first found, identified, and described, which is called their "type locality" in archaeology-speak). They constitute the earliest bona fide evidence of cultural behavior in the long history of life on the planet. These creatures doubtless made other tools of other materials—biodegradable ones such as wood, bone, horn, antler, shell, and even plant fiber—but virtually all that remains are the stone artifacts, and this is a preservational bias that has shaped our thinking ever since.

The earliest tool users whose physical remains we have found left their lithic handiwork at Kada Gona, Ethiopia, about 2.6 million years ago and slightly later at other sites in the Hadar country and around Lake Turkana in northern Kenya. They were smallish creatures, more ape than human, at least to the casual eye, and they had brains about a third the size of ours. However, in the ratio of brain volume to body mass, they were the smartest land mammals of their time. But while we tend to think of these creatures in terms of their brains, it is much more appropriate to characterize them in terms of the opposite end of their anatomy, their feet.

By the time the more gracile of the several kinds of east African australopithecines or the earliest representative of the genus *Homo* began manufacturing stone tools, they had already been walking on two legs for several million years. Indeed, habitual upright posture and bipedal locomotion are probably the most profound single adaptations that our remote ancestors ever made. We may well never know just what feature of the environment or other factor triggered this fundamental and revolutionary adaptation, but a mid-Pliocene cold snap between about 6.5 million and 5 million years ago probably played a role. According to this scenario, expansion of the Antarctic ice cap dropped sea levels worldwide, including that of the Mediterranean. This in turn changed the precipitation pattern of African rain forests and ultimately caused their contraction. This reduction in forest cover caused many arboreal species of primates to pass from the scene, while others became, at least in part, terrestrial.

For at least some of these new ground dwellers, bipedalism offered several advantages. Now they could cover relatively great distances with a low expenditure of energy. Life in the trees can be fairly simple, if today's monkeys are any indication. You need mostly to move around in a fairly leisurely pursuit of the regular and cyclical fruiting of the variety of forest trees. Once on the ground, however, you need to forage much more widely for adequate food. In the same vein, bipedalism frees your forelimbs to carry foods you've collected from one place to another and also to manipulate objects (sticks, for example) that could, in turn, make food getting easier. With freed forelimbs—now arms with distinct hands, in fact—this bipedal creature could also carry its infant young from place to place.

There are yet other advantages of walking on two feet. Standing or walking erect puts your field of vision above the height of tall savanna grass, giving a primate that is largish a bit of an edge, to be sure, but he was no match for some of the savanna's predators. Also, it has been suggested that upright posture helps in using the body, especially the upper body and arms, in threat displays—pounding the chest or other aggressive gestures.

Whatever the primary advantage of bipedal locomotion—and I suspect it relates directly to enhanced mobility with reduced effort—it is virtually certain, as noted by Richard G. Klein, a paleoanthropologist at the University of Chicago, that all of the "benefits" of bipedalism operated in tandem. With all of bipedalism's presumed advantages, however, it did not happen overnight.

Indeed, in many ways, the earliest bipeds were far more apelike in certain respects than is usually realized. They continued for millennia to use trees as sleeping areas, foraging localities, and refuges. But also, and more basically, their bodies retained such "primitive" characteristics as a pronounced difference in size between males and females (called sexual dimorphism). Even so, as noted, by 2.5 million years ago or thereabouts these bipeds *were* making tools. They had crossed, at least in my view, the threshold of humanity.

At about this time, another series of dramatic environmental events again transformed the stage upon which these earliest tool-using actors and actresses performed. Between about 3 million and 2 million years ago, it appears, a series of cooling and drying episodes began in the middle latitudes of the planet. Ultimately they were linked to, if not directly caused by, the onset of glacial cycling in the Northern Hemisphere that began around this time. In Africa, as one result, the forest cover diminished again, the open savanna grew, and the turnover of forest-adapted species to open-ground species continued.

While these changes are ultimately a reflection of cold glacial and warmer interglacial interludes in the north, in Africa and other subtropical settings the most important transformations were a matter not so much of increasing temperature as of a change in the *patterns* of precipitation. Ultimately, shifts in both the volume and the seasonality of rainfall reduced the extent of the African forests and extended the grasslands. However far removed they were, these events still mirrored—albeit with some time lag—the vicissitudes of the northern ice.

Within this changing world, largish, predominantly ground-dwelling, bipedal primates had several adaptive options. One group headed off anatomically and behaviorally in the direction of chewing tough vegetable foods. These were our Pliocene cousins, the so-called robust australopithecines (*Australopithecus aethiopicus, Paranthropus boisei,* and *Paranthropus robustus*). They remained relatively small-brained, apparently made no tools, and ultimately became extinct. The second group remained more omnivorous with, if anything, a preference for the meat end of the dietary spectrum. They developed progressively larger brain cases, as well as the systematic use and manufacture of tools, and later on became you and me.

Once under way in the body of *Homo habilis* ("handy person"), the synergy between increased cranial capacity and enhanced production and use of tools continued and escalated, impelled in no small part by the constantly changing stimuli of a highly plastic environment. By about 1.8 million to 1.7 million years ago, at the last glimmer of the Pliocene and the dawn of the Pleistocene, a new version of us appeared in east Africa—not coincidentally, with a better tool kit.

Named *Homo ergaster* and equipped with a substantially larger body (the males may have reached six feet in height) and a proportionately bigger brain than its predecessor's, this species not only was fully adapted to terrestrial life but could also cope with climatic extremes its predecessors could not survive. *Homo ergaster* appeared in an Africa where the temperature and precipitation regime was changing from coolish and moister to very warm and very dry. They had attained the same body size as essentially modern humans, had lost the hairy body covering of their predecessors, and were probably the first of our remote ancestors to be able to cope with genuinely arid environments. Indeed, with a few minor differences, *Homo ergaster* is anatomically modern—but only from the neck down.

Though still not in our league brainwise, *Homo ergaster* was nonetheless more than intelligent enough to refine, and thereby transform, the Oldowan tool kit into a more sophisticated technology (called Acheulean) and to carry it to parts of Africa where tool-using hominids had rarely or never gone. (This new "Acheulean" tool kit was named for Saint-Acheul in

France, where it was first discovered.) More significantly, especially from the perspective of this book, *Homo ergaster* was probably the first hominid to leave Africa for Europe and the Middle East and initiate the trail that would ultimately end in the New World.

The timing of the initial exodus from Africa into the uninhabited vastness of Eurasia is a subject at least as contentious as that of the appearance of humans in the New World. Based on controversial data from D'manisi in the Caucasus of Georgia, Longuppo Cave in south-central China, and heavily disputed dates from Java, some authorities argue for a very early dispersal out of Africa, as long as two million years ago, well before *Homo ergaster* even comes onto the scene.

A more conservative and traditional view places the first African exodus at about 1 million years ago. This view is based on better-controlled information from Ubeidiya in the Jordan Valley of Israel. However, very few other sites exist anywhere outside Africa that are conclusively as old as Ubeidiya, and sites reliably dated between about 1 million and 800,000 B.P. (before the present) are equally rare. Even if the first diaspora occurred at about 1 million B.P. or even earlier, there is scant evidence for a human presence in much of Eurasia until much later.

Recent reevaluations of the available European evidence suggest only a limited human presence before about 600,000 to 500,000 years ago, though earlier colonizations that failed may have occurred in Spain and Italy. Similarly, with the exceptions noted before, the human penetration of the farthest reaches of middle- and lower-latitude Asia (north China and Java) are rather younger than 1 million B.P.

"When they got there" is actually less important than the simple fact that they did get there. It is that arrival that constitutes a watershed event in the evolution of the genus *Homo*. Whether the first sojourner was *Homo habilis* at 1.9 million years ago or *Homo ergaster* at 1.7 million to 1.0 million years ago is less important than the elementary fact that two of these creatures did leave Africa and did occupy areas of far greater topographic and environmental diversity than anything "back home." That they were able to do so speaks volumes not only to their increasing capacity to use culture—inventions of various kinds—to buffer the variability inherent in new environments, but also to the continuing interplay between cultural behavior and continued increases in brain size and cognitive capacity.

Three factors were critical to the successful penetration of Eurasia. Only one is found in the archaeological record: more sophisticated stone tools such as hand axes and cleavers used for a wide array of chores, the Swiss Army knives of their day. But those foraging hominids needed the ability to control fire and to make tools of wood, bone, and plant fiber, not just stone. All these innovations were needed for subtropical creatures to survive in environments much more severe than any they had ever experienced before. All were essential where episodes of cold, harsh weather were recurrent features of the region—especially at higher elevations in northern latitudes. If, as seems reasonable, the physical and cultural evolution of *Homo habilis* and its immediate ancestors in Africa was conditioned by a more varied regimen of rainfall brought on by cyclic (and distant) cold spells, their more modern descendants had to cope all the more directly with the effects of seasonal cold.

Hand axes and cleavers of stone, the hallmarks of the so-called Acheulean tool kit, were fairly widespread especially after 600,000 years ago, but conclusive indication of the use of fire is vanishingly rare. Given the role fire must have played in coping with colder climates in Europe and Asia, this is surprising. What evidence there is of early use of fire is equivocal at best. All the heat-altered sediments, dispersed ash and charcoal, and burned stone tools that archaeologists have turned up at some early sites could just as easily have been caused naturally, for example by lightning. Presently, the best evidence of the human use of fire is no older than 1.5 million to 1.4 million years ago in east and south Africa. That is well after the proposed (and very controversial) early exit from the continent but considerably before the generally accepted date of human dispersal.

Outside Africa, evidence of the possible use of fire is problematic before about 500,000 to 250,000 years ago, when unmistakable hearths have been documented at a site called Locality 1 at Zhoukoudian in north China. In France, Spain, and central Europe, scant evidence exists, most of it more recent than 400,000 to 300,000 years ago. Actual hearths or fireplaces appear quite late in Europe and the Near East, but this may well reflect inadequate field recognition and recovery techniques, not a genuine absence of fire. Once again, however, the mere presence of humans in seasonally cold areas says more about the capacity of later hominids to adapt than does the incidence of firepits.

Even rarer than hearths are indications of nondurable artifacts of wood, bone, or fiber. While this is hardly surprising given the highly friable nature of such artifacts in most archaeological settings, their absence has lent undue importance to the relatively common stone tools. This bias in what has been preserved and what hasn't has in turn helped create (and sustain) an image of Late Pliocene and Early Pleistocene technology that is not only wrong for that time but for virtually all later periods. To be sure, stone was an important component of the tool kits of the first wayfarers outside Africa, but it is virtually certain that stone was always a minority element in their technological suite.

A dramatic and wholly unexpected glimpse of the nondurable part of early Eurasian tool kits was recently recovered under exceptional preservational circumstances at Schöningen in Germany. There, in lakeside deposits nearly 400,000 years old, a series of carefully made wooden throwing spears (javelins) attest to the role that perishable artifacts must have played in the conquest of midlatitude Europe.

By no later than 200,000 to 150,000 years ago, descendants of the original hominids who left Africa included a variety of forms ranging from robust proto-Neanderthals in Europe and the Near East to "almost" anatomical moderns in Africa and, perhaps, remarkably conservative (at least in an anatomical sense) hominids in southeast Asia. Whatever their appearance, they had much larger brains than their forefathers and -mothers and increasingly sophisticated durable technology, and in most areas had established themselves in virtually the full range of ice-free habitats available across Eurasia. Notable people-free zones were portions of unglaciated central and eastern Europe as well as interior north-central and northeastern Asia, including Siberia. Here the severity of the Pleistocene climate—even in the absence of glacial ice sheets—still posed a formidable barrier to permanent occupation. While it is likely that scattered bands of humans moved into some of these areas during warmer interglacials and milder interstadials, they probably retreated as soon as weather took a downturn.

Of course, at this time (some 100,000 years ago), no human had set foot in Australia—separated from mainland southeast Asia by sixty-two miles of open water—or any part of the entire New World.

The penultimate steps in the trail to these virgin landscapes would be taken not by any archaic representatives of *Homo sapiens* (*neanderthalensis* or otherwise) but by fully modern humans of our own genus (*Homo*), species (*sapiens*), and subspecies (*sapiens*). Paleoanthropologists, archaeologists, and geneticists all disagree intensely over the question of whether we emerged with our current cranial capacity and brainpower, as well as our fully modern physiques, only once in Africa or many times around the world (meaning that one species evolved several times from multiple ancestors in several regions—which is, frankly, pretty hard for some to imagine, perhaps all the more so because it smacks of the nineteenth-century polygenism that was so badly tainted by the contemporary racist worldview). For some scholars, this is a fascinating brouhaha, but it actually has very little to do with the main tale of this book. However many "homes" (or points of origin) our single kind may ultimately be able to claim, it was creatures just like us who constructed the watercraft used to colonize Australia and who ultimately took the first unwitting steps into a new hemisphere.

Unlike their southern seafaring kin, who wound up among the kangaroos and koalas and tropical forests and deserts of Australia, the populations that initially drifted into northeast Asia and Siberia were true children of the cold. They had been shaped by at least nine glacial cycles, at least since they had left Africa, and, armed with a highly elaborated severe-weather technology, these northern colonists were fully equipped to thrive in places where their predecessors would not or could not have gone. Indeed, they had a number of things in common with the woolly mammoths and other gigantic grazers such as oversized musk oxen and now-extinct elklike animals with racks the size of a small automobile that they unknowingly followed into the New World.

To the anthropocentric and even more to the nationalistic among us, appearing on the same list as one of those large—and probably pretty stupid, even smelly—beasts might seem close to blasphemy, but human evolution works by much the same forces that have shaped other creatures.

Many of the creatures that lived in relative proximity to the glaciers were large, even gigantic by today's standards. Large size implies, among other things, plenty of good food at the critical times when the body is in a growth period. The edge of the glacier was a region highly productive of good food, at least seasonally. There were streams of fresh water spreading all over the place, and waterborne silt and windblown loess replenished soils as faithfully as the flooding Nile replenished Egyptian soils until the Egyptians built the Aswan Dam. These were fresh fields, regularly renewed, unlike the old, relatively inert, leached-out realms of warmer climates such as the tropics. Here were plants of many kinds all heavily engaged in rapid and highly intense reproduction, meaning that there was an abundance of especially nutritious parts such as seeds and flowers and new shoots to feed fast-growing young herbivores. (For obvious reasons, if herbivores start growing big, it behooves predatory carnivores to do the same and vice versa in a kind of escalating war.) But something else was going on besides the achievement of sheer size.

In a few places in the forests of Sumatra, one may still run across a goatlike animal called a serow. It is apparently little changed from the earliest pre-Pleistocene progenitors of goats and sheep, and it is characterized by short, straight, sharp horns—offensive weapons. On the other hand, the mountain sheep of North America and the Mongolian giant sheep have huge horns curved into spirals—hardly useful for goring an enemy though fine for head butting. If they serve as offensive and defensive weapons, they also serve another important function: letting a potential female know how good a male is at obtaining nourishment. They are what are called "wrestling" weapons for arguments over females, and they have even been called "luxury organs," meaning that the owner possesses the ability to obtain otherwise scarce resources with such skill that he has some left over to produce what might seem like frivolously elaborate organs such as spiral-shaped horns. (One can think here, as well, of the peacock. It is hard to imagine developing so ludicrously elaborate a feature as its glorious tail on a starvation diet.)

A sheep's horns or a deer's antlers grow only after the animal has achieved its main bodily growth, and most species shed their antlers annually. This means that there needs to be a period of the year when the environment produces a large excess of food over that needed for maintenance (of adults) and growth (of young). Antler growth also calls for special minerals as well as an excess of food availability. Such conditions were fulfilled by the environments near the southern edges of the glaciers.

Large body size and among males, if not both sexes, elaborate luxury organs such as horns, antlers, and tusks, occur in mammal species whose females produce milk high in solids, promoting rapid growth of young, which tend to be large at birth and capable of running soon after birth. Another aspect of this reproductive "strategy" is that the young tend to remain with the parents for a fairly long time. All this, of course, matches the presence of large, fast-moving predators such as enormous bears and large cats. Deer, such as the white-tailed deer that are (comparatively) small and avoid predators chiefly by hiding in the woods and scrublands, don't need huge size or enormous antlers. The big elk and other cervids of the open lands with their extravagant antlers were also long-legged, speedy, high-endurance animals.

Another luxury item that evolved in glacial neighborhoods was the accretion of fat. Clearly, a bear that needs to hibernate through a long period has to build up fat reserves. Any herbivore that needs to survive the sparse cupboard called winter, scraping away snow to find a bit of dried-up forage, is likely to starve to death (and often does) without an ample supply of fat developed during times of plenty.

What does all this—or any of it—have to do with humans? As noted, we went from climatically benign environments that changed little in the short run (though greatly over extended periods) to more severe ones, which varied greatly seasonally, from place to place, and over long periods of time. Our teeth became less for biting as we developed other means of offense and defense. We remain among the largest of the primates, though, until the days of the steroid-laced NFL, one could not call us gigantic in the same sense as the short-faced bear. But we outdid our fellow Ice Age mammals in one area of increasing size: the cerebral cortex. This tended to grow in many Ice Age mammals, becoming an organ permitting far greater sociality among such animals as lions and wolves as well as their prey—herds of horses, bison, mammoths, and so forth. But of course, among humans, this organ became far larger (as a fraction of body size) and far more complex than that of any other terrestrial creature in all of the 3.5 billion or so years that life has existed on the planet. It is this powerful organ that lets us imagine, among other things, that we have slipped past any lowly mammalian origins to become a wholly separate sort of creation.

Other mammalian "luxury organs" of which we are astonishingly fond came about at the same time. Most of us possess to one minimal degree or another a vestigial mammalian covering of hair called fur, which grows only to a certain length and then stops. Fur may have become largely vestigial on hominids during their tropical savanna beginnings. But we have bona fide hair—on our head and, among males, on the lower face— that keeps on growing through life (once it starts). Unique to humans, this is very much a luxury item, calling for a constant amount of nourishment to grow healthily, not to mention vast amounts of attention.

We also happen to be a very fat species comparatively, and not just the couch potatoes among us. Typically, about 15 percent of the overall body

Venus of Willendorf.

weight of a pretty fit adult male human is fat and 20 percent or more among females—not that we need it to hibernate, though it must have been useful when clothes consisted of crudely sewn together hides, not the high-tech thermal wonders of today's mountain climber or skier. Indeed, specialists now consider mammalian fat to be the equivalent of a bodily organ, not only serving as insulation and padding for feet and eye sockets and providing a hedge against lean times, but helping to regulate such important matters as appetite and the immune system. But human evolution added to these functions.

In fit humans, fat is concentrated in three regions—the stomach (where it provides a readily converted source of energy), the buttocks of both sexes, but especially women's, and the female breasts. These features (which are unique in the animal world—no other mammal has permanently large mammary glands or anything resembling buttocks) are both secondary sexual characteristics, as much sexual attractants as an elk's antlers. They bespeak the ability of a woman to feed an infant that needs to be highly dependent for a very long time—unlike, say, a horse's foal—so that its brain can continue to grow in both size and complexity. If the human infant's brain were near adult size at birth, its head would be far too big for the child ever to make it through the mother's pelvis, and if her pelvis were big enough to accommodate an adult-sized brain at birth, she probably wouldn't be able to walk. Like all design, the evolutionary design of the human being has been a series of compromises. Many of the compromises that led to our present design were as driven by the glaciers as those of the woolly mammoth. Taken together, this unspecialized appetite and this particular reproductive strategy are what zoologists call a "dispersal phenotype," a body plan designed for colonizing new territory, fresh fields, relatively unpopulated places.

Another aspect of this type of biological strategy is a considerable plasticity of body type within a species. Zoologists point out that the body type (for example, size) of a deer differs with latitude, typically growing larger and faster in more extreme climates and open lands and smaller and more conservatively in the tropics. Similarly, the human body, over generations, has been highly variable, capable of making extraordinary adaptations to differing environments. Consider the huge lung power of the mountain people of Ecuador or the Sherpas of Nepal. Some Eskimos, now properly called Inuits, live in far more extreme circumstances than the people who lived near the glaciers' edges in the Pleistocene; over time they have developed a circulatory system that provides an increased flow of blood to the hands, feet, and other body parts exposed to the extreme cold. In addition, the Lapps, the reindeer herders of the European Arctic, shunt blood from one artery to another paired one, which results in warm venous blood returning from the extremities to the heart. This means that hands and feet can become seriously reduced in temperature without affecting important organs such as the brain and the heart. A bare-chested Lapp in 40°F weather would complain of the heat.

The malleability of humans' anatomy and physiology, as well as their omnivorous appetite, were other parts of the biological equipment that permitted expansion into varied environments—not just cold ones. They were adapted to cope with the stress of change, and therefore they could move from Africa to Europe and Asia. And once they added the necessary cultural achievements to their remarkably versatile biological heritage, they could take on the very ice that, over a million years, had exerted so profound an effect on them even from a great distance. The populating of the Western Hemisphere, one of the great adventures of all time, was just a late chapter of that wider adventure story, the peopling of the earth. Yet it would take a long time, filled with heated argument, before the world would believe that such an adventure could have taken place more than a few thousand years ago.

CHAPTER FOUR

GOOD-BYE, GLACIAL MAN;

HELLO, CLOVIS

By the mid–nineteenth century in Europe, the scientific scrutiny of very old things was eating away at what most people perceived to be the very foundation stones of European civilization. In England in particular, the correct interpretation of the Bible, the lineage of humanity, and our very place in nature were all being seriously called into question. For many, the fact that such issues were being raised was intellectually and even emotionally devastating.

At this remove in time, it is nearly impossible to understand how devastating it was. Middle- and upper-class Victorians were *au courant* with contemporary science in a way that Americans today might well envy, and the implications of new scientific discoveries were pretty clear and widely debated. Already, in previous decades, the faithful had had to face up to the fact that God had created animals that simply hadn't worked out and had gone extinct—that is to say, parts of the Creation were not perfect. Then the problem had arisen that the world was much older than Genesis seemed to say it was. Genesis now had to be regarded as a poetic way of saying that God had spent up to six separate ages, including the Pleistocene, preparing the planet for his supreme creation, Man, in about 4000 B.C.

Then, in 1859, thanks to a French amateur archaeologist named Jacques Boucher de Crèvecoeur de Perthes and some things he had come across earlier on the Somme River, people had to reckon with solid proof that man himself might be older than the Bible would have it—indeed, that he was a creature of the ice ages (whenever that was, and nobody at the time had any way of assigning dates to the Pleistocene that were much more than guesses, but it had to be older than six and maybe more thousands of years ago).

Beginning in 1837, Boucher, who was a customs official in Abbeville along the Somme, began collecting from the gravels along the Somme canal chipped flints he found in association with the bones of extinct animals. The next year he put his finds on display in Abbeville and then in Paris, and within three years he had published a treatise titled, perhaps a bit ambitiously, *Of the Creation*. The reception of these efforts was cool at best, but Boucher, undaunted, went on collecting. He published another volume calling his finds *ante*diluvian, and this time his reception was not merely icy but derisive. But by the mid-1850s, a couple of other men found what they took to be confirming evidence in Amiens and Saint Acheul, and French geologists began to come around to Boucher's view.

All this while in England, starting in the late 1820s with Father MacEnery's excavations, a few people were finding similar associations of stone artifacts and the remains of extinct animals such as mammoths and woolly rhinoceroses. But as mentioned earlier, cave stratigraphy was thought by most geologists to be almost impossible to sort out. After all, one investigator had found mammoth bones that were, he thought, clearly associated with an implement that was unmistakably from the time of Julius Caesar. So any such findings from caves were pushed aside. But in 1858, some fissures were found in the rock of a cave located on Windmill Hill that overlooks the harbor at a town called Brixham in Devonshire. The fissures suggested that this was a cave in which the stratigraphy had not been disturbed, and before long a high-powered committee of nationally renowned geologists was formed to provide direction to excavations in the cave carried out by a local archaeologist, William Pengelly. The excavations paid off: the following summer, in the fateful year of 1859, they found flint tools in earth that lay below a several-inch-thick floor of "stalagmite" in which and above which were the remains of "lion, hyaena, bear, mammoth, rhinoceros and reindeer." It was indisputable: humans had lived during the lives of what were by then perceived as Ice Age animals.

One of the committee directing the excavation at Brixham Cave, a geologist named William Falconer, had found himself in the summer of 1858 near Abbeville and had gone over to have a look at Boucher's finds. He had found them, as well as Boucher's conclusions, believable and, on returning to London, urged others of the Brixham committee to have a look for themselves. In 1859, they did so and vindicated Boucher. (This ushered in a new feature in archaeological studies—the site visit, usually by a select group of bigwigs in the field, or what one American wag far off in the future would label the "paleo-police.") In that same year, members of the Brixham committee delivered papers at scientific meetings announcing the antiquity of mankind in "this portion of the globe," and later the ultimate arbiter, Charles Lyell, in a presidential address at a meeting of the Royal Society, announced that he was "fully prepared to corroborate the conclusions" of his colleagues.

If that was not enough to satisfy any scientific holdouts, the unflappable and assiduous Boucher continued his efforts in the gravels of the Somme and in 1863 came up with a complete human jaw and some teeth unmistakably associated with tools of worked flint. The town of Abbeville unveiled a statue of this famous customs official in 1908. By 1859, however, the chasm between the ancient world and Bishop Ussher's moment of human creation had been eliminated.

To make matters worse in 1859 for people who still considered the seven days of Genesis the literal, or at least poetic, truth, Charles Darwin published his *Origin of Species*. This landmark book in all the history of science threw the world for a complete loop by stating that animal species had arisen via natural causes. An analogous intellectual shock today would be hard to pinpoint, but it might be equivalent to showing physicists that energy simply doesn't exist. But matters were soon made even more unpalatable for many. Though Darwin did not say much about it in *Origin of Species,* it soon became clear that he and other evolutionary thinkers were implying that human beings had descended from apes. (In fact, we aren't; today it is clear that humans and apes descended from a common ancestor.)

Within four years of Darwin's exposition, many other treatises appeared in the same vein. Thomas Huxley, an especially eloquent student of nature, was forcefully raising the ape issue, and in 1863 the grand old man of geology, Charles Lyell, published *Geological Evidences for the Antiquity of Man,* which put an end to virtually all lingering scientific doubts about the evidence of men among the mammoths. And these Ice Age people, as primitive as they seemed from their crude stone implements, were now taken to be directly ancestral to modern Europeans and not some race utterly—and comfortingly—separated from Europeans by some catastrophe like a worldwide flood. Not only that, but shortly before Darwin's momentous insights, the hunched, thick-headed, seemingly misshapen hulk known as Neanderthal Man had arrived on the scene, his remains recovered in 1857 from a quarry in Germany.

This Neanderthal being, according to one somewhat biased Continental observer, was either a deformed idiot or a Russian. Others saw it as some far more ancient, brutish being on the evolutionary path from ape to human. Before long, with the discovery of many more remains, most ob-

Recent reconstruction of a Neanderthal
depicting the modernity of the species.

servers believed Neanderthals to be ancient, not anywhere near as brutish as on first impression, and indeed a fairly close evolutionary step in our direction. (It is notable that today, with all our brilliant technology and sophisticated ways of looking at such remains, no one yet can say for certain if the Neanderthals—now seen by many as a human subspecies called *Homo sapiens neanderthalensis*—who dwelled in Europe and the Near

East from well before 100,000 years to as late as 25,000 years ago disappeared from competition with Cro-Magnon Man—*Homo sapiens sapiens*—or interbred with these newer and seemingly brighter arrivals and vanished into our gene pool.)

In any event, soon enough the notion became widely understood by European scientists of many stripes—geologists, paleontologists, archaeologists, and anthropologists—not only that humans had evolved biologically over a long period of time from apelike ancestors into their present human grandeur, but that human cultures had also evolved—gradually and certainly—from the primitive savage through successive stages to the pinnacle of human achievement: European civilization and, most especially, its incomparable Victorian English version. In other words, there had been cultural as well as biological evolution. And these several ologies, however upsetting they were to the pious, almost immediately coalesced into a solid and relatively uniform multidisciplinary platform for the scientific study of prehistory, the platform upon which it still rests to this day.

All of this crossed the Atlantic in short order to a United States preoccupied with slavery and secession and soon to be in the throes of the Civil War. Nothing much would occur in America in the fields of science, though armaments specialists would invent the submarine and the Gatling gun. A handful of Americans attended to Darwin's theory of natural selection. Louis Agassiz, the glaciologist who had left Switzerland for Harvard, thought that the possibility of a human presence in the world prior to (or contemporaneous with) the glacier was not unreasonable, but he didn't believe that Darwin's natural selection could replace the hand of God and *create* species. Furthermore, he summarily rejected the notion that all animals were descended from a single ancestor. Asa Gray, the nation's most distinguished botanist, on the other hand, became Darwin's strongest American supporter. Joseph Henry, the multi-interested physicist who was still secretary of the Smithsonian, issued instructions for antiquarians and travelers on what to look for in Indian country to see if people had lived in North America in ages comparable to those in Europe. This putative inhabitant of glacial times in America soon came to be called Glacial Man.

By the 1870s, the astounding revolution in scientific thought brought on by the Europeans had penetrated deeply into the awareness of Americans; amateurs and trained scientists alike scoured the landscape for signs of Glacial Man. They dug around in caves and shell mounds, they probed deposits of river gravel and slogged around in swamps. They found stone tools in such places, to be sure, but not in association with the likes of mammoths, or indeed any other Pleistocene animals. The stone tools themselves looked not at all unlike modern aboriginal specimens; in fact, there was no way to tell a truly ancient lithic tool from a recent one. Agassiz himself was finding extensive evidence of North American glaciation but no artifacts among the gravels and other glacial deposits.

Many people believed that if Europeans had had their Neanderthals and later their Cro-Magnon men, who had done exquisite cave paintings of Ice Age animals, the New World ought to have its own equivalent. It was merely a matter of looking more extensively. Before long, academic war would break out on the fields of American archaeology—a battle even more contentious than the one going on over the identity of the mound builders at the same time. Today, we think of the subjects that reside under the umbrella of natural history museums to be quiet, slow-moving, dusty perhaps, and hardly the thing to get all destabilized about. But in the decades at the end of the nineteenth century, the fields we are concerned with here saw some of the most ferocious disputes in the history of American science. This was the period when a paleontologist at Yale, Othniel C. Marsh, waged a bitter struggle with his counterpart at the Smithsonian, Edward Cope, over finding, identifying, retrieving, and understanding dinosaurs, a long-term dispute that involved accusations of fraud, cheating, and other ungentlemanly activities, and was played out with the intensity of a Kentucky blood feud.

The mound-builder controversies were tame by comparison. They were driven by preconceived views about the identity and character of the contemporary native populations and a host of other (irrelevant) considerations and biases, resolved only after years of painstaking effort using increasingly sophisticated archaeological techniques. Unlike the battles over dinosaurs by the two most powerful professional paleontologists, the mound-builder disputes were chiefly between amateurs and the trained archaeologists, who were just coming into their own as a profession. And while American archaeology was developing a more scientific approach in the years between 1865 and the turn of the twentieth century, it nonetheless lagged far behind the field as practiced by Europeans. It is fair to say that American archaeologists at this time plowed ahead, for the most part following their own lights, only occasionally peering over their shoulders at their cooler and more generally methodical counterparts in the Old World.

THE PALEOLITHIC IN EUROPE

As early as the first decade of the nineteenth century, the more or less systematic collection of prehistoric archaeological remains, or "antiquities" as they were called, was under way in several parts of Europe, notably Scandinavia. By 1806, the Dane Rasmus Nyerup, a librarian by trade and an antiquitarian by avocation, had amassed artifacts from all over Denmark and urged the royal government to create a museum for his and other, similar collections. Soon enough, the newly established Danish National Museum of Antiquities was literally filling up with artifacts, and scholars were trying to fit them into known Danish history.

Out of the disorderly mass of data soon emerged the idea of the so-called Three Ages System—stone, bronze, and iron. In the 1830s, J. J. A. Worsaae conducted stratigraphic excavations in Danish burial mounds and other sites and demonstrated that there was indeed a chronological succession in the manufacture of stone, copper or bronze, and iron tools. With the solitary exception of Jefferson's remarkable but unnoticed use of stratigraphy nearly fifty years earlier in Virginia, Worsaae's work was the first application of excavation by natural levels in the history of archaeology.

As a result of this Danish work, prehistoric archaeology now existed as a field of legitimate scholarly inquiry, at least in one corner of Europe. Not long afterward, the Three Ages System would become the temporal yardstick for not simply northern Europe but the whole continent. By the time the American Civil War ended, the terms Paleolithic (Old Stone Age) and Neolithic (New Stone Age) had been introduced. The Paleolithic was seen to be a very long period of indeterminate beginning when flaked stone tools had been used, followed by a much more recent interlude, the Neolithic, when ground and polished stone technology had made its appearance. Soon, geographically widespread and long-lived tool kits or "traditions," such as the Acheulean with its highly recognizable heart-, lozenge-, or almond-shaped hand axes and rectangular cleavers, as well as more localized tool suites, or "industries," were identified, described, and named—usually after the first sites in which they were discovered.

As Dave Meltzer has eloquently explained in several articles from which the following historical synopsis is partially drawn, soon European and, somewhat later, American scholars were familiar not only with the ancient Acheulean but also with later Stone Age (Upper Paleolithic) cultures such as Solutrean (for Solutré in east-central France) and Magdalenian (after La Madeleine in the Périgord, in southwest France). Shortly thereafter, archaeologists specified an intermediate, or Middle Stone Age, culture, called Mousterian (after Le Moustier, also in southwestern France), which became the name of the period when the recently discovered premodern creature called Neanderthal lived. By the end of the nineteenth century, the idea of a long Paleolithic age, if not yet a household notion, had at least percolated across the Atlantic.

THE VANISHING AMERICAN PALEOLITHIC

In the early 1870s, two American men began careers that would make them major figures on opposite sides of a great archaeological chasm. One was a medical doctor, the other an artist. The artist was William Henry Holmes, who, in 1871, came to Washington, D.C., to study art. There, like any tourist, he visited the Smithsonian, where he was sufficiently taken by a stuffed bird to sketch it. A paleontologist on the staff happened by, saw the sketch, and hired Holmes to draw fossils, which in turn were seen by Ferdinand Hayden, who took Holmes along as an artist on a major government-funded scientific expedition to Yellowstone the following year.

The young artist was soon made assistant geologist and, in numerous trips to the plateau country of the Far West, produced panoramic geological illustrations of the region that, according to one historian, "represent the highest point to which geological or topographical illustration ever reached in this country."

Holmes was thus employed in 1876 when a New Jersey physician,

Charles Conrad Abbott, published a monograph on the "rude" and, he suspected, Paleolithic-age stone tools he had found in riverine gravel beds near his family farm in Trenton, New Jersey (which is, in fact, quite close to the southernmost limit of the last glacial advance). In the quest for an-

Charles Conrad Abbott, M.D., ca. 1875–1888.

cient inhabitants of the New World to match those of Europe, crude tools such as those of Paleolithic Europe were the next best thing to finding remains of humans associated with ancient faunal remains, and none of the latter had been found after a decade or more of frustrating search. The tools Abbott found were mostly hand axes, chipped by bashing them against a rock "anvil" or, alternatively, bashing them with another rock. In any event, they resembled the tools that Boucher had found along the Somme and that had been turning up in Europe ever since.

Abbott's finds caught the attention of a professional, Frederic Ward Putnam, who had been appointed curator of the Peabody Museum at Harvard in 1875. Previous to his appointment, he had been a zoologist, but he would become a major figure in the excavation and preservation of the great mounds of the Midwest, developing sophisticated techniques of mapping, digging, and recording of finds. In a sense, he rescued the Great Serpent Mound from destruction by buying it for the Peabody, which later ceded it to the state of Ohio to maintain. But Putnam's other interest besides the mound builders was proving that humans had lived in North America before the end of the Pleistocene. And so it was that Abbott's report on his "paleoliths" from the Trenton Gravels was published by the Peabody Museum, the tenth in its series of annual reports. And once a Harvard geologist journeyed to Trenton and went over the ground with Abbott, confirming the artifact-bearing deposits to be of Pleistocene age, Abbott crowed to himself that he had discovered America's Glacial Man.

For two decades, Glacial Man wowed the reading public in books both technical and popular and in lectures and other presentations. Abbott was pronounced America's own Boucher. Similar finds were pouring in from all over the East and elsewhere. Americans could rejoice that the New World had not been slighted by the Paleolithic hunters of the Ice Age, and some scholars would suggest that humans had found their way to this continent even earlier.

Meanwhile, at the Smithsonian's Bureau of Ethnology and at the U.S. Geological Survey, both by 1877 under the directorship of John Wesley Powell, scientists were altogether unfriendly to the idea of Glacial Man. It was theoretically awkward. The government scientists were virtually all followers of pioneer anthropologist Lewis Henry Morgan, whose *Ancient Society* postulated a simplistic series of stages that humans had gone through, from savagery through barbarism to civilization. This was seen as a gradual (but not glacially gradual) process, and the notion of Glacial Man in America left a huge gap in the archaeological record with practically nothing occurring between Pleistocene times and the American Indians, who were, of course, in Morgan's and other schemes, still savages.

By 1882, the artist turned geologist William Henry Holmes had turned from exploring the geology of the Far West to another interest: ceramics. He set out to catalogue and categorize all the known forms of American aboriginal pottery, a task he continued well into the 1890s and that formed the foundation of most other such research by archaeologists to this day. (It is worth noting that Holmes was one of the very first scholars to record that baskets, fabrics, and nets were sometimes impressed onto pottery, providing insights into the nondurable plant-based technologies seldom preserved in many parts of North America. These perishable technologies were generally far more important to their makers than the much more often recovered items made of stone.) Before his ceramic studies were complete, however, Holmes received another assignment, this from John Wesley Powell, which was—in essence—to destroy all the loose talk about Glacial Man. Powell, who was essentially responsible for putting the U.S. government into the business of science, and who had hired the largest single array of professional scientists anywhere in the world under one roof, was convinced that science was no place for the amateur. He insisted that science was threatened by such unscientific procedures as simply sticking a chipped rock from a riverbed of unknown age next to a Paleolithic tool from clearly Pleistocene Europe and calling them the same thing.

Powell suggested that Holmes start with a deposit near Washington, D.C., where a proponent of Glacial Man had recently discovered Pleistocene tools. There is an old photograph of Holmes, ever a calm and distinguished-looking fellow with a luxuriant brushy mustache, wearing a jacket, vest, tie, and narrow-brimmed hat, seated among a small surface quarry of cobbles located in the sun-dappled ground of a second-growth forest. It is a picture of elegant calm, not of paradigm destruction. It was here, however, that Holmes determined that these were not paleoliths but preforms—that is, the rocks from which recent Indian hunters had flaked off pieces to be made into arrowheads. Some of them, indeed, bore some resemblance to the turtle-shaped paleoliths of the Somme and other European sites, and Holmes promptly crafted a few such turtlebacks with his own hands, dramatically letting the air out of the Pleistocene claims.

He went on to study the geological settings in a host of locales, starting with the Trenton Gravels, where Abbott's evidence of Glacial Man had arisen, and he consistently found that the deposits were young, not Pleistocene, and that the artifacts present were merely Indian quarry refuse. Any that were found in old deposits had gotten there, Holmes asserted, by falling down rodent holes or being moved by other natural causes. The entire issue of the American Paleolithic, Holmes asserted, was "hopelessly embarrassed with the blunders and misconceptions" of people who were more like amateur relic hunters than serious scientists.

William Henry Holmes.

Naturally enough, proponents of Glacial Man were not pleased, nor were they persuaded. There have been, by the way, many studies made by science historians and other scholars suggesting that few people are likely to have their minds changed by mere argument and reference to the facts. More often than not, adherents to one scientific view do not give up when a new view arises replete with its own evidence. Instead, opposition to a new theory finally dies out when the adherents to the old theory themselves die out—a paradigm shift by the grim reaper.

Certainly, Charles Conrad Abbott was not about to throw in the towel. At scientific meetings, Abbott railed and fumed while the elegant Holmes remained cool and calm. Abbott wrote nasty poetry about Holmes. A supporter of Abbott was vilified as a "be-tinseled charlatan." Abbott accused the government scientists of a kind of federal conspiracy "foisted on the unthinking to secure the scientific prominence of a few archaeological mugwumps." The government scientists, it is true, were comparatively well funded, while the others had to struggle for research funds, and there was a sense that the members of Powell's empire—the U.S. Geological Survey and the Bureau of Ethnology—were arrogantly squashing any disputants. There is, in fact, some evidence that the government scientists did engage in efforts to keep opponents from getting their reports published in the scientific journals that were coming into being in this period.

Holmes continued to argue his view into the 1920s, having acceded to the position of director of the Bureau of Ethnology on Powell's death in 1902. By now, a new generation of archaeologists was coming of age in the twentieth century. They were loath to call attention to artifacts that might arguably be of Pleistocene provenance lest they find themselves cut to shreds by Holmes's elegant, swift sword. Indeed, the calmness that Holmes always displayed even when his opponents were at their most outraged and outrageous must have merely added to their frustration as they watched Glacial Man being systematically sliced to ribbons. In 1920, now in his seventies, Holmes accepted a position as director of the newly established National Gallery of Art, leaving science to return to his artistic roots. He held that position until a year before his death in 1933, a man who had moved with powerful grace between what later generations would perceive as two separate, even irreconcilable "cultures"—art and science.

Meanwhile, throughout the period when irrepressible, nongovernment archaeologists scoured the land for signs of Glacial Man, another line of evidence occasionally cropped up: bones. And by the turn of the century, an adjunct to Holmes had also cropped up, a man who soon gained a reputation as the most utterly implacable, even terrifying commentator on the notion of a deep human antiquity in North America that the nation had ever seen, or in fact has seen since. This was Aleš Hrdlička (pronounced approximately "Herdlishka"), a medical man who ultimately lodged at the Smithsonian and who was given to writing marginal notations like "mindless dolt" on other investigators' site reports.

Hrdlička was born in 1869 to a Bohemian family in what is the present-day Czech Republic, and was brought to New York at age thirteen. Trained in two medical schools, he practiced medicine briefly before taking a position at the New York Hospital for the Insane in Middletown, New York. There he began a study of the physical characteristics of the inmates,

Aleš Hrdlička.

and this led in turn to an interest in pathology that took him briefly to Paris and back to New York, working on large skeletal collections of European origins. He then caught the eye of none other than Frederic Putnam, who had gone on from Harvard's Peabody Museum to help found the Field Museum of Natural History in Chicago and the anthropology departments at both the University of California (Berkeley) and the American Museum of Natural History in New York. Putnam plucked Hrdlička out of New York's College of Physicians and Surgeons and sent him off on an 1898 American Museum expedition to the Southwest and Mexico, where he studied the physical characteristics of several Native American tribes. Thus did Putnam set in motion the man who (with Holmes) would put to death his dream of the existence of Glacial Man.

The quest for "paleoliths" was largely over in 1899, but then one of Putnam's people found a human femur in the Trenton Gravels and hope glimmered again. Putnam turned the bone over to Hrdlička, who pronounced it no different from a modern Indian femur. By then the Trenton Gravels were so controversial that the femur was soon forgotten. With some more studies of controversial skeletal material in the Midwest, Hrdlička was fully into the fray, and in 1903 he was hired by Holmes to head the newly formed Division of Physical Anthropology at the Smithsonian's National Museum, now the National Museum of Natural History.

As more and more supposedly Pleistocene human remains came to light, Hrdlička became The Man. Indeed, he had a severe-looking visage, a strong jaw, and a perpetual frown: dress him in western apparel, and he could easily have been a no-nonsense lawman bringing order and tough justice to a frontier town. (One can, a bit wildly, think of Holmes and Hrdlička as the Doc Holliday and Wyatt Earp of early-twentieth-century anthropology, running all abusers of the proper scientific method out of Tombstone.) Simply stated, Hrdlička's position was that if people had been here in the Pleistocene, they should look different from modern folks. They should be more like Neanderthals. Both Hrdlička and Holmes were convinced that the human presence in North America could be no more than 4,000 or 5,000 years old, while there was a general sense that the Pleistocene ended some 15,000 to 20,000 years ago.

Hrdlička trashed virtually every "discovery" of so-called Pleistocene human remains, pointing out that they were hardly different from modern ones, and often called in geologists to throw doubt on the age of the geological deposits in which the remains were found. Peripatetic in the extreme, his researches carrying him to many exotic parts of the globe, Hrdlička surely knew his bones, knew about human variability, and few were likely to contradict him successfully when he arrived at a site of Pleistocene man and found just a modern Native American. In his wake, he often left embittered provincial archaeologists, warring factions snarling at one another over geological evidence, with otherwise normally courteous people accusing others of untrustworthiness and even deliberate falsification. The federal juggernaut rolled on, crushing all such claims. For those involved, it must have been an unpleasant time. As David Meltzer has written of the period:

> Anthropologists bickered among themselves—but mostly with Hrdlička—over what a Pleistocene-aged human fossil should look like, then argued with paleontologists about the timing of mammalian extinctions. Paleontologists wrangled with geologists about where to draw the line between Pleistocene and post-Pleistocene formations. Geologists fought with one another over the number, timing, and evidences of glacial history. Even linguists got into the act, clucking their disapproval at everyone's failure to provide them with sufficient time to account for the great diversity of native North American languages.

Just as a new generation of archaeologists had given up raising the issue of European-like paleoliths lest they be cut down by Holmes's rapier, yet another generation of scientists learned to lie low about Pleistocene human bones lest they be bludgeoned by The Man. But, of course, there was more to it than that. Throughout the debate about Glacial Man that raged from the 1870s into the 1920s, a number of subtexts lay darkly behind the argumentation.

Most of the Paleolithic supporters knew little about contemporary Native Americans and couldn't have cared less, while the government scientists insisted that there had to be a direct line from the earliest migrants to the continent and the living aboriginal populations, which, they were convinced, had arrived not so long ago as the result of a single migration from Asia. Further, many of the Paleolithic supporters were easterners by birth and education—and in the East there was a tendency to want American discoveries and science to fit into European models. On the other hand, many of the Washington scientists came from more western areas and disdained connections to Europe in science as in many other things. At the time, a German-born American, Franz Boas, whose work among the Eskimos and Pacific Islanders had made him much more than the nominal founder of modern American anthropology, insisted on a direct link between anthropology and archaeology, and the Washington archaeologists agreed. On the other hand, the Paleolithic supporters saw little reason for it.

As we know now, glacial-age humans *were* present in North America; the Paleolithic supporters were right. We now have innumerable artifacts from this period; Holmes was wrong. And they were *not* Neanderthal-like; Hrdlička's hard line was wrong as well.

It may seem that these two men were professional naysayers, blindly holding to dogma, slowing down progress. But in a very important way, Holmes, Hrdlička, and the others who hammered the Paleolithic supporters of the era were right. For no one in that period did find legitimate evidence of Pleistocene humanity in North America. The Washington scientists established some hard-and-fast, wholly reasonable scientific criteria for judging such archaeological evidence, and these standards still apply. One had to find (1) undeniable artifacts or osteological remains that were unmistakably human; (2) an indisputable context (such as direct stratigraphic association with extinct Pleistocene animal remains); (3) a valid and reliable control over chronology—which in those days meant undisturbed stratigraphy. None of the sites so virulently attacked by Holmes and Hrdlička met all those criteria when they were announced or even when, in some cases, they were reexamined in more modern and technically proficient times. It is important to iterate that the general criteria they established then are neither unreasonably harsh nor unreasonably lax—and, as we'll see, they are basically the same criteria that are in effect in archaeology today.

Until the late 1920s, these criteria were never met in the quest for Glacial Man. Establishing exact chronologies was impossible at the time; only relative chronology could be determined, and, given the state of the art of stratigraphy, that was iffy at best. Stone artifacts such as crude hand axes could also be nothing more than broken cobbles or, as Holmes had shown several times, discards from recent Indians. The three hard-nosed criteria set a bar that was a bit high for the archaeological techniques of the time. So the issue remained at best a Mexican stand-off, the two sides glowering at each other over an apparently unbridgeable chasm. Then, at a time when most educated Americans were preoccupied with more urgent matters such as Prohibition, the stock market, mobs, movies, and the illicit delights of the Roaring Twenties, an excavation in an insignificant arroyo in a remote part of New Mexico changed the world of American archaeology.

FOLSOM AND CLOVIS

Jennings, Meltzer, and many other archaeologists have "reconstructed" the scene that might have occurred at Folsom at the very end of the Pleistocene, but it is a tale worth telling again. At some point about 10,000 years ago, a herd of very large bison thundered down a narrowing arroyo, came around a curve, and were ambushed by a group of people armed with what were most likely wooden-shafted throwing spears or atlatl-propelled darts tipped with extremely fine, even elegant stone points. Some of the big animals probably escaped, thundering on, bellowing. A number of the bison may have perished instantly, the fierce projectiles striking through ribs to a vital source of life, the heart or lungs. Some would not have been so lucky. The hunters no doubt promptly fell to finishing off the wounded and then began butchering this wonderful kill with the enthusiastic help of the other people, probably mostly women and children, who had watched from the bank above as the noisy and extremely dangerous melee took place.

Stretching away from this joyous and bloody scene were grassy meadows, broken by copses of trees. Beyond, forested hills rose to the horizon. It was a salubrious place and probably remained so over the years when similar events took place. Eventually, dust from the surround blew into the arroyo, covering the area and its bones and other signs of feasting. Some ten thousand years passed.

Chances are that in modern times the arroyo was visited by cattle that had strayed through the ever-fragile fences of ranchers who came to inhabit the valley in the nineteenth century, now a bit drier than when the huge bison had met their end, but otherwise little changed. Clearly it was straying cattle that brought the foreman of the Crowfoot Ranch near the tiny town of Folsom to this scene in late August of the year 1908, a day or two after heavy rains had flooded the area and sent torrents through this and other arroyos in the neighborhood, among other things freeing cattle to roam.

The foreman, George McJunkin, was a black man who had been born into slavery and, like so many people freed from servitude by law or by flight, had migrated west and taken up the life available to such drifters in the business of cattle ranching. Besides being a capable manager of a cattle operation, McJunkin was something of a naturalist, it seems, or at least a sharp observer of his surroundings. While out on his horse checking fences and looking for strays, he paused near the curve in Wild Horse Arroyo, noticing some bones that had been partly uncovered by the torrent of water. They were too big to be the remains of cattle, and they seemed even large to be bison bones.

He showed the bones to a blacksmith from the nearby town of Raton, Carl Schwachheim, who, over the years, tried to interest the Colorado Museum of Natural History in McJunkin's find. Not until 1926, four years after McJunkin died at age sixty-six, did the blacksmith prevail on the director of the Colorado museum to come and have a look. It does not appear to have been any mention of a stone point that brought Jesse D. Figgins, the director of the museum, to the site. But come he did, bent (he said in a memorandum) only on collecting enough fossil bones of the ancient bisons to produce a mounted skeleton of one in his museum.

There may have been more to it than that, however. In 1925, Figgins had become involved at a dig at Lone Wolf Creek near Colorado City, Texas, where it seems that stone points had been found in association with the remains of ancient mammals. In fact, Figgins had made three such claims for signs of human activity associated with Ice Age creatures, but the Washington establishment had dismissed all of them with a shrug, pointing out that the dig had not been run by "responsible archaeologists."

In the summer of 1926, Figgins found a delicately made stone point among the ancient bison bones in Wild Horse Arroyo, and in 1927 he wrote up a preliminary report designed to "stir up all the venom there is in" the Smithsonian's Hrdlička. Then he learned that a meeting had been arranged with the great man and met with Hrdlička in Washington that spring. Figgins was surprised to be received cordially by Hrdlička, who regretted only that the points had not been left *in situ* so others could have seen them there. He suggested that in the event that Figgins made another such find, he let the professionals know by telegram so they could come quickly and see with their own eyes a human artifact embedded in the remains of an Ice Age mammal.

In spite of a certain western bravado on Figgins's part and the fact that this was Hrdlička's way of saying that a western rube could hardly be deemed competent to handle such a matter, Figgins was humble enough—not claiming to be either an archaeologist or a paleontologist—to think this admonition quite reasonable. And in the following summer, near Folsom, when he and his party came across a stone point imbedded between the fossilized ribs of an Ice Age bison, he left it there and hastened to telegraph Hrdlička, and then others at the Smithsonian and other major museums: ANOTHER ARROWHEAD FOUND IN POSITION WITH BISON REMAINS AT FOLSOM NEW MEXICO HAVE INVITED HRDLICKA TO MAKE INVESTIGATION.

Eagerly, the big shots from the East showed up. Hrdlička was otherwise engaged, so a young colleague of his from the Bureau of Ethnography, Frank Roberts, came, arriving with Alfred Vincent Kidder of Washington's Carnegie Institution. Kidder and Roberts were at the time putting together the cultural sequence of the Pueblo country only a hundred or so miles south of Folsom, based on a major excavation of the ruins at Pecos, New Mexico, but the two did not arrive at Folsom before Barnum Brown of the American Museum of Natural History in New York (the first man to uncover a *Tyrannosaurus rex*) got there and began dusting the matrix away from the stone point and the bones. There was no doubting that the point and the bones had arrived in place simultaneously, and other scientists who arrived subsequently all got to see the same thing (in modern archaeological parlance, the artifacts and bones were in direct association). In all, Brown went on to discover some seventeen points in association with Ice Age mammal bones as the summer progressed. Within a month of his visit, Kidder—recognized widely as a, if not *the*, major figure in the field—pronounced the find to be some 15,000 to 20,000 years old. And later, Brown wrote up a report which, a bit ungraciously, did not mention Figgins at all.

Even with these panjandrums of the field weighing in about the site's authenticity, there was room for disagreement. When, it was asked, had this particular bison species gone extinct—in the late Pleistocene or the early Holocene? Was the geology consistent with a late Pleistocene date? The matter was not settled until geologists had pored over the site and pronounced the deposits to be at least late Pleistocene in age. Even then, William Henry Holmes would refer people to the "prevailing" opinions, and Hrdlička grumbled that there still were no prehuman remains (which is true to this day and irrelevant), thereafter maintaining a silence on the whole affair. In short order, however, virtually everyone agreed. The three criteria the Washington elite had long insisted upon had been met. Humans had dwelled in North America at least by the end of the Pleistocene.

The discovery of an Ice Age existence of humans was not without its ironies. Hrdlička himself, by telling Figgins to call in the eastern cognoscenti, had helped things along in the gainsaying of his own theory of a far more recent human arrival. And also, the Pleistocene artifacts—which came to be called Folsom points—were hardly the "crude" cobbles that Abbott and others had assumed were all Glacial Man would technically have been capable of making. Instead, they were exquisitely made implements—delicate, with finely chipped edges and a large central area on each face chipped out to make the smooth groove called a flute or channel flute. Clearly they were the work of skilled artisans, people who had mastered the fine art of flint knapping by pressure flaking, not a bunch of Pre-Mousterian oafs banging rocks together. And, importantly, no one had ever seen anything like these points; with the fluting, they were unique in the known archaeological record, something that was peculiarly American.

The Folsom discoveries were a watershed event in American archaeology, and more discoveries were on the way. Another find in New Mexico a few years later would usher in the period called Clovis that would dominate the study of early man in North America for about seventy years. The traces of the man—yes, the man—who would bestride the late Pleistocene continent and points south as a veritable colossus were discovered in an out-of-the-way town in the arid badlands near the Texas border. And Clovis Man, soon perceived as the mightiest hunter ever to appear in the Americas, might have been called Riley had it not been for a girl who was fascinated by medieval French history. For in 1906, the daughter of a Santa Fe Railroad official was given the opportunity to rename the obscure little railway stop of Riley's Switch. Enamored of a fifth-century Frankish king who had converted to Christianity, she named the place for him—Clovis— and it grew into a small agricultural and commercial center. By the 1930s, Clovis was in the western side of the Dust Bowl, a place of ferocious summer heat and little promise for the cattlemen who were trying to raise beef in the neighborhood. Over the years, ranch hands had been finding large bladelike pieces of chipped stone here and there in the dusty ground, and word of this reached a genteel man with a fancy address on Philadelphia's Main Line and a soft accent from his birthplace, New Orleans. This was Edgar Billings Howard, a wealthy patrician who in his early forties had taken up archaeology as a second career.

According to a young graduate student named Loren Eiseley who worked with Howard one summer and who would later be lionized more for his poetic writing style than for his work as an anthropologist, Howard had a "driving mania" to find the skeletal remains of Folsom Man. To this end he began searching three hundred miles due south of Folsom in the Chihuahuan desert near Alamogordo and later Carlsbad, New Mexico, backed by Philadelphia's Academy of Natural Sciences. This was cave country; in addition to Carlsbad Caverns, there are an estimated two thousand caves in the old limestone formations, a huge ancient reef that lies north of the extremely craggy and hostile Guadalupe Mountains. The conditions were frightful—heat, dust, unpleasant rock, and the heavily armed plants of the desert. But in 1932, Howard found a hearth and the bones of Ice Age animals (caribou, horse, camel, and so forth) that depended on a grassy environment. This showed that the region had once been a relatively lush part of the southern plains. Then, in that same year, Howard heard from relic hunters about the appearance near the town of Clovis of stone implements among the bones of huge Ice Age mammals, and he moved his operation there for four years beginning in 1933.

While the town of Clovis had grown since it had ceased being Riley's Switch, even becoming something of a center of aviation, the surrounding area had suffered from the long drought and the nearly constant winds that were scouring the land, occasionally revealing long-buried bones. A local collector, Ridgely Whiteman, took Howard to a place called Blackwater Draw fourteen miles south of Clovis, where the winds had uncovered a large bone bed of bison and mammoth remains, and soon enough Howard secured the area for the Philadelphia Academy.

Many tantalizing finds were made in a gravel bed there by Howard and his multidisciplinary team, which even included a specialist in mollusks (a malacologist) to study fossil snails as indicators of environmental conditions. Indeed, Howard's was essentially the first such broad-based team to undertake a major archaeological excavation in the United States. In the fourth year of work, 1937, Howard and his team found Folsom points associated with the remains of Pleistocene bison. Beneath that layer, they found larger and somewhat less finely made stone points associated with the remains of mammoths.

Here, then, were late Pleistocene mammoth hunters, who had lived in this area even earlier than the Folsom bison hunters. Their characteristic stone points were larger and longer than Folsom points, with slightly cruder

General view of a portion of Blackwater Draw
(South Pit excavations), ca. 1933.

and shorter flutes. They eventually came to be called Clovis points, rather than some early and cruder version of the Folsom tradition. And what came to be called the Mammoth Pit in the gravel bed in Blackwater Draw— a place scientifically known as Blackwater Locality No. 1—became the accepted "type" locality for Clovis culture. For there, in addition to the Clovis points, Howard's team found a number of other stone and bone artifacts that made up the basic Clovis tool kit soon found practically everywhere across the United States.

The tool kit included large blades from which other tools could be made: distinctive end scrapers, tools that are beveled on one or both ends that may have been hafted and used for defleshing hides before they were tanned; handheld side scrapers used for various scraping and cutting chores; gravers (beaked tools used to incise wood and bone); large and small fluted projectile points; and bevel-ended shafts made of bone that may have been attached to wooden spear shafts, with the projectile point hafted to the other end. Another typical Clovis tool, though not found at Blackwater, is what amounts to a bone wrench putatively used for straightening out spear or dart shafts but more likely used to make cordage from various plant materials, such as its analogs are still used today.

The stone tools from Blackwater Draw were clearly not made of any local stone. Instead, as later analysis showed, they were fashioned from materials located, in some cases, hundreds of miles away: Edwards chert, found some twenty miles to the east in present-day Texas; Tecovas jasper from north of the Edwards chert; Alibates agate from the Texas panhandle. Presumably, these people traveled far on arduous treks to specific places for specific preferred materials—or, less likely, they were participants in far-flung trade networks. Did they plan these trips ahead, or were they merely taking advantage of rock that lay along the seasonal migration routes of Columbia mammoths and other herds the hunters followed?

From plant materials found in the gravel bed of the Mammoth Pit, Howard's people were able to determine the climate around the time the Clovis hunters had thrived here in the southern plains. Evidently, just before the Clovis hunters arrived on the scene, the region had been a cool, dry savanna ringed with spruce and pine forests on higher ground. In Clovis times, the area was moister—damper soils and a good deal of standing fresh water from springs and perennial streams. The grasslands and forests would have persisted, but summer and winter extremes of temperature were somewhat moderated. There was plenty of game, both large and small, easily stalked at the many watering places. In short, it was a perfect place for hunter-gatherers. But this wonderful late Pleistocene world was already changing even as Clovis people arrived.

By the time Clovis culture in this region had ended—a time we can now peg as extending no more than seven hundred years after it all began—the big mammals, including horse, camel, and mammoth, but not bison, were gone, extinct in the area. It may have been a period of prolonged drought that did in both the big herbivores and their carnivorous predators such as dire wolves and saber-toothed cats. There is evidence that the water table began to drop in this period, with springs and year-round streams beginning to disappear. The Clovis people in Blackwater Draw would have found themselves in a highly stressful situation, suggested by what appears to be an attempt to dig a well.

By the time the people present in the area were producing the smaller Folsom points and hunting bison, many ponds had turned into marshy areas, most streams no longer ran year-round, and many were gone altogether. It was by then well into the Holocene, and the entire climate was undergoing big changes as the glaciers in the north receded. On the southern plains, it was hotter and drier, the temperature extremes greater. Ancient bison and pronghorns congregated at the edges of the dwindling water holes with their little surrounds of lush vegetation. The forests of the higher ground were mostly gone, deep-rooted trees clinging only along old watercourses in the lowlands. The winds increased and may well have been comparable to the spring winds that assault this region today, laden with yellow dust, roaring over the land, rendering plant life horizontal, and eroding hope.

Was the short-lived Clovis culture a kind of apex in the art of the North American big-game hunter? Certainly at Blackwater Draw, the Clovis people appear to have killed mammoths, which were not only huge but hugely powerful and probably extremely dangerous when aroused. But how? Did they drive them to the ponds and the muck, where the great beasts got stuck and were possibly further immobilized by wrapping ropes made of grasses around their legs? Or were they more like scavengers, waiting for the mammoths to get stuck in the mud on their own, then bringing them down? Or did they simply scavenge dying mammoths? The evidence at Blackwater Draw, and the many other places where the artifacts of the Clovis people soon began to be found, was not and is not conclusive.

In any case, by the late 1930s, while the nations of Europe were about to start another world war, the tool kit of the Clovis culture emerged in the minds of American archaeologists and then percolated into the public mind as the earliest sign of human habitation in the New World. No sign of human habitation had by then been found underneath any assemblage of Clovis material. Clovis appeared from the limited evidence to be a culture that had apparently spread with lightning speed across the continent and then south into Latin America. In a nation given to setting records—on foot, in automobiles, or in flying machines—these Clovis people had what it takes. Speed. Daring. Inventiveness. The pioneering spirit writ large. Conquerors of the frontier. People could cheer for these First Americans.

By now, the field of archaeology was a far more professional arena. Numerous graduate schools offered archaeological degrees. Journals for the reporting of new finds were beginning to spring up in the subfields of the discipline. Obtaining a degree in archaeology now called for the mastery of a tremendous variety of information. Finds in Africa and soon Asia would revolutionize knowledge about the long course of human evolution, bringing to light humanoid creatures with strange names such as Australopithecus. Systematic ways of studying the astonishing ruins of the Southwest such as Mesa Verde were coming about. Studies of the Pleistocene and earlier eras in Europe and elsewhere were turning up exciting new data and insights into life in the three ages: Stone, Bronze, and Iron. A student of archaeology had too much to learn as other fields enriched his or her own—such as geology, of course, botany, hydrology, and zoology. The answer to this dilemma had already been found: the multidisciplinary excavation, like that of Blackwater Draw. This would become the norm and would add considerably to the data an excavation could generate. But, as is so often the case, a gain in one area can be accompanied by a loss. Not many noticed at the time, but more and more, students of archaeology learned less and less of the field from which archaeology had originally sprung: geology. It was a new era—one of increasing specialization.

But not even the shrewdest geologists of the era could determine exactly when those exemplary first Americans—Clovis people—had lived. The dates of their perceived sovereignty over all the other creatures of North America remained ambiguous, and the matter would stay that way until after World War II, when some more peaceful uses were found for the mysterious force that ended the war: radioactivity.

CHAPTER FIVE

———

TIMING IS EVERYTHING

From the dawn of prehistoric study, archaeologists were hamstrung by the fact that no one knew exactly when anything prehistoric had actually happened. A few exceptions existed. In temperate-zone areas, where the seasons differ considerably from winter to summer, one could count tree rings on recovered wood beams or posts to establish the age of the wood and, by extrapolation, the building of which the wood had once been a part. The recognition that tree rings were annual growth markers goes back to no other than Leonardo da Vinci and is now an elaborate and technical field called dendrochronology. It depends on the fact that trees in such areas exhibit clearly defined rings added annually when new growth occurs in the spring. Then growth slows through the end of the summer and ceases altogether in the winter. The width of the growth ring varies depending on many things, notably the amount, duration, and delivery periods of rainfall during the growing season. The patterns thus formed can lead you from tree to tree back in time as much as 10,000 years into the past—to the beginning of the Holocene.

With only such techniques available to them, by the time World War II ended, about all archaeologists could say was that Clovis Man had evidently abided here and there across the United States around the end of the Pleistocene, maybe 10,000 to 20,000 years ago, but more likely 10,000, and had been succeeded by Folsom Man and then other Paleo-Indians and later Archaic Indians and so on, all in a vaguely perceived and imperfectly defined sequential chronology.

After Folsom Man, by the way, none of these lithic cultures got a "Man" moniker. So-called Eden points were found in Wyoming north of the first Clovis finds, and Yuma points had been found to their west. Soon yet other points were discovered, including unfluted Folsoms called Midlands, eastern varieties called Dalton and Cumberland, and many other types, all clearly old but of very uncertain or inexact vintage. In any event, with other similar but not identical points, and some that were not so similar but still old, showing up all over the country, things were getting complicated. This condition was, of course, exacerbated by the fact that none of these ancient items could be assigned a "real" age.

Relative age was another matter, and in some cases stratigraphy could establish which type of artifact was older or younger than another. The basic principles of stratigraphy had been known, if not widely practiced, since 1668, when Niels Stensen (a.k.a. Nicolaus Steno) had articulated his stratigraphic "rules." The first rule is the law of superposition, which simply says that in an undisturbed geological situation, the younger layers and any materials in them are superposed or lie above the older layers and their contents. Put most simply, the deeper layers are older than the shallower ones. But the world and therefore stratigraphy is more complicated than that in many areas.

In practice, establishing stratigraphic relationships is a very difficult and notoriously tricky process, especially for many modern archaeologists, who are remarkably ill trained to comprehend or perform this critical chore. Whole textbooks have been devoted to the subject of stratigraphy, and many careers have been spent sorting out the most important ways to establish stratigraphic relationships and avoid the many and often subtle pitfalls of interpreting complex stratigraphic sequences. Using an old and shopworn but still useful analogy, strata are like chapters in a book; the stratigraphy is the story told by those chapters.

To give you an idea of how complicated reading the story told by the strata is, imagine you find a projectile point in what had once been a hole or pit. Obviously, it had to have entered the pit after it was dug. Similarly, the pit had been dug into a stratum, which had to have been there before the pit could be dug. If there are other pits, say, four pits all intersecting one another, establishing the sequence in which they were dug and the sequence of their contents is going to be difficult, to put it mildly. Few archaeologists today are trained to do this kind of thing properly.

Even today, when such instruments as lasers and electron microscopes capable of showing what an *atom* looks like have been brought to bear on the matters of stratigraphy and dating, people can still find reason to disagree. Certainly I learned this (to my dismay) as the years went by and the grousers about Meadowcroft groused on. Archaeology, which in the United States has been essentially a subdiscipline of anthropology since the time of Franz Boas, is thought of at least by some scholars as a social science—which means almost automatically soft and imprecise, like sociology and economics, as opposed to the "hard" sciences such as physics and chemistry and molecular biology. In these fields, you can frame an experiment to test a hypothesis—say, about light waves—and prove or disprove the hypothesis. Another researcher can create the same original conditions and perform the same experiment, and he or she should get the same result. But archaeology, however soft a science it is (and theoreticians have spent lifetimes fretting about this), was soon to benefit from the hardest of all sciences.

Another means of telling the *relative* time of things found in the ground came along around the time of World War II: the fluorine method. Bones that are buried in the ground take up fluorine from the groundwater over time, so a collection of bones found in one place that were buried at about the same time should have the same concentration of fluorine in them. On the other hand, if they have gross differences in fluorine content, they were not buried at the same time. The method is of little use in determining the age of bones in different sites since the amount of groundwater and the amount of fluorine it contains can vary widely over fairly small areas, but it came in handy in solving a major problem in early human evolution.

In 1912, a paleontologist named Charles Dawson found in a gravel bed near Lewes, England, the remains of extinct Ice Age animals, chert artifacts, and the skull and jawbone of what appeared from association to be an early Pleistocene humanoid. Called *Eoanthropus dawsonii*, this "dawn man" also seemed to be a different strain altogether from the *Homo erectus* remains that were roughly contemporary with it. By putting a wholly unexpected branch on the human genealogical tree, this anomaly threw what the British call a "spanner" into the human evolutionary works until the 1950s, when J. S. Weiner and others subjected the skull and the jaw to the fluorine method. It showed that the two skeletal items were not of the same age and that both were much younger than the legitimately early Pleistocene animal remains. It soon became known that this creature, called Piltdown Man, was a hoax; in fact, it was a fairly recent human skull and the jawbone of an orangutan, cleverly doctored to look old and planted in the gravel with the animal fossils and artifacts so that the hapless Dawson would be sure to come across them. Just who had perpetrated the hoax and for what reason remains unclear, but speculation about who this hoaxer was is as spirited as that about Jack the Ripper. There has even been speculation that Jack and the Piltdown hoaxer were the same man, none other than Arthur Conan Doyle. Of course, Conan Doyle has since been "cleared" of this charge, but the accusation made the entire matter all the more titillating.

Informed speculation continued to be the primary means of assigning an age to any prehistoric material until about this same time, the 1940s and 1950s, when physics revolutionized archaeology and other fields that probed the prehistoric past. Long before, it had become clear that various elements, such as uranium, potassium, and carbon, come in various forms called isotopes. Isotopes of a given element all have very much the same properties, differing only in having different amounts of neutrons in their nuclei. And many isotopes are radioactive, emitting energetic particles into the surroundings at an average rate peculiar to that element. As each atom of a particular radioactive isotope loses particles, it turns into something else—either a different element or another so-called daughter version of itself. And this brings up the notion of a half-life, a concept that is often misunderstood.

A RADIOCARBON PRIMER

The chemical basis of most life on earth is the element carbon, and each living thing consumes a bit of carbon all the time it is alive. Plants get it from the carbon dioxide in the atmosphere, herbivorous animals get it from plants and the atmosphere, carnivores from the herbivores and the atmosphere. A certain small percentage of all this carbon is a radioactive isotope of carbon called carbon-14. The rest of it is called carbon-12. (There is no need to protest over the presence of radioactive carbon in all of us; it is simply part of nature, not a nefarious plot by the government or the nuclear power industry.) All of us living things take in carbon—both carbon-14 and carbon-12 (which is basically inert)—until we die. Then the carbon-14 present in our tissues decays, transforming itself into another element, nitrogen-14. It takes 5,730 years for half the carbon-14 in, say, a dead geranium to turn into nitrogen-14. In another 5,730 years, half of that *remaining* carbon-14 will have become nitrogen-14. And so on. All this came to be known in 1947 through the work of a chemist, Willard Libby, who was rewarded with a Nobel Prize in 1960.

So suppose you took a bit of a scraping from a wooden tool used by a potential ancestor you found in the family rockshelter and measured how much carbon-14 was still in it compared to nitrogen-14. If it was half and half, you could confidently say that about 5,730 years had passed.

In the early days of radiocarbon dating, one needed fairly large samples to get a measurement, and even in such a case the measuring techniques were comparatively rough. So a radiocarbon date was given in years B.C. or in years before the present (B.P.) plus or minus a smaller number of years. A radiocarbon date would appear in a report like this: 12,000 ± 120 years B.P. (before present, which is, by long established convention, actually A.D. 1950).

This of course meant anywhere between 11,880 and 12,120 years ago, a difference of 240 years, which is still in a sense relative, but less relative than mere guesswork or even informed speculation. The amount of years plus or minus is a statistical measure of the confidence one can place in the date—and that confidence depends on several things, but chiefly the size of the sample being analyzed. Bigger is better.

Carbon-14 dating has become so important a feature in studies of early humans and other prehistoric events and phenomena that it is best we go a bit further in explaining some of the technicalities involved. For despite the application of high-tech methods and ever-increasing confidence in the technique, serious scholars still can—and do—argue about the results. And of course people like fundamentalist Creationists or some Native Americans will point to the complexities and occasional ambiguities involved and say the entire technique is flawed and therefore meaningless, thus preserving their belief that the Genesis story is verbatim history or that humans arose in North America and spread to the rest of the world.

Carbon-14 dating is possible thanks to cosmic processes. In brief, the constant rain of cosmic radiation into the earth's atmosphere causes the isotope of nitrogen, nitrogen-14, to turn into carbon-14. *An assumption here was that the amount of carbon-14 thus produced in the atmosphere has remained constant over the past 50,000 to 100,000 years.* Carbon-14 reacts with oxygen in the atmosphere and becomes carbon dioxide. *The assumptions in this case were that C-14 is as likely to be oxidized into carbon dioxide as is nonradioactive carbon (mostly carbon-12) and that all this takes place fast enough to make the ratio of carbon-14 and carbon-12 the same everywhere.* Because most organisms—plants and animals—do not discriminate between the two forms of carbon present in the overall carbon budget they take in from their surround, *it was assumed that the plant or animal would have the same ratio of the two carbons as are present in the atmosphere.* Once the plant or animal dies and stops absorbing carbon, the radioactive carbon begins to decrease, half of it turning back into nitrogen-14 after 5,730 years. One can measure the amount of carbon-14 by counting its atomic emissions over a brief period of time with equipment similar in essence to a Geiger counter.

After radiocarbon dating was first tried out, some of the assumptions in italics above proved to be not quite perfect. First of all, the industrial age has pumped a whole lot of very old carbon into the atmosphere from the burning of fossil fuels—fuels consisting of little else than dead plants that died several hundred million years ago and were buried, where time and pressure and other forces turned them into coal, oil, and natural gas. Because the dead plants have long since lost all their carbon-14, when burned they add huge amounts of carbon-14-*deficient* carbon to the atmosphere. Happily, adjustments for this can be made by using tree-ring dating and other dating systems to figure out the ratio of C-14 to C-12 before the Industrial Revolution. Similarly, by comparing the carbon ratios with calendrical methods of dating, one can make adjustments for such monkey wrenches in the works as changes in the earth's magnetic field (which affect the amount of cosmic radiation striking the atmosphere and thus the amount of carbon-14 available to be soaked up by plants).

Another complexity that must be considered is that some creatures, such as certain mollusks and water plants, take up "dead" carbon from old rocks, chiefly limestone, as well as from the atmosphere, and thus appear older than they are. Also, carbon can enter a dead creature after death from such contaminants as humic acids in the soil. These considerations put a premium on the preparation of the specimen to be tested.

Even with all of the needed precautions taken, radiocarbon dates tend to *underestimate* the calendrical age of specimens, and the amount of underestimation tends to grow with time. Something that is 22,000 calendrical years old will test out to be only 18,500 radiocarbon years—or 3,500 years "too young." At 33,000 calendrical years, the radiocarbon years can be as much as 4,300 years "too young," or 28,700. The practical limit for radiocarbon dating is about 45,000 years, and in fact, beyond 22,000 (calendrical) years, the entire method gets considerably more relative. But for specimens that are 22,000 years old or less, there are straightforward gauges for relating the radiocarbon years to calendar years. When encountering prehistoric dates in the scientific literature or the press, it is important for obvious reasons to know if the figures are given in raw radiocarbon years or calibrated years, that is, adjusted to calendrical years.

More recently, a far greater accuracy has been achieved in radiocarbon dating thanks to a device called an accelerator mass spectrometer (AMS). Previously, the way to measure the amount of carbon-14 in a sample compared to its decay product, nitrogen-14, was to count the sample's emissions over some reasonable period of time. This counted only the amount of radiocarbon that decayed in that interval, and from this one could do the math and determine how much was present. In AMS dating, which amounts to putting the sample in a kind of linear accelerator like the ones used to smash atoms, one counts all the atoms of carbon-14 present, not just the ones that decay. This permits far greater accuracy; theoretically, it should provide accurate dates up to 100,000 years ago. In actuality, achieving accurate dates of such great age is not practical even with AMS dating. The reason is that any sample that is 35,000 years old will have only 2 percent of its original carbon-14 left. Even a tiny bit of a recent contaminant—say a 1 percent increment of modern coal dust in the sample—is enough to skew the radiocarbon date seriously. So AMS dating has proven a boon to archaeologists not so much in extending the process back in time as in making it possible to date ever-smaller samples with ever-increasing accuracy. In earlier days, the way to increase one's confidence in a date (and reduce the number of years plus or minus that followed the date) was to use a bigger sample. Now this is no longer much of a consideration—as long as there is enough money in one's research grant to afford the more expensive AMS technique.

There are other, similar means of dating materials. The potassium/argon method, wherein naturally occurring potassium-40 decays into argon-40, is especially useful for dating the minerals within rocks. The half-life of potassium-40 is a whopping 1.35 billion years, so in theory and practice it can be used to date the very origin of the planet Earth, approximately 4.6 billion years ago. On the other hand, it is not much good at dating rocks that are any younger than a few hundred thousand years old, which leaves a large gap of time where most isotopic dating techniques do not function very well. In certain circumstances the gap can be filled by dating inorganic carbonates such as limestone and the stalactites and stalagmites of caves in which case isotopes of uranium that decay into various "daughter" isotopes at given rates are used. But this isotopic technique is of less value dating once-living things represented by shells or fossil bones since these objects absorb uranium unevenly from their burial surround, thereby skewing the date.

Yet other techniques have been developed, in particular thermoluminescence. This takes advantage of the fact that certain crystalline substances imprison extra electrons in the interstices of the crystals (called "traps") when the substance is subjected to irradiation from naturally occurring elements, normally uranium in the ground. When the substance is bombarded in the laboratory with a dose of thermal neutrons, the trapped electrons are released in the form of light. In other words, they glow. The intensity of the glow is directly proportional to the number of trapped electrons. If you know the intensity of irradiation from the ground (which is essentially constant, given the long half-life of the substances, such as uranium, that generate it), you can then estimate how long ago the irradiation began, thus dating the object. This has proven especially useful in dating pottery sherds and some thermally altered or heated chert artifacts, particularly those that are between a few thousand and a few hundred thousand years old. Thermoluminescence has been used, for example, to show that humans were present in Australia 40,000 or more years ago—which would be an iffy call for radiocarbon dating.

Soon enough, by the late 1950s and early 1960s, carbon-14 dating had established an interval during which Clovis Man had flourished in North America. His tools had been found chiefly south of the Canadian border all the way into northern Mexico and extending from the eastern foothills of the Rocky Mountains all the way to the east coast with several glaring and still intriguing gaps. Other, similar tools had been discovered as far south as the southern tip of South America. By 1967, it was thought that this amazingly expansionary Clovis interval had lasted from 11,500 uncalibrated radiocarbon years B.P. to 11,000 B.P., a mere half millennium. This was an amazingly short period for such widespread exploits. And radiocarbon dates were showing that this was the very same half millennium in which more than sixty species of large mammals were wiped out in the New World. This was the first circumstantial evidence that the first Americans were the heedless destroyers of the continent's most dramatic wildlife.

THE GREAT EXTINCTION

Scientists have found some seventy-six giant ground sloths in the zoological treasure trove of the La Brea tar pits, and the last—meaning most recent—one perished 13,800 years ago. Called a *Glossotherium,* this was a huge creature with long forelimbs, massive back legs, and a thick tail. Like the anteater, another edentate to which it is distantly related, it walked on the outsides of its feet, which measured up to nineteen inches in length. An awkward, even clumsy vegetarian of the open grasslands, it was small-eyed and small-brained and most likely would have suffered extinction sooner had it not been for its large claws and the bony nodules that turned its skin into something akin to chain mail. A more recent one was found in Florida, dating to about 10,000 years ago, indicating that these big sloths were not among the first to go in what seems to be a terrifyingly sudden extinction event in which almost all the large late Pleistocene mammals of North and South America vanished from the planet forever.

Earlier by a bit more than two millennia, the short-faced bear disappeared from the fossil record, a vanishing act that seems to coincide with the appearance on the scene of the grizzly bear. Some say the grizzly drove the short-faced bear out, but how a smaller, slower creature overwhelmed a bigger, faster one is not clear. Perhaps the grizzly, and the black bear as well, gained an advantage by being omnivorous, while the short-faced bear was limited to meat. But when *Arctodus simus* vanished, there were still herds of bison and the horse had not yet gone extinct in the Americas, nor had the mammoths and mastodons. And the vegetarian cave bears of the late Pleistocene, much the same size as the short-faced bear, went extinct at this time as well, in both the Old and New Worlds. So what happened in the kingdom of the bears? What made the world a rotten place for huge bears? We simply don't know.

Similarly, the stag-moose died out about the same time fossils of today's moose appear; was this a matter of competition for the same ecological niche? And what was it about the moose that made it more successful than the stag-moose? Again there is no answer here, just a correlation. Correlations between events or phenomena are not the same thing as causation. One can show that with the increase in the number of streetlights in cities, the crime rate has gone up, but to suggest that light on the streets at night causes crime might not be a tenable conclusion.

In all, some thirty-three genera of mostly gigantic late Pleistocene mammals were extinct not too long before or not long after the glaciers had receded into Canada. (A genus—plural, genera—is a classificatory group that includes one or more species, so many more than thirty-three species went out of business in this catastrophic period.) The animals that disappeared were almost entirely large—even extralarge—animals. A handful of rodents and other small mammals were extinguished at around this time, but nothing that would otherwise be noticed against the normal background buzz of extinctions that occur all the time. It is clear that the expiration of these thirty-three genera took place in a fairly compact period of time—largely between 12,000 and 8,000 years ago, an eye blink in geological time, though a very long period for a human lineage with only an oral tradition to keep the past alive. After a couple thousand years, who

TIMING IS EVERYTHING | 119

would remember the *Glossotherium* except in a generalized way as a monster of myth time? In any event, pinning down exactly when each of these genera was finally lost to the world is now much more feasible than it was a half-century ago, though it remains tentative. The following table provides a glimpse of some of the devastation:

COMMON NAME	GENUS	MOST RECENT DATE BEFORE PRESENT
CHEETAH	*Acinonyx*	17,000
PECCARY	*Platygonus*	13,000
SHORT-FACED BEAR	*Arctodus*	12,600
PRONGHORN	*Stockoceros*	11,300
WOODLAND MUSK OX	*Symbos*	11,100
MAMMOTH	*Mammuthus*	10,500
MASTODON	*Mammut*	10,400
LION	*Panthera*	10,400
HORSE	*Equus*	10,400
CAMEL	*Camelops*	10,300
STAG-MOOSE	*Cervalces*	10,200
GIANT BEAVER	*Castoroides*	10,200
GIANT GROUND SLOTH	*Glossotherium*	9,800
SABERTOOTH	*Smilodon*	9,400
TAPIR	*Tapirus*	9,400

In this list, as in more complete ones, the apparent extinction dates cluster between 11,000 and 9,500 years ago. This was the time that the climate, local weather, and ecosystems of North America were undergoing a spectacularly rapid upheaval. It is also the time when other creatures that could also be called charismatic megafauna thrived—the hunters of the Clovis culture and the ensuing Folsom culture. Both factors—climate change and the mighty hunters of Clovis and Folsom—have been indicated in the cataclysmic end of the giant mammals of the New World.

What was left after the major extinctions had occurred was a host of medium and small mammals ranging from beaver and raccoons to mice and moles; largish prey animals consisting of today's bison, bighorn sheep, mountain goats, pronghorns, mule and whitetail deer, elk, moose, caribou, and musk ox; and predators consisting of polar bears, grizzly and black bears, mountain lions and other relatively small cats—such as ocelots, lynxes, and bobcats—foxes, coyotes, and a handful of wolves. For the first Americans, things had changed dramatically from those grand adrenaline-filled millennia south of the ice sheet when the world was new and terrifyingly aswarm with giants.

Because the timing of the extinctions, particularly as they were understood in the 1960s (that is, as almost simultaneous), coincided with the presence of Clovis Man, the conclusion to be drawn was elementary, at least to a certain professor of geochronology at the University of Arizona, Paul S. Martin, and a colleague of his in Tucson, C. Vance Haynes, who would soon become the bêtes noires of anyone who even dreamt of pre-Clovis archaeological sites.

PLEISTOCENE OVERKILL

In the late sixties, Paul Martin was a rawboned, crew-cut gent with a high, domed forehead and the squint lines of someone who spends a lot of time out of doors. He boldly announced a theory that pegged Clovis Man, the earliest known progenitor of the American Indians, as the most voracious and insatiably reckless hunter of game the world had ever seen.

This was a time when the word "ecology" was escaping from the journals of science into the public mind and the American Indian was beginning to be revised into something of a natural ecologist or, as Martin put it in a December 1967 article in the popular magazine *Natural History,* "the noble savage, a child of nature, living in an unspoiled Garden of Eden until the discovery of the New World by Europeans." That same year Martin published a technical work, *Pleistocene Extinctions,* on which his article was based.

Now, Martin was not the first to point out that a lot of big mammal species had gone extinct toward the end of the Pleistocene, and of course it had been known since the 1930s that Clovis Man had killed at least some mammoths. Indeed, long before Martin, an environmental scholar named Carl Sauer had proposed that early man had wiped out the big-game animals in North America by using fire drives. This was before radiocarbon

Ludicrous reconstruction of Clovis hunters confronting an Ice Age bear.

dating began to pin down the dates, so most people had rejected the idea, based as it was on virtually no evidence except accounts of historic Native Americans burning grasses to hunt and to encourage new growth the following year. Still, the general understanding before Martin's announcement in 1967 was that the extinctions had been caused by sudden climatic change brought on by the retreat of the glaciers. Hotter summers and colder winters would have upset the breeding seasons, with reproduction coming at a season when the young could not survive. Accelerated competition among the big mammals would also have occurred, and they would have wiped out their food supply. When Clovis Man showed up, having recently crossed the Bering land bridge, he administered the coup de grâce to the remaining badly depleted herds.

Paul Martin, however, pointed out that habitat such as grassland appeared to be improving as the Pleistocene ended. Why would such grass-eating species as horses go extinct when there was plenty of grass? Why would spruce-eating mastodons go extinct when spruce forests were ex-

Clovis hunters sprinting south, leaving a trail of projectile points and dead megafauna.

tending northward, following the receding glacier's edge? The unprecedented snows of severe winters could hardly be blamed for these mass extinctions since numerous tropical species had gone extinct in this period. Indeed, Martin looked at the matter globally, quoting Pleistocene experts as all agreeing that the big climatic changes of the previous 50,000 years had occurred simultaneously around the world. But, he said, the extinctions of large mammals had coincided with only one thing: the arrival of humans on the different continents and islands. Martin pointed out that in Australia, for example, various big marsupials had vanished around 14,000 years ago, just after, it was then thought, people had arrived. He pointed to the giant birds called moas that had survived the Pleistocene on New Zealand but had been extinguished by the late-arriving Maoris on those islands about a thousand years ago. Examples abounded.

"My own hypothesis," Martin wrote, "is that man, and man alone, was responsible for the unique wave of Late Pleistocene extinction—a case of overkill rather than 'overchill' as implied by the climatic change theory."

Africa stood out in most minds at the time as an exception; the great wildlife spectacles of that continent were often billed as comparable to those of America's Ice Age landscape—and of course, humans had been in Africa long before the late Pleistocene extinctions had taken place around the world. Martin explained that some 30 percent of Africa's wildlife had indeed gone extinct in the late Pleistocene—such creatures as giant pigs, giraffes with antlers, and giant sheep. This was a significant extinction, if not as severe as that in the Americas, and Martin ingeniously pegged it to the development of fire as a tool and hunting strategy by African people around that time. As for North America, when people first swept in through the

melting ice corridor east of the Cordilleras, we can be confident that they were old hands at hunting wooly mammoths and other large Eurasian mammals. In contrast, the New World mammoth and other species of big game had never encountered man, and were unprepared for escaping the strange two-legged creature who used fire and stone-tipped spears to hunt them in communal bands. . . . In any case, radiocarbon dates indicate that North American extinction followed very closely on the heels of the big game hunters. The Paleo-Indians easily found and hunted the gregarious species that ranged over the grasslands, deserts, or other exposed habitat. As the hunters increased in number and spread throughout the continent, large animals whose low rate of reproduction was insufficient to offset the sudden burden of supporting a "superpredator" soon perished.

The migration of humans into the Americas soon came to be seen as a blitzkrieg wherein a band of as few as a hundred wandering Eurasians, led by maybe twenty-five male superpredators, burst through the ice-free corridor into midcontinent. Overnight they invented the Clovis point and, in an unprecedented (among hunting societies) population explosion, swept across the continent at a spectacular pace, reaching the tip of South America—a distance of some six thousand miles—in five hundred years or less, along the way wiping out practically everything that both moved and weighed more than a hundred pounds, as they colonized (and then extinguished) the previously innocent animal kingdoms of North and South America.

How was it that any big species survived the superpredator? Those that went into the woods—bears, moose, woodland bison, deer—could have evaded Clovis Man, hidden away while Clovis and Folsom hunters slaughtered the last big herbivores in open country. Musk oxen, those shaggy beasts of tundra and snow, were wiped out in Eurasia but survived in North America only, Martin suggested, because part of the population was stranded *north* of the glacier in what was called the Greenland Refuge when Clovis Man went blitzing through. When the ice finally melted back to its current configuration some six thousand years ago, musk oxen were again exposed to humans. But by that time these humans—mostly Eskimos—had fortunately learned about sustained yield. The wandering superpredators were no more.

While it never found anything like unanimous agreement among the scholars concerned with that era, the Pleistocene Overkill theory swept the country with Clovis-style speed. Conservative pundits, sportsmen's groups, and right-wingers in particular found it especially useful, while American Indians and their supporters not surprisingly found it totally disagreeable. As late as 1995, Vine Deloria, Jr., the sometime political scientist and full-time activist from the Sioux Nation, railed against the idea. In *Red Earth, White Lies,* an impassioned (and largely ill-informed) diatribe against the matter of human evolution, the existence of the Bering land bridge, and the continuing failure of the sciences to confirm the creation stories of Native American myth time, he attacked Pleistocene Overkill as merely another politically motivated assault on the moral values of his people. In response to such assaults, he denied the underpinning validity of any and all science, its findings, and its methods, including any result whatsoever from radiocarbon dating—except one he quoted of 38,000 years B.P. that apparently embarrassed scientific dogma. (As we have seen, a carbon-14 date of that

age is by its very nature unreliable.) To unshakeable true believers like Deloria, biblical creationists, and others who are *selectively* antiscience, there
is, of course, simply nothing to say.

In science, however, theories are put forth as hypothetical explanations
of certain observations, not as "facts." They are then tested against the
world in a variety of ways and almost always revised a bit or a lot (or
thrown out) in the light of new information—new observations or new
light shed on old observations. Science is less a matter of creating facts than
a process of reducing ignorance, but some people always prefer the bliss of
ignorance. Scientific theories and propositions can be upsetting to established beliefs, and Martin knew from the outset that his idea was going to
be upsetting—and not just to Native Americans.

In the late 1960s, people were beginning to talk about the unfortunate
results of importing species of plants and animals into one continent that
had evolved elsewhere. Starlings, for example, were brought into New
York City by a romantic in the late nineteenth century who had the idea of
importing every bird mentioned in Shakespeare to this country. They soon
became a terrible menace to native songbirds all across the continent, taking over their territories and nesting sites. Tumbleweeds, the scourge of the
arid West, had arrived accidentally as seeds on ships. Mynahs, goats, and
other alien animals were eliminating the native fauna of Hawaii. The wisdom of bringing in game animals from places like Africa—such as
oryxes—and setting them loose for sportsmen to chase was under serious
scrutiny.

According to Martin, however, the evolution of new species and the
extinction of old ones go hand in hand. In normal times, he said, all the
available niches are filled, and as a new species evolves, it outcompetes an
old one for the same ecological niche and the old one is extinguished. But
in North America, with some thirty genera extinguished practically
overnight, new species did not evolve to take their place. Thus, he pointed
out, when horses were returned to North America by the Spanish and some
of them escaped into the wild, they found plenty of room on the grasslands
they had once inhabited and formed large wild herds. So perhaps bringing
in the likes of oryxes was a good thing, he suggested, filling in niches left
empty for millennia by the marauding of Clovis Man.

The growing number of ecologically minded wildlife biologists and range managers did not think much of Martin's notion, and it turned out to be a major oversimplification of ecological and evolutionary processes. But that is not our concern here. It is sufficient to point out that what can seem to be merely an academic matter, of little relevance in the real world, can on the contrary have considerable ramifications outside the academy. People in the late sixties and beyond who were resisting the growing environmental movement were happy to see the American Indians—something of an environmentalist icon—discredited as the descendants of ecological ravagers—and this did no one any good.

H. L. Mencken, who knew very little about science and its methods, said something wise that applies to science as well as many other fields of endeavor. "For every complex problem," he wrote, "there is a solution that is simple, neat, and wrong." By now, the Pleistocene Overkill theory has lost credibility, except, of course, with Martin, who believes it more firmly than ever, and a handful of acolytes who are not attempting its resuscitation. However, not everyone in the field bit even in 1967, and virulent disagreement has continued for decades. Martin continued to argue that a small group, bursting on the scene and being well fed by the slaughter of huge and even wasteful amounts of meat on the hoof, could have reproduced at the astonishingly high rate of 3.4 percent annually, thus increasing the overall population size dramatically and far beyond the average rate (0.5 percent) of any ethnographically documented hunter-gatherer group. Not only would they have had to be copulating machines to accomplish this, they would also have had to have much lower infant mortality rates than are typical of hunter-gatherers. If they also managed to migrate on average some ten miles a year, they would have constituted an expanding wave of amazingly efficient and fecund killers that could have reached Tierra del Fuego (and every other part of the hemisphere) in less than a millennium.

But many scholars wondered how Clovis hunters could in truth have reproduced at a rate so much greater than other hunting and gathering societies are known to reproduce. Martin evidently got his 3.4 percent rate from the experience of the mutineers who fetched up on Pitcairn Island after throwing Captain Bligh off H.M.S. *Bounty*—and apparently they were copulating machines! (Why Martin chose the Pitcairners is hard to imagine except for the fact that precise data existed about them, whereas it was harder to come by in the ethnographic literature about tribal people.) Furthermore, hunters and gatherers typically move before all the resources in an area are used up, largely because the obtaining of food becomes arduous enough to make moving worth the extra effort. Also, small groups of people, such as little daughter bands, tend to stay within reach of the mother band so they can reassemble periodically to find mates or to replace those lost to fatal accidents. And of course fatal accidents would be all the more likely among people who hunted mammoths on any regular basis. These animals were almost three times as tall as any Clovis hunter, weighed as much as seven tons, and (if they were anything at all like modern elephants) unpredictable and even vengeful, as well as immensely powerful.

Martin cites a nineteenth-century account of some five hundred African tribespeople surrounding a herd of eighteen elephants with fires and then killing off the herd with spears as they stood dazed amid the smoke. However, there is no evidence that Clovis people ever assembled in such numbers or employed fire drives. It is literally inconceivable that humans could gang up and drive mammoths off a cliff, as they would learn to do with bison, and it is barely conceivable that they could—in a communal group—have selected a member of a herd, perhaps an old or infirm member, somehow isolated it, filled it with spear points, and finally run it down, perhaps with the assistance of dogs as distractions. But that this scenario would ever be common beggars the imagination. This sentiment was shared by other archaeologists, notably Scotty MacNeish and James B. Griffin, the late longtime authority on the prehistory of the eastern United States.

Of course, Clovis people did in fact kill mammoths. In all, archaeologists have found perhaps twelve sites where hunters and mammoths definitely tangled and at least one mammoth probably died as a result. These are all in the West, mostly in Arizona and the mountain states north to the Canadian border, with one site as far east as Missouri. In addition, there are another twelve sites where men may have killed mammoths—the evidence is not conclusive—the farthest east of these being in Michigan. That there are so few actual sites of mammoth kills (and virtually none of horse, camel, or sloth kills) is a major embarrassment to the overkill theory that Martin lamely explains by saying that anything that happened that fast would have left little evidence. On the other hand, almost no evidence has ever turned up of man killing a mastodon—those loners of the East—and one has to wonder why not. In a recent account, David Meltzer of SMU cites Jim Judge, another Clovis scholar, for his last word on the Pleistocene Overkill theory: "each Clovis generation probably killed one mammoth, then spent the rest of their lives talking about it."

As more and more became known about the nature of the environmental changes that took place as the Pleistocene came to an end, it seemed more and more plausible that the rapidly changing climate and fragmenting ecosystems, as well as in some places the creation of the opposite— monolithic ecosystems such as the huge area of tall-grass prairie—could all have put many populations of large mammals into seriously stressful situations. It is clear that before the ice receded, populations of animals in a given place could have included some we now know as northern species and some we know as southern. They evolved together in these habitats, and as the climate changed and localized habitats changed, some species had to move out and did, and others—if they couldn't move out—went extinct. The slower reproductive rates of larger animals—cited by Martin as a disadvantage in the face of human assaults—would have been equally disadvantageous in an assault brought about by loss of habitat.

A few other researchers have recently suggested that people invading the pristine lands of the Western Hemisphere could have brought with them viral diseases that in turn could have jumped across species lines and devastated animal populations across the board. It is known that epidemics can spread very quickly and wipe out huge segments of a population—Europe lost nearly half its people to the Black Plague in less than a century. It is also well known that viral diseases can leap from species to species—AIDS evidently arose in chimpanzees, and the Spanish flu of 1918 arose in chickens, jumped to pigs, and thence to humans. In all, it killed 21 million people—twenty thousand in New York City alone—and wiped out such remote populations as Eskimo villages. Why couldn't Asians, reaching the New World, have brought some virus that could do the reverse— leap species lines to infect at least all the herbivores? The large ones would have been most likely to suffer the most, since they not only reproduce more slowly but are always much fewer in number than smaller mammals such as mice. Thus it would have been the smaller ones that survived long enough to develop immunity. On the other hand, there is no known virus that could accomplish such mayhem, none known to leap from humans to other mammals, and no trace of such a virus has ever been located in any remains of mammoths or any other now-extinct Ice Age animal. Part of the reason could be that we have only recently developed the techniques for spotting the DNA of a virus amid the DNA of its host—for example, in the tusks of a mammoth—and it is hard with such tests to find something you haven't already identified.

In any event, all the evidence for what killed off the New World's megafauna is circumstantial at best. None of it would be sufficient to actually condemn Clovis hunters, viruses, or even climate change as the sole terminator. More than likely it was a combination of at least two forces: climate change and the human coup de grâce to some (but not all) species that were greatly reduced, stressed, weakened, and isolated. For example, mastodons could well have become isolated in eastern coniferous forests, which had once been extensive but became smaller islands of forest surrounded by deciduous trees as the climate changed. Small, isolated populations of mastodons would soon have been forced to inbreed, and such inbreeding often produces drastic failures of the animals' reproductive system, leading ultimately but in relatively few generations to extinction. Hunters could, in the case of isolated and weakened mastodon populations, have administered the coup de grâce, and the fact that no one has found any human spear points or other weapons in association with mastodon remains does not prove that such kills did not happen.

Some species might have been weakened by diseases brought by humans, but it seems pushing it a bit to imagine a virus that would be equally lethal (and practically overnight) to thirty-six *genera* of large mammals. But various combinations of climate change (and its many deleterious effects) and selective hunting of relict populations could. At Blackwater Draw in Arizona, where Clovis points first came to light in association with mammoths, the world of the Southwest was experiencing a considerable drought. Formerly perennial streams were drying up seasonally or altogether, forcing herbivores to congregate at dwindling water holes, where they probably overgrazed the surrounding forage and, according to a persistent but mistaken myth, quite possibly got stuck in the mud at the pond's edge, and in any event were far more easily preyed on by a small band of hunters who—no matter how elegant their stone points—were not heavily armed in comparison with a behemoth of several tons.

Logic aside, however, the real problem with Martin's theory turns out to hinge greatly on timing. The overkill theory depends to a great extent on the megafauna of North (and South) America being almost wholly wiped out in the brief interval when Clovis tools were in use. To begin with, succeeding and presumably more accurate radiocarbon dates have shortened the Clovis interval down to well under a half millennium, while other such dates have widened the period in which the megafauna were extinguished—now evidently an interval of several thousand years beginning 17,000 years ago with the cheetah and ending about 9,000 years ago with the end of the giant tapir.

CHAPTER SIX

THE PRE-CLOVIS QUEST

When different lines of inquiry begin to coalesce and point in the same direction, and when the direction they point to is in favor of one's own cherished hypothesis, one rejoices. One also tends to guard that hypothesis with some of the attention a mother bear devotes to her cubs. Once the Pleistocene Overkill theory was enunciated in the late 1960s, an explanation existed for exactly *how* Clovis Man had managed to cover so much ground in so short a time. Those archaeologists who were already convinced that Clovis had been the first American culture could rejoice. After all, it was widely known that seabirds that had evolved on islands, such as the booby, had no fear of humans whatsoever. Because it had no idea how dangerous humans could be, the dodo was eaten to extinction by sailors, and the booby got its name for the same reason, though it survived. The giant mammals of North (and South) America were no different. They stood there, either astonished and presumably mute, or hardly even noticing these little bipeds, until—alas—the last of their kind went extinct.

Not everyone agreed with the overkill hypothesis, however, and well before it and radiocarbon dating came along, plenty of archaeologists believed for various reasons that Clovis could not have been the first group of humans here. Other kinds of points, many of them large and well made though not fluted, were coming to light in numerous other locales. Some of them appeared (in those preradiocarbon days) to be contemporaneous with Clovis or nearly so. The Clovis adherents held firm, however, buoyed by many other Clovis finds elsewhere in the West and all the way to the east coast, with some—though fewer—south of the United States. Many of the finds consisted of caches of Clovis points, leading to speculation that those highly mobile people had left what amounted to toolboxes here and there against the day they returned. Dave Meltzer and others have speculated that the caches had served some religious or ceremonial purpose. To this day, no one has satisfactorily explained the caches. Whether Clovis was first in this hemisphere or not, it remains a highly mysterious group, its characteristic tools appearing so suddenly and without evident precursors, the fluting on its points not serving any purpose that we can be certain of, not to mention the relatively abrupt end of the use of Clovis points. To people today, making the same tools for half a millennium may seem like an absurdly long time of inventive failure, an unimaginable mental stasis. But in the long, long run of human prehistory, it is really quite a small interlude, and when daily life is as dangerous as it must have been, one quite rationally hesitates to change anything as important as a tool that has so far worked well enough. Perhaps, people have suggested, the big Clovis points were made for killing truly huge beasts such as mammoths, but they fell out of use when the chief target became bison and other similarly sized prey, for which smaller points like Folsom points were better suited.

The mysteries surrounding Clovis continued to plague—or rather, puzzle and entertain—archaeologists as the decades passed, and most remained unshaken in the growing certainty that Clovis indeed represented the first Americans. The overkill hypothesis in the late 1960s made it seem all the more likely, as did the generally accepted idea that an ice-free corridor between the Laurentide and Cordilleran glaciers had opened up at just the right time to admit the first Americans. Perhaps the most important factor adding to the general sense of certainty had been present almost from the time the Clovis points at Blackwater Draw had been put into the archaeological record. That factor was the utter failure of anyone to find any site anywhere on the continent that showed people arriving here earlier than Clovis.

The failure was not for lack of trying; from the 1930s through to the end of the century, literally hundreds of pre-Clovis sites were announced—and soon fell by the wayside. They fell by the wayside for very good reasons—indeed, for the same reasons that Holmes and Hrdlička, the

Smithsonian's deadly duo, had shot down all the sites presented for Glacial Man until the finds at Folsom. Their criteria still applied and, modified only to take into account such tools as radiocarbon dating, still apply today. It was against this long cascade of failures that the pre-Clovis dates from Meadowcroft would be judged when, willy-nilly, I found myself in the predicament of tilting at the Clovis Bar, which by the late 1960s was well established. And to make matters worse, by the mid-1970s, a new version of the Smithsonian's old deadly duo was present—in the form of C. Vance Haynes, Paul Martin's colleague at Arizona.

Vance Haynes was trained as a geologist and has long taken an interest in what today we call geoarchaeology. Over the years he has done highly acclaimed work in the Nile Valley in Egypt. One of his major contributions, in fact (and one that is often overlooked), is simply that he has returned a geologist's perspective to archaeological work, a perspective that most archaeologists of the twentieth century have not themselves possessed because they were not trained in it with any depth. Early on, he became a knowledgeable student of the geological subtleties of archaeological sites in the American West, and by the early 1960s he was one of the chief arbiters of any pre-Clovis claim. His perspective on pre-Clovis sites was strongly conditioned, at least in my view as well as in his own published admission, by his experiences at Tule Springs, Nevada. Tule Springs was a paleontological and archaeological site located about ten miles north of Las Vegas. Originally excavated in the early 1930s, the site was one of the first after Folsom to produce evidence of the contemporaneity of early humans and Ice Age mammals. Subsequently excavated again in 1933, 1955, and 1956, the site yielded a radiocarbon date of 23,800 B.P. and what was thought to be charcoal from an apparent "firepit." This date suggested to some that this was far and away the oldest archaeological site yet discovered in the New World.

In 1962–63, the Nevada State Museum conducted a major multidisciplinary excavation at Tule Springs involving archaeologists, paleontologists, a botanist, a radiocarbon specialist, and several geologists, one of whom was Vance Haynes. The objective of the excavations was to establish once and for all the age of the human presence at the site and the nature of the association of such materials with Ice Age mammals. Suffice it to note that Haynes initially bought into a great antiquity for humans at this site before it was realized that the allegedly early dates derived *not* from charcoal in firepits but rather from ancient carbonized plant material—lignite—from the bottom of spring chambers that mimicked the appearance of firepits.

Haynes was badly stung by this incident and soon afterward became one of the staunchest supporters of the Clovis Bar as well as one of the most ubiquitous critics of anyone who dared to try to move it. The Tule Springs incident also burned into his mind the twin specters of contamination and misinterpretation of supposed relationships between artifacts and dates, points that he has faithfully raised ever since. Over the years Haynes has debunked more supposedly early sites and their excavators than even Hrdlička could have imagined. And in at least some minds, he became a second incarnation of that implacable figure.

NEW MEXICO JONES

In the early sixties, Vance Haynes was turning the cold shower on another claim of pre-Clovis habitation in North America, made by a colorful archaeologist and zoologist (and big-game hunter) at the University of New Mexico, Frank C. Hibben. Something of a legend in his younger days, Hibben married rich (running off with a benefactor's wife) when he was quite young, made regular safaris to the best big-game hunting grounds, and was considered an unparalleled shot. He hobnobbed with the rich, famous, and powerful, often slipping away on undisclosed missions that added a patina of mystery to his life. A superb raconteur, he entertained people endlessly in his large house full of taxidermy and artifacts on the edge of the university campus. But for a stocky build, he would have been a fine model for Harrison Ford's Indiana Jones (though one hears that that honor resides elsewhere). Like that celluloid character, Hibben longed to find the holy grail—in his case the holy grail of American archaeology—namely, inhabitants of North America who had arrived before Clovis and Folsom.

In 1936, a student of Hibben's returned to the campus in Albuquerque bearing some artifacts he had found in a cave partway up into the Sandia Mountains, a ten-thousand-foot range that looms on the eastern edge of the mile-high city. The artifacts were nothing special—probably relics of Pueblo Indians from historic times—but Hibben was intrigued by the existence of any cave that had been frequented by people. "The human animal," he was convinced, "has from earliest times been a cave animal." This was clearly the case in Europe and Asia, where generations of people "cowered" during thousands of years, looking nervously out at a world teeming with fearsome animals. Yet all the remains of early hunters in North America, Hibben would write later, had come from "open camp sites . . . along stream banks and around the edges of marshes and ponds." Evidently, Hibben said, the earliest Americans had been unafraid of the large beasts that had roamed their world and had been unfazed by "the chilling winds that whistled down from the glacial ice walls" of their era. Or—the earliest Americans were, like Asians and Europeans, cave dwellers who simply had not yet come to light.

So Frank Hibben undertook the exploration and then the excavation of Sandia Cave, a 453-foot-long tunnel located high up in the limestone wall of Las Huertas Canyon. And there, in due course, he came across the signs of Sandia Man. He would propose that Sandia people had been the first Americans, a group of hunters who had roamed parts of the American West probably some 25,000 years ago.

Throughout most of its relatively cramped (nine feet in diameter) length, Sandia Cave was filled with rubble and dust, as well as bats and the remains of pack rat activity. Early on, the team came across the claw of a giant ground sloth, and, Hibben wrote later, if they found evidence of people living in the cave at the same time as the sloth, they "might yet find an American cave man." They pressed on, excavating during four successive summers and coming across several different layers of material. Throughout the length of the cave, a layer of dust (sometimes six feet thick) had accumulated in the dry interval since the last glacier had receded. Below that was a layer of dripstone—the sort of limestone accumulation that creates stalagmites—forming a floor as hard as cement. Sledgehammering their way through it, the team found an "ancient cave floor" with scraps of flint and charcoal, the shattered bones of bison, horse, and camel, fragments of mammoth tusk, and the characteristic spear points called Folsom points. Folsom points dated back to about 10,500 years B.P. and came after Clovis points. Hibben had found his cave man. But he was only a cave-dwelling member of an already known group known collectively as Folsom Man, and therefore not so big a deal. So Hibben went deeper.

Below the Folsom floor was a layer of yellow ocher, a chalky substance that is a mineral oxide of iron and which Native Americans often collected for paint or dye. Hibben interpreted this level to represent a wet, cold period, a time of glacial advance, perhaps. And below that was yet another ancient cave floor, with the fragments of wolf and other carnivore bones along with bison, camel, mammoth, and so forth. And among them were flint points that were utterly different from the Folsom points: they were leaf-shaped with a pronounced shoulder, less skillfully made, with a single notch on one side for attaching them to a shaft of wood or bone. These points vaguely resembled much earlier leaf-shaped points found in many parts of western Europe and attributed to a culture called Solutrean. With the points were a variety of other tools, including what appeared to be hide scrapers.

Below the Sandia Man level was another layer, this one of white clay—from another wet period. Geologists working with Hibben suggested that the alternating layers of wet and dry origin corresponded with the oscillating advance and retreat of the glacier over thousands of years and thus came up with the date of 25,000 years for Sandia Man, plus or minus some 30 percent—which is a margin large enough to call the entire matter into question. At the time (1946) that Hibben published a popular book about early humans in the New World called *The Lost Americans,* there was still some doubt as to whether Folsom points were earlier or later than Clovis points, but his date of 25,000 years certainly made Sandia Man older than anything previously found. In a book called *Early Man in the New World,* updated and reissued by the American Museum of Natural History as late as 1962, the authors wrote that "there can be no doubt about the meaning of Frank C. Hibben's discoveries in Sandia Cave, New Mexico, in 1936. . . . The Sandia point is, of course, definitely older than Folsom."

Alas and alack for Frank Hibben and others who put their money on Sandia Man, the aforementioned Vance Haynes and his colleague George Agogino began in 1961 to reinvestigate Sandia Cave. Already there had been a good deal of controversy over Sandia Man, some saying that a mere handful of artifacts was hardly a basis for postulating an entire "culture," while others wondered if the Sandia excavators had gotten the geology of all those layers right. Meanwhile, only one other Sandia site, known as the Lucy site, had been discovered—also in New Mexico and also excavated by Frank Hibben. By then as well, the Solutrean connection had been deemed unlikely if not impossible. But many were still comfortable with the notion that a Sandia Man could exist.

Haynes and Agogino did not complete their written report for nearly twenty-five years, but in 1986 it appeared in *Smithsonian Contributions to Anthropology,* and it was devastating. In brief, the Sandia "cultural" layer immediately below the layer of yellow ocher—with its scrapers, projectile points, and animal bone fragments—was the result of what is called "bio-turbation," meaning in this case that animals had been burrowing verti-cally through several layers, carrying bones and artifacts down below through the ocher from the Folsom layer to the so-called Sandia layer. Nothing was found in the Sandia layer that dated earlier than about 14,000 years ago at most. Haynes and Agogino suggested that the "San-dia" scrapers and points had probably been used in more recent times by people mining ocher. Probably they had used the points to etch ocher blocks that could then be lifted out to be taken away and traded. In short, there was no Sandia Man.

The authors wrote that they had a "hope that this work will restore Sandia Cave to its rightful place in American archaeology," by which they no doubt meant the scrap heap. Of course, within the archaeological com-munity, the word had gotten out long before the Haynes and Agogino re-port saw the light of day, and there was considerable talk—not for public consumption—about the unstated conclusion Haynes and Agogino had reached.

Looking into the murk in 1994 for *The New Yorker* (which, it goes without saying, is a far cry from a scientific journal), writer Douglas Pres-ton interviewed as many people as he could reach who had been present at the original digs at Sandia Cave. When early questions arose, Hibben had insisted, for example, that his findings had been independently confirmed by a leading geologist, Kirk Bryan, and an experienced archaeologist, Frank H. H. Roberts, who had both worked extensively at the site. But eyewitnesses told Preston that Roberts had been there perhaps twice, and the same for Bryan. It turned out also that each time Hibben had sent ma-terial from Sandia Cave off for radiocarbon dating, he had sent mislabeled artifacts or committed other errors. Hibben had evidently made similar in-explicable goofs in other areas such as Alaska, where he claimed to have found a Clovis point on a pebbly beach in process of being washed away but later investigators found no such beach, much less any other sign of human habitation.

Lewis Binford, a man who turned out to be a major figure in archaeology, who was hired by the University of New Mexico over Hibben's objections, and who had been the one in the radiocarbon lab who had pointed out Hibben's earliest Sandia samples were flawed, was quoted by Preston as thinking of Hibben as a "curiosity." Binford wondered why "he went through all these *charades* to make himself important?" In all, the weight of the evidence, however circumstantial, points to at least one, if not more, instances of what could charitably be called "scientific license" committed by the great old storyteller. Sandia Man, in the end, has now vanished from all but long-out-of-date textbooks.

THE MAIN MAN

Louis S. B. Leakey, the grand student of early human evolution from Kenya, was legendary at spotting archaeological treasures. So proficiently did he find the remains of early hominids from millions of years ago in such places as Tanzania's Olduvai Gorge (in particular, the diminutive two-million-year-old *Homo habilis*) that he was considered to have a special attribute: Leakey's Luck. That it had something to do with perception, not just luck, and that his perceptiveness was not restricted only to fossil remains, is attested to by his plucking a young Englishwoman essentially out of a crowd and sending her off to Africa to see what she might be able to find out about the then wholly mysterious lives of wild chimpanzees. Thus he set into motion the twentieth century's most accomplished observer of animal behavior: Jane Goodall.

That Leakey's luck in finding fossils may also have had more to do with his wife, Mary, is highly likely. She was, it turned out, by far the more technically proficient of the two and made some of the fossil discoveries that Leakey named and interpreted. However, she preferred to stay out of the limelight. As Meltzer succinctly put it, whatever its source, Leakey's luck ran out in the Mojave Desert, and again Vance Haynes would play a role.

Leakey was among those Old World archaeologists who thought their American colleagues were a bit narrow-minded, a bit provincial in their certainty that Clovis Man had been the first American. Leakey saw no reason why human beings had not lived in the Americas long before the current American party line said, and he took great delight in saying so to American archaeologists. In 1963, while lecturing in California, he met Ruth de Ette Simpson of the San Bernardino County Museum, who had come across what she thought looked like some very old, primitive stone

Louis Leakey (right) and Ruth Simpson examining alleged artifacts from Calico Hills, California.

artifacts near Calico Hills in the Mojave Desert. Leakey enthusiastically accompanied Simpson to the site, a great fanlike accretion of soil, rock, and other debris that had washed out of a canyon. Called the Yermo Fan, it was at the time thought to be the product of the recent ice ages. Leakey marched around the site, finding Ruth Simpson's artifacts (which were chipped cobbles) unimpressive, but then he spotted a couple of chalcedony fragments in a trench someone had dug with a bulldozer.

"Dig here," he said, somewhat in the manner of Babe Ruth pointing his bat to the left field seats of Yankee Stadium prior to hitting a home run, and went back to Africa. Returning to the Yermo Fan later, Leakey chose three rocks from the thousands excavators had meanwhile selected as possible artifacts. On a later trip he chose forty-three as probable artifacts and, seeing burn marks on some cobbles that appeared to have been placed in a circle, pronounced them a hearth. All the stone "tools" Leakey found worthy were made of chalcedony, a form of quartz, suggesting that the toolmakers had been selective about materials. A geologist calculated that the rocks in the Yermo Fan were some 50,000 to 100,000 years old. To Leakey, the notion of the ancientness of mankind in America was demonstrated. (It is said that, in regard to the Calico Hill finds, Leakey's wife, Mary, thought her husband was nuts.)

In 1968, Leakey arranged to have about a hundred archaeologists and geologists meet in San Bernardino to evaluate this exciting evidence, which suggested that human beings had arrived in the New World about the time when anatomically modern human beings were emerging in Africa. In other words, the first Americans had to have been Neanderthals or some as yet unknown Neanderthal contemporaries. This was perhaps the biggest site visit in history, making the visits of the Brixham Cave experts to Abbeville look like small potatoes. Among the visiting geologists was C. Vance Haynes. Haynes was highly skeptical of the Calico Hills tools, which, he said, evidenced edge angles more appropriate to naturally shattered rocks than those created by human hands. He also faulted the interpretation of their geological setting. In fact, Haynes thought the desert fan environment a poor choice for human occupancy but an ideal setting for the creation of what archaeologists call ecofacts or nature facts. In this, Haynes was right, just as Hrdlička had been right.

Thereafter, except for the San Bernardino excavators and Leakey himself, no one put much stock in the Calico Hills artifacts. That the "tools" all had the artificial look of something handmade could as easily be explained by the fact that only artificial-looking rocks had been selected from the hundreds of thousands of broken ones. And the breakage was most easily explained as the result of rocks clattering and tumbling out of the canyon in a great rock-crushing cascade—that is, they were broken by natural forces. (Decades earlier, a French paleontologist, Marcelin Boule, had grown impatient with a great number of claims about such putative "paleoliths" in Europe. He threw a collection of flint cobbles into a cement mixer, which soon cranked out a splendid collection of prehistoric "artifacts.") As for the fact that the Calico Hills "artifacts" were all made of chalcedony, it was pointed out that chalcedony was chipped more readily than the rest of the stone types in the fan and thus looked most artificial. Finally, the circle of stones Leakey had pegged as a hearth turned out to be just that, a circle of stones deposited naturally, the burn marks being the result of a brush fire. Later, the last nail to be driven in, the Yermo Fan was discovered to be 200,000 years old, meaning it had come into being prior to the existence even of Neanderthals. Into the eighties, some die-hard believers soldiered on, excavating at Calico Hills, but virtually no one today thinks of the Calico Hills site as anything but a bunch of rocks. But not all sites that were taken to be pre-Clovis needed Vance Haynes to shoot them down.

THE DEFLESHER THAT WASN'T

For centuries, it has been widely assumed, with good reason, that humans arrived in this hemisphere via the Bering Strait. Even without being a land bridge, it is the shortest distance (ninety miles) between Asia and North America. Logic long suggested, and still does, that signs of this human migration should be visible, at least on the North American side of the strait. Somewhere up there one should find some stone projectile, a precursor of the strange and beautiful Clovis point. And in fact numerous sites of temporary human habitation have been found in Alaska. (For reasons that should be obvious, archaeological work was fairly slow to take place in Siberia.) In 1966, an Alaskan find promised to show a pre-Clovis human presence in the far north.

That year a Canadian paleontologist, Charles R. Harrington, was searching for mammal bones in the Old Crow Basin, the remains of an ancient glacial lake in the Yukon, where he soon found a caribou leg bone that had been fashioned into a deflesher, a tool used in hide processing. About ten inches long, one of its ends had serrations or teeth carved into the edge. Harrington also found some mammoth and other bones that might also have been altered by humans; they had cut marks that appeared to have been made by sharpened implements of one kind or another. He obtained a radiocarbon date on the caribou bone that said it was 27,000 years old. That meant people had to have been in the Yukon 15,000 years before the first known appearance of Clovis Man—a real shocker.

Almost immediately the skeptics were at work, casting a blanket of doubt over the entire matter. One problem was that the deflesher and the other bone objects had been found in sediments that themselves had been transported some distance by floodwaters, so exactly where they and the supposed artifacts had come from was not known. The flake scars on the bone "tools" might have been made by human hands, but they might also have been the result of predators or even just the natural grinding from glacial geological processes. Why, some asked, would the people alleged to have made the markings have only bone tools and not stone tools? There arose a quasi-experimental side dispute over the bones; Robson Bonnichsen, an archaeologist then at the University of Maine (now at Oregon State University), said that the Cree Indians left the same kinds of markings on bones from which they extracted marrow, and presumably other tribal people did the same in the Yukon. Lewis Binford, then at the University of New Mexico and known to be an implacable foe of what he considered mushy, nonscientific thinking in archaeology, pointed out that in Africa and Asia scavengers and carnivores such as hyenas and lions leave the same spiral markings on bones from which *they* extract marrow.

An ever-darkening shadow of doubt loomed over all the "artifacts" except the deflesher, which no one disputed was a real artifact. But then another radiocarbon date was obtained on the deflesher, and it appeared that a major error had been made in the original dating. It was difficult in the early days of carbon dating to date bone accurately, bone presenting an array of problems—then and now—that charcoal does not. For one thing, labs were not sure at the time what fraction of a bone to date. The deflesher was deemed a mere 1,300 years old, quite likely a tool made by the not-so-ancient ancestors of the local Kutchin Indians. As the years passed, even Harrington himself came to doubt his early interpretation. The Old Crow site became a textbook example of the difficulties in interpreting very early American sites.

THE FAITHFUL OPTIMIST

A man who had no apparent difficulties interpreting early American sites was Richard Stockton "Scotty" MacNeish. A former Golden Gloves cham-

pion and as colorful a figure as existed in New World archaeology, Mac-
Neish worked for sixty years from the High Arctic to the Peruvian highlands and from the Atlantic to the Pacific on sites spanning the length and
breadth of North and South America. By his personal estimate Scotty
logged more than 5,600 days in the field.

In the 1950s and 1960s, he gained fame by mounting one of the most
successful multidisciplinary projects ever in order to track the history of
the domestication of maize (corn) back to the Tehuacán Valley in Mexico.
Though he retained a strong interest in early domesticated plants (when he

R. S. "Scotty" MacNeish (left) and J. M. Adovasio at Meadowcroft Rockshelter.

died in an auto accident in 2001, at the age of eighty-two, he was on the
trail of the origins of rice), he also turned his attention to caves, rockshelters, and open sites where he hoped to find very early artifacts.

He was convinced that there was no reason why people could not have
been in the Northern Hemisphere at least 30,000 or 40,000 years ago, and
he began searching for pre-Clovis sites. Much of his work in subsequent
years was in South America, and we will look in on Scotty in Chapter 8 on
that major arena in the quest for the first Americans. There he would make
a series of discoveries that were all met with a great deal of skepticism. Un-

daunted, he headed for New Mexico in the 1990s and a promising cave that had been discovered in 1975 and had long been on his list of places to dig. Called Pendejo Cave, it sits at the foot of a limestone cliff some three hundred feet above a normally dry arroyo near the town of Orogrande. The arroyo is part of a drainage that debouches into the eastern part of the huge, desolate Tularosa Basin. This is the home of the deathly white gypsum sands of White Sands National Monument, and not far to the west lies the White Sands Missile Range. The cave itself is thirty-six feet wide, running approximately north–south, and is some twenty feet deep and eight feet high at its highest.

In the early 1990s, newspapers blazoned the news that MacNeish had found in this cave evidence that humans had been in New Mexico as early as 35,000 years ago. Subsequently, MacNeish and his staff identified some twenty-six separate layers containing an abundance of faunal remains as well as what MacNeish believed were unequivocal indications of a human presence. These included firepits and hearths, stone, bone and fiber artifacts, human fingerprints on unbaked clay pellets, and even a human hair. A remarkable sequence of *seventy-two* radiocarbon dates indicated that the cave had been used by humans from the recent past to beyond 51,000 years ago. However, as was usual with MacNeish's discoveries, what appeared unequivocal to him was extremely problematic to most other archaeologists who visited the site.

Many believed the fireplaces were really the result of natural blazes, most thought that the early artifacts either were not man-made or had sifted down from later deposits, and virtually all questioned the hair (rumor has it that it came from a bear) and the origin and dating of the alleged fingerprints. In short, while there are definitely indications of a human presence at this locality *after* about 12,000 years ago (which would still make it a pre-Clovis site, by the way)—including fiber artifacts analyzed by my colleague at Mercyhurst College, David Hyland—few believe the site was occupied before this time.

The Pendejo Cave discoveries came after the early dates I received at Meadowcroft, but they illustrate the tendency on the part of some archaeologists to find just what they are looking for, to perceive in the world before them exactly what they want to see. Indeed, it has only too often surfaced in scientific debate, such as the infamous cold fusion controversy of the recent past. This all-too-human quality is hardly restricted to archaeologists—it can be found among gamblers, lovers, salesmen, CEOs, and many others. The four digs I have described here—and of course one could fill several volumes with the details of all the others that have sought to set a much earlier date than 11,500 years ago for the onset of the peopling of America—violated one or more of the dicta long agreed upon by American archaeologists for judging the authenticity of an allegedly early site: (1) the presence of undeniable artifacts (2) in indisputable context (3) with valid and reliable chronological control.

The Canadian paleontologist Harrington found an artifact, to be sure, but he initially received the wrong date for it. The rest of the "artifacts" turned out to be quite deniable, and they all were found in what are called "redeposited" sands and gravels, meaning that the context was disputable. MacNeish had the habit of consistently interpreting anything that bore any resemblance to an artifact as unequivocally the work of humans, a case of enthusiasm and expectation often outrunning reason and technical analysis. Having long expected that the earliest Americans would be very ancient, Leakey got his ancient dates all right (for a while), but he put faith in a handful of highly questionable artifacts found in a context that was otherwise highly suspect—an alluvial fan. Desperately wanting to find an early cave dweller, Hibben blew all three criteria—and perhaps worse. In his book on early man, Hibben wrote of finding his mountain-dwelling, pre-Clovis pioneer: "by accident, we came upon a New World cave man, a primitive hunter that satisfied all our expectations as to how ancient man should act and live." Frank Hibben's Sandia Man is perhaps the most extreme, not to mention egregious, example of finding evidence to fit one's expectations.

It was against this background, this literal roar of failed attempts, that I discovered in 1974 and 1975 that I had become another of these Don Quixotes, taking on the windmill of conventional wisdom and established dogma.

CHAPTER SEVEN

MELEE OVER MEADOWCROFT

Now that I can look back on some forty years as a student and then professional archaeologist, I have become very much aware that a good deal of my career—far from being a smooth, well-planned trajectory, one thing leading logically to the next—might better be described as a series of ricochets, one of which led me to the Meadowcroft Rockshelter in south-western Pennsylvania, where my career has been rattling around for three decades.

I can say that I always wanted to be an archaeologist. I made up my mind about that when I was four or five years old, growing up an early reader in Youngstown, Ohio. My mother, a single parent (my father died in World War II), kept me supplied with books of all sorts, my favorites being anything on archaeology and geology. I knew before I graduated from grade school that I wanted to go to the University of Arizona to pursue archaeology, and by the time I got there in 1962, I was also deeply into motorcycles. So I ended up riding around the desert a lot (which, among other things, forces you to learn to appreciate the subtle differences in landscapes), graduating after three years and spending a fourth year in graduate school. I then returned to Youngstown to teach for two years at what would become Youngstown State University.

In 1968, I headed off to the University of Utah, where I became a graduate student of a legendary archaeologist named Jesse D. Jennings. Jennings was probably the finest field archaeologist of his part of the twentieth century—and also at times one of the rudest, most abrasive human beings I have ever met. Evidently he was even more so in his earlier days, but shortly before I arrived he had suffered a horrendous heart attack. The story went that when he was lying gray-faced on the gurney, a doctor approached and asked if he wanted someone to fetch a priest to administer

The Dark Lord, Jesse D. Jennings.

last rites. Jennings reached out, grabbed the doctor by the collar, pulled him down, and snarled, "Do you seriously think I intend to fucking die here?" The story may be apocryphal, but it definitely is "him."

Jennings never praised anyone in my hearing. Instead, he was occasionally so brutal as to be repellent and, in fact, in some thirty years of teaching, he turned out only a handful of Ph.D.s. Most of his students simply couldn't take the abuse, and left to study and finish their graduate work elsewhere. One of his teaching techniques was to take his students to other archaeologists' digs, where he would point out all the flaws in technique loudly and as brutally as he pleased. I was with him once when he asked the archaeologist at one site, "What did you use to excavate this place, egg-beaters and hand grenades?" He objected strenuously to having both males and females on a dig, since he was convinced—and said so out loud whenever he ran into this—that nothing could be done right what with everyone spending their time copulating. He was known to his creatures (his students and ex-students) by many epithets, among which perhaps the most used was "The Dark Lord" (after the grim and terrible figure in Tolkien's *Lord of the Rings*).

The Dark Lord had very little time or use for archaeological theory. When I was a student, something called New Archaeology had recently been born. This was a complex and allegedly revolutionary new way of looking at the archaeological record, explicitly calling for a more "scientific" approach. That is, you pose a hypothesis and then, in the manner of a physicist or chemist, try to prove it or disprove it by the evidence in the ground. It also called for carefully attending to the patterning of things found in the ground (such as where a feasting group threw picked-over bones), the crunching of archaeological data via what were at the time mainframe computers, and a great deal of theorizing about the nature of archaeological evidence. Jennings thought this was, put very simply, bullshit on the part of people who didn't really know how to do the basic fieldwork of archaeology. "If you don't collect the data right," he would say, "who cares what you *think* about it?"

Very early in my graduate career I was "assigned" to work for Mel Aikens (a former Jennings student who had completed his Ph.D. at the University of Chicago) on the material culture remains he had recently recovered from a site in Utah called Hogup Cave. After I had labored through Christmas break in 1968 on the lithic assemblage from the site, Jennings then bluntly suggested that perhaps I should analyze the basketry from the site, "as there was no one else around to do it." This was scarcely an honor or reward. The Dark Lord held a low opinion of baskets, at least compared to stone tools, and, I assumed, an even lower opinion of those who analyzed such stuff. Significantly, though he never said so explicitly, I was quick to realize that if I elected to ignore his "suggestion," I should probably pack my bags and pursue my graduate career elsewhere. Indeed, I had actually heard him utter such an order to one of my fellow students before he exiled him into the Outer Darkness.

After the Hogup basketry analysis was completed, late in the spring of 1969, I decided I wanted to finish at Utah as soon as was humanly possible. Mel Aikens suggested that I reanalyze the many other basketry collections that Jennings and others had excavated in Utah over the previous half century and that were curated at the university museum. I could, Mel thought, use this data as a basis of a dissertation project that would ultimately involve the comparative study of similar collections housed at other institutions as well.

By late in 1969, I had visited nineteen institutions across the length and breadth of the United States and had looked at virtually every perishable artifact ever found in a proper archaeological site in western North America. I was well on the way to becoming one of *the* experts on this arcane kind of thing. Of course, expert or not, Jennings had doomed me to doing something that he himself did not consider "real" archaeology. Eventually I applied for and received a postdoctoral fellowship at the Smithsonian Institution, and continued my comparative study of prehistoric perishables from western North America. Before I actually went to the Smithsonian, I was asked to analyze a large collection of early perishables from the Andes, which led in 1973 to a conference in Albany to report on the Andean material at the behest of its excavator, Tom Lynch (himself, coincidentally, soon to become deeply involved in the Clovis wars). When the conference was over, Jim Richardson, a scholar of South American prehistory at the University of Pittsburgh, asked if I could give him a ride home, as I was on my way back to Youngstown to visit my mother. On the way, we ran into a blizzard and my windshield wipers went out, so I had to lean out the window and wipe the windshield clear by hand while we plummeted along in a near whiteout. Jim chose that moment to tell me that they were looking for a North Americanist in the anthropology department at Pitt, and would I be interested? And I was thinking, my inner voice rising in pitch, here we are in this blizzard and we're both probably going to die, and this guy is asking me about a position at Pitt? I didn't think about it until later.

What they wanted was someone to teach the hard-nosed, multidisciplinary techniques of field archaeology. I couldn't come right away since I was scheduled to do some fieldwork in Cyprus that fall, but I got the appointment anyway. Before leaving for the Mediterranean, I let the word out that I would like to find a place for teaching fieldwork the following summer that met various criteria: the prospective site needed to be reasonably accessible from Pittsburgh; it should be a place where little digging had been done before so that while the students were being instructed in field techniques, they would also be uncovering something new about the prehistory of the area; and preferably it should be a rockshelter. Much of what I had learned about excavating had come from working in and observing Great Basin rockshelters under Jennings or one of his students—and, of course, listening to The Dark Lord sneer at other rockshelter digs.

Somehow, in the spring of 1973, Phil Jack, a historian at California State College in California, Pennsylvania, heard about my requirement and contacted me, saying that he had a friend named Albert Miller, a big landowner in southwestern Pennsylvania near the West Virginia border and only a few miles from the Ohio River. On his property, or, more accurately, on the property of a foundation he and his brother Delvin (an illustrious harness racer) had created, was a large and largely untouched rockshelter that almost surely would make an ideal archaeological site. The property was called Meadowcroft, and as soon as I saw the Meadowcroft Rockshelter, perched among the trees about forty feet up from Cross Creek, a small tributary of the Ohio, I knew that generations of people through history and back into prehistory would have seen in it the same thing I did. It was a prime place for a temporary camp.

THE DIG AT MEADOWCROFT

People leaving the Ohio River to go hunting or collecting in the uplands would have found the channel of Cross Creek a pleasant and useful pathway, leading as it does gradually upward through very steep and hilly wooded country. Some seven and a half miles west of the river, the rockshelter would have provided a comfortable stopping-off place for such travelers. I climbed up the embankment and found, in the rockshelter's embrace, evidence that modern wayfarers had also found it a prime place for

*General view of Meadowcroft Rockshelter before excavations,
facing west, ca. 1973.*

*Close-up of the Early Holocene stratigraphy at Meadowcroft. The tags mark
microstratigraphic layers, occupation surfaces, fire pits, trash and refuse pits,
and the loci of geological sampling.*

*Close-ups of Holocene microstratigraphy at
Meadowcroft. Images were taken under different
lighting conditions to show the flexibility of the
lighting system used at the site.*

their trips. There on the rocky floor was a crude stone fireplace, really just
a circle of stones, and in the circle were beer cans, hash pipes, and syringes.

Carved into brown sandstone, the shelter is located on the north shore
of the creek, with a southern exposure. The prevailing winds, running from
east to west, provide nearly continuous ventilation, blowing noisome
smoke and insects away. The shelter itself is now about forty-nine feet wide
and twenty feet deep, and the ceiling is about forty-three feet above the
floor. In earlier times, the floor was lower and the overhang projected far-

ther out; in other words, the rockshelter was once substantially larger. In the intervening millennia, parts of the ceiling have fallen, in some cases in a rain of large chunks, or boulders, moving what is called the dripline (the line inside of which the site remains dry and outside of which the site is wet) farther and farther back (or north). This is typical of many rockshelters, as is the slow and steady, grain-by-grain attrition of sandstone from the ceiling, a product of the daily weathering of the cement that holds the sand grains together. Added to the rockfalls and the constant rain of sand grains was a lateral flow of sheetwash from the hillside that brought with it yet other sediments into the shelter, through apertures created at both ends of the collapsing roof.

The shelter is about 700 feet above sea level in a region of the Appalachian (or Allegheny) Plateau where the maximum elevation is some 1,200 feet. The elevation and southern exposure turned out to be more important than we could initially have imagined when we, students, and a small band of specialists from other fields descended on the rockshelter on June 15, 1973, for two months of excavations.

Below the beer cans and drug paraphernalia on the surface, we found steel beer cans, then old-fashioned beer bottles, then colonial glass bottles that Indians had flaked into tools. Before long we were into the era before European contact. At the outset, we thought that maybe the bedrock basement (or culturally sterile floor) of the shelter would be about three or four feet below the current surface, extending back maybe to 1200 or 1300 B.C.—just a guess based on other rockshelters in western Pennsylvania. That would be perfectly sufficient for our training purposes. It would take students down through a bit of complicated stratigraphy where they would, we hoped, encounter cultural features such as fireplaces and trash pits, objects of human manufacture, as well as natural unmodified objects or ecofacts such as plant and animal remains. By the middle of the summer, as we dug through progressively older strata, it was clear that the site was going to be both deeper and considerably more ancient than we had previously estimated.

The following summer (1974), we returned and by early July had penetrated through layers more than ten feet deep. We had come across some twenty levels of prehistoric fireplaces, showing that at this spot for literally thousands of years people had been taking it easy, sitting around the fire, munching. We plowed on down through layer after layer, finding the remains of successively older and more or less familiar cultures, known from other digs in the Northeast. We reached a stratum that was in excess of 10,000 years old—we knew this from the kind of spear points we found in it, called early Archaic and known to date back to that period. Below the early Archaic levels, we recovered still more cultural material that was more or less familiar. Then we encountered a layer of rocks from a major spall (rock fall) from the shelter's roof that had thoroughly sealed off the sediments below.

Breaking through the rock seal, we began to turn up decidedly unfamiliar but undeniably human-made things—artifacts. This was in levels

The Miller Lanceolate Projectile Point, in situ at Meadowcroft. The point is named after Albert Miller, who discovered the site. The point dates to between 11,300 and 12,800 B.P.

Late Pleistocene artifacts from Meadowcroft. All were found on the same surface as the Miller point and date to between 11,300 and 12,800 B.P. From left to right: the Miller point; two blade fragments; two biface thinning flakes; a broken biface.

Close-up of small blades from
Meadowcroft. Such items were used
in sets, hafted into bone or wood
handles/shafts, and at Meadowcroft
date to between 11,300 and 16,000 B.P.

that we knew were getting close to—and even deeper and therefore older than—the time period when current archaeological thought allowed humans to be. At a level that appeared to date to about 12,000 years ago, we found an intact spear point. It was about three inches long, evidently a tool that had once been bigger but had been repeatedly resharpened to its present size and perhaps simply left behind as too small. It was what archaeologists called lanceolate in shape and was unfluted (unlike Clovis points). It did not look exactly like anything else we had ever seen from the New World.

So we immediately decamped to our favorite bar in town and polished off ten kegs of beer. We named the point the Miller lanceolate to honor Albert Miller, the generous owner of a site that now looked as if it was going to make a lot of waves.

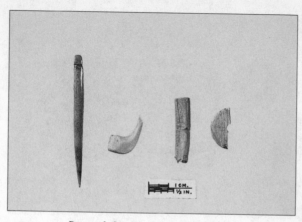

Bone tools from Meadowcroft Rockshelter.

And there was more. Below the Miller point were more firepits dating back as far as 15,000 years ago. In these lower levels we also found remains of bones, wood, shell, basketry, and cordage. The basket was a fragment, so fragile that we needed to spend two days injecting it with a polyethylene glycol solution (PEG) before we could pick it up. We were in what we called Stratum IIa, and from it we eventually extracted several

Ice Age blade cores from the Cross Creek drainage.
These date to between 11,300 and 16,000 B.P. and are highly
reminiscent of material from north China dating to 30,000 B.P.

Simple plaited basket fragment from Meadowcroft. This basket, like the others, is of birch bark strips and was used to produce containers of various configurations. This specimen dates to ca. 3,000 B.P.

dozen stone tools along with hundreds of small pieces that had been flaked off to make tools (such flakes are called "debitage"). Among the tools were rhomboidal "knives," unifacial choppers and scrapers (meaning only one side had been chipped off), sharp-pointed gravers, and microengravers.

The people who made these tools were no novices. Instead they imported high-quality materials: Kanawa chert from West Virginia, Flint Ridge material from Ohio, Pennsylvania jasper, and Onondaga chert from New York. They used sophisticated knapping techniques to make elegant tools. In other words, these were no simple-minded "rock-bashers" but instead highly skilled craftspeople. Most of the blades we found were small, almost microblades. In other excavations elsewhere, archaeologists had found similar items, a widespread technology in which, for example, a spear or dart might be made by fitting several of these small blades into slots around the end of the spear, making a multiedged weapon of considerable effectiveness. So here had been people familiar not only with that technology but with the flaking of larger points as well. The Miller lanceolate was, we learned, vaguely similar to examples found in Oregon and Texas and not totally unlike examples found in the Great Plains. But the

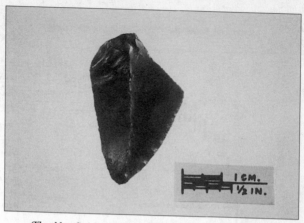

The oldest finished lithic tool from Meadowcroft. Called the Mungai knife, after a local farmer, it was recovered from a ca. 16,000 B.P. living surface.

Miller point antedated all those other examples, and this led us to wonder if it might be ancestral to all or, at least, some of them.

The other tools we found were similar to one degree or another to those found at other sites, though earlier. The rhomboid "knives" were like those found elsewhere in both eastern and western Pennsylvania; the graver and retouched flakes resembled those found in Nova Scotia as well as New Mexico's Blackwater Draw, where fluted Clovis points were first found in the 1930s.

In all, from all eleven levels we would eventually collect 2 million artifacts and plant and animal remains, and spend years sorting through it and making sense of it all. But midway through the second season, on July 13, we got the first radiocarbon dates. We had requested eleven dates to be run from five different strata, and that, in itself, is a lot of dates to be run. Doing so is expensive, and it was not uncommon for a dig to be "completed" with only a handful of radiocarbon dates, or even as few as one, which as often as not called such data into question. I wanted to avoid that, among other things.

The deepest date derived from a stratum that contained no cultural associations (that is, nothing man-made like a tool or hearth) was anywhere

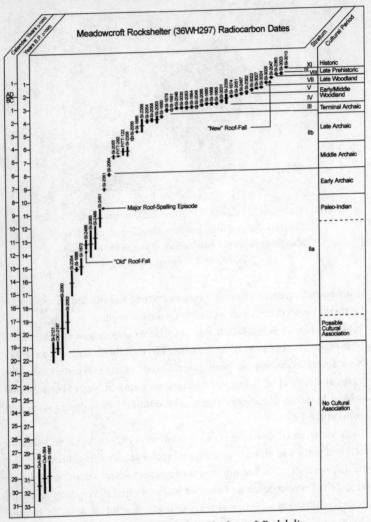

The radiocarbon chronology from Meadowcroft Rockshelter.

from 19,000 to 28,000 years old. The most recent stratum we dated went back to only 375 B.C. plus or minus 75 years, and others ranged as far back as 2870 B.C. plus or minus 85 years. And then a huge leap—the next two dates were shockers: 12,900 B.C. and 13,170 B.C.

And that meant three or four thousand years before Clovis.

Excavations at Meadowcroft, facing southeast. Dr. David Clark,
site supervisor, is in foreground. Students in the background are working
on Pleistocene living surfaces.

Maybe, we all thought, because the gap was so great from about 3000
B.C. to 12,000 B.C., the early dates had to be wrong. On the other hand, the
radiocarbon lab was utterly professional and almost always totally reliable. And so also, I knew, were the diggers at Meadowcroft.

One of these was David T. Clark, our first crew chief—a former U.S.
marine who had gone on to graduate from Ohio State University. The prototypical hard case, he was the most meticulous fieldworker I have ever
seen or probably will ever see. An enormous amount of closed-site, rockshelter, and cave excavation involves slowly unearthing material microlayer by microlayer with a trowel. It can seem endless, finicky, and tedious,
but it is upon the care with which this task is done that literally everything
else of archaeological importance rests. Clark was an utter genius with a
trowel, which he wielded like a laser scalpel, and the students he taught became so proficient that they could *hear* it or *feel* it when the trowel hit another microlayer—a subtle shift, an almost imperceptible transition,
marked only by a textural change from silty sand to sandy silt or vice versa.

Clark was taciturn, severe, rigid, and uncompromising. If a student

General view of excavations at Meadowcroft, ca. 1976, facing southeast.

made the same mistake twice, he or she would not work another day for him. He had no patience with screwups and expected the people working in his particular area—the so-called Deep Hole, which contains the deepest and oldest levels—to start work a full hour earlier than everyone else and stay on an hour later. Illness or hangover was no excuse. Given his almost monomaniacal concern with precision, I had no doubts that the samples we had sent to the radiocarbon lab were absolutely kosher in terms of context and association.

After straw-bossing the major excavations at Meadowcroft, Dave eventually moved on, doing his dissertation work at Pyramid Lake out in the western Great Basin in 1977. I got a call from him a little while later.

"It's gonna be tough here," he said. I asked him why.

"The crew chief is sorta different," he said. I asked him what he meant.

"Well, she—uh—uh—she doesn't wear a shirt."

I told him that he'd just have to deal with it. Dave completed his dissertation, got his Ph.D., and wound up teaching elementary school in Washington, D.C., and working part-time in the archaeology department of Catholic University there. In some ways, I suppose, the high point of his career was his years as crew chief at Meadowcroft. We replaced him there with a former student of mine from Youngstown State University, Mike Beckes. Beckes was another man of superb technical skills, a former Hell's Angel type and more than a bit of a hard case himself, but one who was somewhat more approachable than Clark.

Another regular was Joel Gunn, a quiet, patient, and insightful man who had a thorough knowledge of cave stratigraphy from working in Europe on several digs, as well as a thorough appreciation of how people used caves and rockshelters again and again over long periods of time. He had, and indeed still has, a high regard for the profound effect climate and climatic change can have on the nature of human cultures. He kept us attuned to these questions as the excavations continued and various kinds of material—including huge quantities of climatically sensitive plant and animal remains—turned up.

We called Joel Dr. Jekyll or Mr. Hyde depending on whether he had spent any time with a container of John Barleycorn. A thoroughly charming and usually mild-mannered guy, he was much married (and much divorced). Once into the "loon water" (as we always called it), he was capable of a Fredric March type of face change and no end of outrageous activity.

Interestingly, when Joel retook possession of his body, he usually had no recollection whatsoever of any of Hyde's excessive behaviors. In fact, over time, I became convinced that the two Joels actually did not know of each other. Though today he would probably be locked up for some of his deeds, this was the seventies and we were not members of a department of classics or art history. Most of the archaeology students of the time were people who would be more comfortable on a front-end loader or in a roadside saloon than at the Princeton Club in a Hepplewhite chair.

The Dark Lord had been among the first field archaeologists to insist that other specialists be on hand from the outset of an excavation, such as geologists, sedimentologists, and floral and faunal experts—people who could assess the many kinds of evidence on the spot as well as later in the lab. In this, the Meadowcroft Rockshelter dig was especially blessed. We had the services of geologist Jack Donahue from the beginning and on through virtually all the years of the dig. More on him later. Another specialist who was with us throughout most of that period was John Guilday, a vertebrate paleontologist who identified the hundreds of thousands of animal remains we came across. He was a polio victim and spent his professional life in an iron lung. His expertise was so great that the Carnegie Museum of Natural History was happy to build him a lab in his house, and there, with grad students or, more often, his wife, Alice, holding up each bone and turning it for him as he directed, he identified every creature with a backbone that we found at the site. He was, to put it simply, the very best in his field.

It is important to have this kind of continuity of personnel in a dig that extends over a long time. Otherwise, you can get people with different criteria and different agendas, and the turnover can be a plague to the final assembling of all the data.

From the outset, well before we discovered that we were going to be shoved into the Clovis/pre-Clovis wars, I had wanted this excavation to be a model of its genre, an unsurpassed use of the finest and most precise archaeological excavating techniques, including any new technique that came along. In the secret recesses of my brain, I actually wanted it to be the best piece of field archaeology ever undertaken.

To that end and from its inception, the Meadowcroft/Cross Creek project was a multidisciplinary undertaking. The central goal or theme of the operation was the systematic acquisition, analysis, and integration of any and all data bearing on the archaeology, history, paleoecology, geology, geomorphology, pedology, hydrology, climatology, and floral and faunal succession of the entire Cross Creek drainage. Moreover, I wanted the data gathered, analyzed, and interpreted with as great a degree of precision and with the most sophisticated methodologies of which any of the project staff were cognizant. Also, crucially, we were fortunate that the project could be carried out virtually without temporal or fiscal constraints. Heavily funded from the beginning to the present, it was designed to epitomize the so-called state of the art.

ROCKS, DIRT, AND DUST

Again, from the outset of the Meadowcroft/Cross Creek project, and even before the first trowel full of sediment was ever removed from the rockshelter, we wanted to learn as much as possible about this small stage upon which any prehistoric actors and actresses might have played out some of their own particular destinies. That meant, of course, understanding the geology of the rockshelter itself and the drainage of which it was a prominent part, not to mention whatever effects on the shelter's climate and condition the waxing and waning of the glaciers had produced.

Geology, of course, is not simply about the grand events of the past—the great movements of the earth's plates, the forging of mountains, the eruptions of volcanoes, the carving by water's inexorable hand of the Grand Canyon. It is also about much smaller and, in geological terms, shorter events. Even in 1973, it was possible to identify microgeological events and processes that had taken place not over eons but rather in actual calendar years and even far briefer periods. It was, and remains, my contention that to understand the activities of humans in the past you must first define and understand the landscape with whose trajectory they have intersected. In short, without knowing what has happened to the stage over time, how can you study the prehistoric performers?

Even as a freshman back in the sixties at the University of Arizona, I had never understood why such a huge chasm (pedagogically) existed between geology and archaeology. I took huge doses of geology as an undergraduate and later as a graduate student. I learned everything I could about sedimentology, erosion, microgeology. My first lecture before a class was actually as an unpaid assistant in geology, not anthropology. My archaeology mentors, notably including Emil Haury, often stressed the importance of geology, and of course Vance Haynes was already teaching geoarchaeology at Arizona at that time. The importance of the geological stage was further hammered into my head at Utah by both Jennings and Aikens, as well as fellow students such as David Madsen. Small wonder, then, that for me the elucidations of the geology and archaeology of prehistoric sites were inseparable activities.

This perspective was not particularly unique then and, indeed, stretched back to the beginnings of both fields in Europe in the nineteenth century. At that time, those engaged in prehistoric archaeology often were trained first as geologists. Today, regrettably, geology has been sharply deemphasized in the training of most undergraduate and graduate archaeology students, with profoundly negative consequences. Indeed, while the last several generations of American archaeology students may be much more theoretically elegant than I or my generation, many are methodologically bankrupt. In any case, it is often easier simply to summon a compliant geologist to a site and then employ his or her services on an as-needed basis. Regrettably, most geologists (willing or not) are not normally trained to address issues important to the archaeologist or to think in much more temporally circumscribed terms than eons or millennia. In such situations, the geologist and archaeologist can be likened to ships passing in the night without significant communication or meaningful interchange.

In any event, before fieldwork began at Meadowcroft, I knew what we wanted to ascertain geologically. First, we needed to understand the long

Meadowcroft senior geologist Dr. Jack Donahue (left) and excavation supervisor Dr. David Clark sampling sandstone in the Meadowcroft Rockshelter cliff face.

history of the Cross Creek drainage itself and how long it had been in its present configuration. Next, we needed to know in as sharp a detail as could be managed the precise evolution of the rockshelter over time. How and by what means had sediment been introduced or "emplaced" in the rockshelter? Had the larger rocks, which littered the hillside below the site, once been part of the overhang or roof? If so, how big had the site once been? Material from small grains to boulders will, over time, fall from the ceiling of a rockshelter, a process called spalling. We wanted to develop a record of spalling incidents and how they had affected the human use of this shelter.

To help answer these questions, I recruited a more-than-willing Pitt geologist, Jack Donahue, who along with his students remained active at Meadowcroft for decades. Jack was at the time a coal geologist, a field that by then was not likely to develop much more deeply or widely than it already had. Jack was ready for a career switch, and he threw himself into what he would in many ways help to develop—the field of geoarchaeology. Indeed, he would become the first editor of that subfield's main scientific journal, *Geoarchaeology*, and he remains active in geoarchaeological research to this day.

General view of the latest late Pleistocene living surface at Meadowcroft prior to the removal of roof blocks, facing southwest.

To unravel the complex history of Cross Creek, Jack and his students initiated a geological assay of the Cross Creek drainage and the rockshelter that was (and still is) unparalleled in scope, scale, and resolution, at least in the realm of cave and rockshelter excavations. To all of the previously published geological material about the area, they added the findings

*Late Pleistocene Clovis-age living
surface with rock fall removed,
facing south.*

of field reconnaissance on foot and by air. They studied backhoe trenches and deep-core borings in the surround (activities that were part of a conveniently timed soil conservation project).

As for the rockshelter itself, we first mapped it in detail, including all the rocks lying on the surface. We extracted a series of rock samples all the way up the seventy-two-foot-thick sandstone rock unit that made up the walls and roof of the rockshelter, and from this we could see, via microscopic study, even minute changes in the composition of the sandstone.

These changes would let us "fingerprint" rocks we found as we dug down and match them with the places on the roof from which they had spalled.

Again, before the excavation process began, we inventoried all the plants growing around the rockshelter and up the slopes above, and we stripped an area up to seventy feet from the rockshelter of all vegetation, the better to understand the nearby topography.

Once excavation began, with a north–south trench running from outside the dripline to the back wall of the shelter, an exhaustive series of collecting and sampling protocols was invoked. We made three-dimensional maps of the site every foot or so as we descended, showing not only any sign of a human presence, but also rock spalls down to the size of a silver dollar and anything else that indicated the amount of floor space that was available and used. We cut twelve sampling columns straight down through the site to the shale bedrock below, to keep track of such things as the ratio of sand to silt particles over time. We looked in these samples for pollen, for elements such as nitrogen, phosphorus, and others that result from the decay of plant materials, and for the remains of small animals such as rodents and snails that are sensitive to small climatic changes. We studied individual sand grains at the atomic level with scanning electron microscopes to see if they had been moved around by water at any time.

Perhaps the most novel (and at the time unprecedented) geological effort began in 1974, when we placed an aluminum tray on the sloping roof of a protective wood structure we had by then erected over the rockshelter floor to protect it from rain, curious hikers, or vandals, as well as permit work to proceed in foul weather. Into the tray we swept sand and rock fragments from the roof—a job we did daily for the next four years of fieldwork. With this material matched daily to the weather humidity, temperature, and so forth, we had a useful gauge of weather conditions during earlier times at the rockshelter. In this same vein, we used holding tanks to trap all sediment washing into the rockshelter's ends during rainstorms, another way of studying the thick sediment pile that accumulated in the rockshelter over time.

We soon became the first archaeological excavation to have a hookup at the site to a mainframe computer (at Pitt) and certainly one of the first ever to have such complete computerized records of every detail of the excavation.

As happens at most professional excavations, we sieved virtually everything through a series of increasingly tiny meshes via water flotation. If the sample came from a fireplace or had any charred material, we processed it using hydrogen peroxide, the very thing used to create blondes in beauty parlors. The British archaeologist who invented the technique told us about it and, in keeping with the plan to use any useful technique, we ordered up two fifty-five-gallon drums of the stuff. The student we assigned to draw some peroxide from the barrel put on a protective rubber

Dr. Andrea Fitting mapping at Meadowcroft, ca. 1975.

apron and gloves and nevertheless soon found that the peroxide was eating through them and his shoes. We thus learned the difference between the highly diluted solution used as hair dye and antiseptic and 100 percent laboratory-grade hydrogen peroxide, which is a component in some rocket fuels and was actually tried out as a propellant for British submarines.

In our earthbound arena, the hydrogen peroxide flotation process not only efficiently broke down the clay or silt bonds in sticky sediments, but it sharply reduced the damage to any charred items, meaning, among other things, that we could send much cleaner samples to the radiocarbon labs for dating.

Implementing all these procedures was time-consuming in the extreme and very expensive. Indeed, by 1975, the "summer" field season at Meadowcroft went from two months (mid-June to mid-August) to four months with six-day workweeks and twelve-hour workdays. People would still be working at the site when the weather turned cold and the leaves began to change in late September. Fortunately, we enjoyed heavy financial support virtually from the outset. This included funding from the University of Pittsburgh and the Miller family via the Meadowcroft Foundation, plus grants from the National Geographic Foundation, the National Science Foundation, the Buhl Foundation, the Leon Falk Family Trust, and several private sources. These not only included a former student of mine from Youngstown State University and a longtime friend, John Boyle, but also his father, Edward (who passed away as this chapter was being written).

The actual research all this funding made possible was tedious, painstaking, highly technical, and very slow moving. In fact, it was as far from the Indiana Jones stereotype of instantaneous and spectacular discoveries as imaginable. Through the twenty-seven years of the entire Meadowcroft project there were very few dramatic discoveries, but instead the agonizingly slow accumulation of minute bits of information, the full significance of which is only now emerging. One of the most important aspects of all we accomplished at Meadowcroft is the often overlooked fact that it provided a nearly unique sequence of human habitation over a period of some 16,000 years.

In retrospect, it is easy to see that this kind of archaeology is not for everyone, and I can fully understand why some archaeology students (and their postmodernist professors) would prefer to debate whether the world exists from the comfort of a cozy bar rather than spend a four-month field season excavating microstrata with razor blades or staring through a microscope at sand grains or flotation samples. It takes a special sort of mentality to engage in the kind of unremitting, tedious labor we insisted on, and it is not difficult to see why the Meadowcroft/Cross Creek project was filled with strange personalities. After twelve hours of troweling thin layers of dirt and dust, you go crazy at night. Running, weight lifting, drinking, fornicating, staring off into space and babbling incoherently— you do almost anything for relief. It takes a truly bizarre person to live that way for months on end, and we had tents full of them.

Whatever the toll all this took on young and eager psyches, the precision we wanted to teach at Meadowcroft—the extent to which one could use the most modern and sophisticated techniques to obtain, refine, and analyze data—paid off in ways that we certainly could not have imagined when we began. For once the pre-Clovis dates came out and some of the

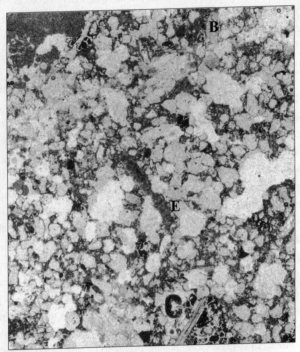

Photo micrograph of sediment sample from lowermost Stratum IIa at Meadowcroft Rockshelter. Sample shows bone fragment (B) and eggshell fragment (E) and also indicates that the sediments were not affected by groundwater percolation.

profession went into attack mode, we were well armed with the most precise close-focus data ever extracted from a North American archaeological site of this or probably any other time period.

While the ultimate "payoff" of our high-resolution data-recovery methods in terms of the pre-Clovis/Clovis wars was years away, there was also an immediate return. By the end of the second year of the project, we knew that the Cross Creek drainage had not assumed its present form until late Pleistocene times. Specifically, we determined that the actual genesis of Meadowcroft Rockshelter had begun between 40,000 and 23,000 B.P. But, assuming that anyone was around to visit it in these early years, Meadowcroft was probably not a very attractive place to hang out in much before 23,000 to 21,000 years ago. Up until then, it was subject to periodic flooding by a Cross Creek that had not yet cut down to its current bed level. After 21,000 years B.P., the flooding ceased, leaving the site high and dry, and by 20,000 years ago people could have lived there quite comfortably. But this, of course, was also the time when the glacier had reached its most southerly growth, a phenomenon called the glacial maximum. What of the great glacier towering just to the north of Meadowcroft Rockshelter?

Even before all of our geological and other analyses, we knew that forty-seven miles north of Meadowcroft lies Moraine State Park, which marks the southern terminus of the last glacial advance at the height of the last glacial period. We also knew that by 14,000 years ago, the glacier had receded to where the city of Erie now lies, 125 miles to the north. And the presence of the glacier in our general neighborhood would become an enormous and a nearly endless bone of contention once we published those pre-Clovis dates from Meadowcroft. I would drastically underestimate, in fact, how geologically naive many of my colleagues were (and still are in many cases).

At the time, I did not think much about my nearly fanatical drive to make Meadowcroft the best excavation ever, but I realize now with utter clarity that it was me showing Jennings that I could be even better than he at his own game—fieldwork. My dissertation had involved no fieldwork (just the study of collections of materials), but I had stayed the course under his ferocious rudeness, as so many others had not. Maybe I wanted to hear him say something that sounded like approval. He never did. Once, years after the first Meadowcroft data was published, he allowed as how he thought my excavation was "evidently" done with great care, but he never visited the site.

Recently, a friend of mine was talking to an amateur archaeologist in Pennsylvania who said that among those folks and some of my students, *I* have now become known as The Dark Lord. "Very demanding," the amateur said. That came as a big surprise and brought to mind Gandalf's admonition to the hobbit who likened one of his companions to the evil Lord of the Rings. "There is," Gandalf said with finality, "only one Dark Lord." I confess I am very demanding, but, compared to Jennings, at least some people think I'm a hell of a lot nicer.

ECO-SQUABBLE AT MEADOWCROFT

When my colleagues were confronted by the state of the natural world in the immediate vicinity of the Meadowcroft Rockshelter beginning 16,000 years ago, the Clovis Firsters simply couldn't believe it. Far from being the barren tundra they expected, what with the proximity of the glacier, the area around Meadowcroft could not even have been characterized as a boreal or northern forest, though some boreal tree species like spruce were present. In fact, what with the oak and hickory trees and white-tailed deer, it was not all that different from today. Since this evidence from Meadowcroft did not accord with the maps the paleoecologists had drawn up, many of them and their archaeological friends said the radiocarbon dates from the earliest strata at Meadowcroft had to be wrong

What all this told me was that these critics were basically ignorant of glaciers, glacial geology, and even the nature of the paleoecological record, as well as the methods by which paleoecologists gather and interpret data. I also realized they apparently had an unusually hard time simply reading the geological and other reports emanating from Meadowcroft.

If you stand next to an alpine glacier of the sort that persist to this day on mountaintops in the Pacific Northwest, at noon on a cloudless day you can often go shirtless. To insist that a white-tailed deer (or, at least, its black-tailed western counterpart) couldn't live in the vicinity is just silly. To this day, some critics haven't got it through their heads that at the time in question the glacier was not looming up on the nearby horizon, it was more than a hundred miles away. But back in the late seventies, when the pre-Clovis dates from Meadowcroft were announced, some people were pursuing the craft of paleoecology, or, more accurately, examining its conclusions, with a set of built-in blinders. It was simply taken as a given that open land next to a glacier had to be uniformly frozen—underlaid by per-

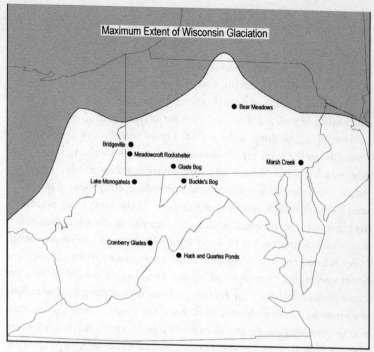

Maximum Extent of Wisconsin Glaciation

Bear Meadows

Bridgeville
Meadowcroft Rockshelter
Glade Bog
Marsh Creek
Lake Monogahela
Buckle's Bog

Cranberry Glades
Hack and Quarles Ponds

*Unglaciated sites with late Pleistocene botanical material near
Meadowcroft Rockshelter. Note: The map shows the ice front during
the glacial maximum, ca. 20,000 B.P.*

mafrost and overlaid by bleak treeless tundra. But all the evidence at that
time in the Northeast came from relatively high elevations, which is to say
places where it is always colder. Lower down, warmer temperatures are the
norm and growing seasons are longer. Today Meadowcroft, which is 853
feet above sea level, enjoys fifty-nine more frost-free days than Pittsburgh,
which is only thirty miles north and east but, much more important, 370
feet higher.

Evidence of the ecosystems in glacial times was, and still is, derived
largely from fossil pollen grains and other plant remains extracted from
former bogs and lakes, and in the seventies and eighties very few such sites
had been analyzed for data from as far back as 20,000 years ago. (And
those were all high-altitude sites.) In 1980, only some eight sites in the entire unglaciated American Northeast had yielded plant material of Pleis-

tocene age (see map on page 175), hardly a sharp-focus picture for an area of more than 290,000 square miles. By the early 1990s, the picture remained soft. Data from fossil pollen for 15,000 to 18,000 years ago had been obtained from only about twenty-five sites in the entire eastern half of the North American continent, from Texas to Hudson Bay and points east.

To this day, much of the paleoclimatic data from eastern North America consists of pollen grains, and even for palynologists, fossil pollen can be tricky. For one thing, some pollen is more recognizable than others—especially pollen from the coniferous trees such as hemlock, spruce, and pine, which include a great many northern species. Pine pollen is especially resistant to decay. As a result, pine will often be overrepresented in a given sample—both in fact and in interpretation. At the same time, deciduous trees that occur in warmer climes, such as maple and chestnut, have pollen that is particularly subject to decay from microbes and natural oxidation. Pollen is best preserved when there exists a consistent pattern of either wet or dry conditions, of cold, or of acidity. These are all conditions that are scarce in the Northeast. Yet another problem with making interpretations of climate based on such remains is that many kinds of trees do not indicate, or circumscribe, a particular set of climatic conditions. Today's white pine can indicate cool or warm or even boreal conditions, depending on the species, and identification at the species level is often difficult with fossil pollen grains. Beyond all that, the pollen of many tree species is easily caught up by the wind and transported considerable distances. This is an excellent strategy for spreading your kind if you are a plant, but it makes it hard for a palynologist to say that the tree that gave rise to the pollen he has found used to grow nearby.

Pollen analysis, in other words, tends to be better for giving a general and fairly soft-focus climatic picture of a large region rather than for providing details about the local microclimate in a specific locality. Yet even with all of those caveats about the pollen record, and despite a good deal of other evidence to the contrary, many palynologists today still insist on the unbroken, solid, uniform stripe of tundra along the edge of the Laurentide glacier, based on the high-elevation sites they are most familiar with.

The paleoecologist may, however, have other evidence with which to work. In the assessment of ancient ecosystems—preservation permitting—

you may recover bigger pieces of botanical evidence in addition to, or even instead of, pollen. At Meadowcroft, pollen is poorly preserved but macro-botanical remains are not. In fact, the site yielded more than 1.4 million items, including everything from seeds to moderately large portions of tree limbs with and without bark. Since most of the bigger stuff is not designed for long-distance travel, it is a pretty fair indicator both of what was grow-ing near the site as well as what humans and other animals were bringing into it. Significantly, while most of the plant remains postdated 10,000 B.P., enough charred remains were present in the lowest levels to show that de-ciduous trees were present at the time humans first visited the site some 16,000 years ago.

Back in those early days of the Meadowcroft excavations (and to some extent still today), critics sought *any* conceivable way to shoot down our results. So one early line of attack was that the radiocarbon dates for all this material had to be wrong because such temperate creatures as deer and deciduous trees simply couldn't exist that near the glacier. It was all tundra and/or boreal forest near the glacier in those days, they said. Q.E.D., *quod erat demonstrandum*. Thus is demonstrated Adovasio's folly. The critics could ignore the elevation factor because the local experts in palynology also ignored elevation. This confusion, by the way, is a hang-up mostly among eastern paleoecologists. In the West, people such as David Madsen at the Utah Geological Survey understood at least two decades ago that el-evation plays a key role in localized climate and weather, a bit of Unifor-mitarianism that remains a principle that it is unwise to overlook. As a matter of fact, the critical role of elevation was thoroughly understood by the 1890s, when C. Hart Merriam, a Yale-trained biologist on a govern-ment science expedition to the Southwest, elucidated the concept called Merriam's Life Zones. This showed that, on the mountains and mountain chains of the West, there are essentially stripes of vegetation types as you go higher and higher, ranging from hot desert cacti to boreal trees such as Engelmann spruce to windswept tundra. Moisture tends to increase, and temperature to decrease, the higher you go. Indeed, you can travel the eco-logical equivalent of two thousand miles from, say, Arizona to Hudson Bay, simply by climbing the mountains ranged east of Tucson where I went to college.

Even so, in the late seventies and early eighties, the scoffers were bay-ing like coyotes over what they thought was the dead meat of Meadow-croft.

Enter Kathleen Cushman, a young Pennsylvania woman who had majored in art history at Ohio Wesleyan University, then gotten a master's degree in Old World prehistory from the University of Chicago. In 1976, at Texas A & M, she began to work on a Ph.D. degree in biology, in particular in paleoecology, and even more in particular in the state of the environment just south of the Laurentide Ice Sheet at Meadowcroft, which she knew was "one of the few well-documented archeological sites in the northeastern United States from which several types of fossil botanical material have been recovered." Five years later, in 1981, she had proved my point about the "reality" of that alleged stripe of tundra tucked up against the ice from the New Jersey shore to the Rockies.

Her comparative analysis of the eight other sites in the Northeast where plant remains had then been analyzed suggested that elevation above sea level might well be as important a factor as proximity to the glacier. High on the Allegheny Plateau, conditions tended then to be more boreal (as they do today). Yet, in all eight sites, there was clear evidence of the presence of some deciduous trees such as hickory, birch, beech, and oak among the pines and spruce. Even at the glacial maximum, in many instances the forest composition was not unlike its modern composition. Elsewhere, she noted, a site from south-central Illinois showed that some 11,000 years ago, oak, elm, and ash were growing amid the spruce a mere fifteen miles from the limit of the glacier. She concluded, in the cool language of science, that the ice's influence "on vegetation may not have been as great as has been previously believed."

Clearly, then, the countryside along the edge of the glacier must have been a mosaic, a patchwork of different ecosystems. Depending on elevation, local weather conditions, even which way a gorge faced, it varied from tundra to at least partly deciduous woodland. It varied enough to support many kinds of life from mastodons to deer, from boreal owls to songbirds and of course to enterprising humans, who, while probing the inviting tributary to the Ohio River called Cross Creek, would have looked up at one point and noted an inviting rockshelter nestled into the hillside, facing south, sun-dappled, a good place to tarry a while.

But such a picture continued to be anathema to many of my colleagues. As late as 1989 and even on into the 1990s, this confusion of expectations with facts continued. In that year, Dena Dincauze, already a persistent critic of Meadowcroft and card-carrying Clovis Firster from the University of Massachusetts, complained in a review of the then-available scientific literature devoted to Meadowcroft about the "absence of the extinct Pleistocene fauna" in the controversial pre-Clovis level called Stratum IIa and the "presence of hardwood species macrofossils" there. Once again, at least, in Dena's mind, in spite of evidence accumulating to the contrary, there should not be the likes of oak trees and deer so close to the looming edge of the glacier; thus the dates had to be wrong. This is about the same as saying that because Frenchmen usually speak French and I have reported and even tape-recorded a Frenchman saying something in English, he cannot be French. In other words, her complaint is not reasoning in any sense normally ascribed to the process of science. In science, facts are facts, and expectations are continuously adjusted in the light of facts.

Why many eastern scholars have not given up their belief in the map is beyond me. But you can still see it in textbooks despite the fact that Meadowcroft and other sites have now shown conclusively that it never existed. I recall asking John Guilday once, after he had examined tens of thousands of animal bones from the site, if he was disturbed by the fact that temperate species had turned up at Meadowcroft just after the glacial maximum, and he said he wasn't. Clearly, at Meadowcroft, he said, the transition from Pleistocene to Holocene was something of a nonevent—a near-perfect echo of the conclusion reached by Kathy Cushman with the plant remains.

Far from limiting herself to climatic considerations in 1989, Dincauze raised yet again the great specter earlier brought to the fore by Vance Haynes.

The specter was, of course, contamination. According to Dincauze, the samples we sent off to be dated had not been pure and good.

Which is why I was so lucky to have such generous funding for the excavation of Meadowcroft Rockshelter. Throughout the excavation, I had been ferocious about our radiocarbon dates and the technical perfection on which they had to rest, lest I wind up the subject of ridicule and insult.

Well, that happened anyway, but here is how the true believers, those who worshiped at the Shrine of the Sacred Fluted Point, dealt with my radiocarbon dates.

CARBON-14 AND MEADOWCROFT

None other than Vance Haynes himself wrote not long ago that nowadays archaeology is, essentially, all radiocarbon dating. At the same time, Vance has had the worst time swallowing the radiocarbon dates from Meadowcroft. Vance read the earliest reports on Meadowcroft and was an early visitor to the site. At one point, he actually wrote me to tell me that the work was unexceptionable and that he had found no holes in our data. I could scarcely believe it, and in fact I have saved his letter to this very day. But then a chain of events occurred that have, like his original letter, lasted to the present.

In a conversation with our radiocarbon specialist, the late Bob Stuckenrath, who was a friend of his, Vance thought he heard Bob say that all of the early radiocarbon samples had to be arrested during the pretreatment process lest they completely dissolve or, as the technical jargon has it, "go into solution." This in turn suggested to Vance that all of the early dates were contaminated with dissolved materials from some unknown source(s). He immediately became suspicious and freely and aggressively voiced his doubts to all and sundry who would listen. The old Tule Springs specter of contamination had arisen again, this time almost 2,180 miles to the east.

Never mind that what Bob had actually told him was that the pretreatment of *two* very small samples had been arrested and that all the rest had behaved normally. Never mind that Bob clarified his remarks with Haynes on several occasions, and never mind that the distinguished Oxford Radiocarbon Dating Facility in England had explicitly stated that no indications of contamination could be found in an early Meadowcroft sample it dated.

Once raised, the shadow of contamination has never died, at least in the minds of Haynes and some of his acolytes. This is not science, but, I suppose, neither was Bob Stuckenrath's reaction to all this. He said, "If they don't believe the evidence, fuck 'em"—definitely not scientific discourse, but not ill considered, either!

Since then (1974), Vance has employed every ounce of creativity in finding ways to blow out of the water any dates from Meadowcroft that place humanity on the scene before 12,000 B.P. or—essentially—before Clovis. As were others at the time (including some of us even before the rest of the pack), he was quick to point out the large discrepancy in millennia between the pre-Clovis Paleo-Indian dates and those of subsequent people (Archaic Indians), and he recommended that more samples be taken and many more dates be run—and at more than one radiocarbon-dating laboratory.

No one then, by the way, and no one since has questioned any of the dates obtained first or in subsequent tests that are *younger* than the semi-mystical date of 11,500 years B.P. That is, no one with the exception of two Haynes disciples, Ken Tankersley and Cheryl Munson, who have intimated that *all* of the dates were wrong. Paradoxically, Haynes never even questioned the date of 11,300 B.P., which is of Clovis age. All the dates that are *post*-Clovis came, it seems, from perfectly obtained samples from perfectly determined stratigraphy and were perfectly tested in the lab. Whatever must have gone haywire to produce the pre-Clovis dates suddenly became magically inoperative after the magic moment of 11,300 B.P., and critics like Haynes have come up with some astoundingly creative, if unscientific, explanations for this astonishing timing.

By the later 1970s, we had obligingly obtained nearly forty dates from two different laboratories, which had told us essentially the same story. Since then the total number of dates we have run is fifty-two, with thirteen from the pre-Clovis strata. What they show—and this is really the most important thing about Meadowcroft—is the longest continuous use of a single place in all of North American prehistory.

I should point out here that none of the hundreds of American or foreign archaeologists who actually visited the site between 1973 and 1978 questioned the rigor or precision of the excavation, the data-recovery techniques, the stratigraphy, the context, or the association of dates, artifacts, and ecofacts. In other words, the dig at Meadowcroft matched the criteria that Hrdlička and Holmes set forth more than a century ago and that have been only slightly updated in the context of modern technology.

I repeat them yet again:

1. Artifacts of indisputable human manufacture recovered in primary depositional contexts
2. Clearly defined, unambiguous stratigraphy
3. Multiple radiometric determinations showing indisputable internal consistency

Practically no one has ever found these criteria to be too stringent or, as one commentator put it, "legalistic." Nor are they so lax that they require amendment. However, there have been a few suggested amendments. In fact, Paul S. Martin (of overkill persuasion) and a colleague, Frederick Hadleigh West, have insisted on what they call "replicability." Now, replicability is a very important word in the hard sciences. In a physics or chemistry experiment, replicability is the sine qua non. The way an experiment is set up and carried out must be able to be done by someone else exactly the way you did yours, so that your results can be checked. That, of course, cannot be done exactly in the case of an archaeological dig, and what Martin clearly implied by the word was that lots of pre-Clovis sites need to be found before any one of them can be considered real. And that is, of course, not science at all, however much comfort it brought to those who have lived or died by the Clovis Curtain. (It took the discovery of only one live coelacanth, a weird fish of the Indian Ocean then thought to have been long extinct, to prove that the species still lived.) And perhaps more to the point, even *without* some sort of replicability, the criteria above have long been successfully used to doom hundreds of alleged but flawed pre-Clovis sites to a deserved oblivion.

In any event, my dates were internally consistent and few sites have ever yielded more. There was really only one way left to invalidate the dates that had come out of Meadowcroft, and that was, as noted, contamination.

Something had to have dribbled or floated or drifted into the lower strata of the rockshelter that rendered all (and only) the older, improper, even impolite radiocarbon dates not just wrong but too old by thousands of years. We had numbered the various strata in the nearly sixteen feet of material that overlay the shale bottom of the rockshelter with roman numerals, with Stratum I being the lowest and therefore oldest. We had received dates on material from Stratum I as old as 30,000 years B.P., but there was no cultural (meaning human) material in that stratum. It was what we call sterile.

Next up (and younger) was Stratum II, which was in fact separated into two smaller units, with IIa being the one with dates from 19,000 to 11,000 B.P. that were so offensive to the Clovis lobby. This level just *had* to have been contaminated by something. The obvious candidate—this being Pennsylvania anthracite country—was coal. We knew that the nearest actual outcrop of coal was about a half mile away from Meadowcroft, making transport of coal into the rockshelter pretty unlikely unless humans had actually carried it in. Nevertheless, we had searched for coal particles in every sample taken for carbon dating with both optical and scanning electron microscopy, finding no contamination. None of the dating laboratories or other independent researchers who had looked at the samples had found any contamination by coal particles. We had also checked all these samples for any paleobotanical evidence, chiefly spores, of the sort that typically occur in the coal common to the area (coal that dates back to the Pennsylvanian age). None turned up.

Another compromising candidate was vitrinized wood or vitrite, ancient Pennsylvanian-period wood fragments that had become fossilized. We found two highly localized occurrences of vitrite on the north wall of the shelter immediately below the interface or boundary of Stratum IIa and the sterile Stratum I. The vitrite was horizontally or spatially separated from the earliest occurrences of human activity by a distance of more than twenty feet and vertically separated from it by almost two feet of sterile sandy deposits. In order to get vitrite into the culture-bearing levels, it would have had to be physically transported to the early firepits by someone who had dug it up and then added it in exactly the right doses to render the pits older than they actually are. They would have had to add just enough vitrite, for some unknown and unimaginable reason, to sequentially skew the age of each of the pits in precise chronological order—one hell of a feat! This, of course, would also apply to any coal brought into the site from elsewhere.

Never mind our responses to the critics' objections. Vance Haynes repeatedly suggested that contamination must be present. Perhaps it had percolated up into the site via groundwater.

We knew it could not have, based on our nuanced understanding of what had brought sediments and other materials into the rockshelter throughout its history. The eleven separate natural strata that exist above the rockshelter's shale floor were all the result of three sources: occasional rockfalls from the ceiling, providing fragments from fist-sized rocks to boulders; a steady rain of mostly quartz grains, also from the ceiling; and what is called sheetwash, meaning sediments coming down from above the rockshelter during rainstorms.

Nothing was entering the site from below. Indeed, any water movement from a fluctuating water table would have erased the chemical signature that marks the dripline, which moves toward the back of the rockshelter with the ever-retreating rockshelter roof. Inside the dripline, there is a high concentration of calcium carbonate ($CaCO_3$) from mussel shells or the sandstone, while outside, this calcium carbonate signature has been removed by rain percolating into the sediments. The continuing presence of $CaCO_3$ inside the present and to a lesser extent former driplines demonstrated that no upward water movement that would have erased the $CaCO_3$ signature has occurred. In other words, the trail and track of the dripline could still be plainly seen. Additionally, our excavations conclusively showed that after 22,000 years ago, groundwater levels fell, never again to rise within thirty feet of the deepest occupation surface.

Never mind. Vance Haynes wanted more reassurance, more proof that the site was not contaminated, and continued to call for it in various scientific journals. Others chimed in, notably the aforementioned Haynes disciple Ken Tankersley, then an associate professor at Kent State University in Ohio. Ken's life trajectory has not, it seems, included much by way of notable archaeological findings; instead he has made a career mostly from being a professional naysayer. Tankersley offered some fairly tortured reasoning to come up with contamination at Meadowcroft, including an astonishing wrinkle on the notion of "replicability." He noted that contamination from vitrite had occurred at two other alleged pre-Clovis sites, so therefore it probably had happened at Meadowcroft. He too pointed to groundwater as the culprit.

I would not be honest if I said I did not find all of this irritating in the extreme. Here were a handful of Clovis First critics hypothesizing a lot of contorted, even fanciful, scenarios by which the radiocarbon dates at Meadowcroft could be wrong—scenarios we had already systematically ruled out by the most painstaking methods available to us. We responded with what I now look back on as a somewhat (no, very) smart-ass paper in *American Antiquity*. We called it the "Yes, Virginia" paper; in it we ridiculed Vance Haynes and his acolytes and what we knew were ill-informed criticisms. A colleague, upon reading it, told me that we would surely be vindicated, but it would take a long time and even longer now that we had insulted Haynes, who was by now widely considered the chief arbiter of such matters. Indeed, he was at the time a member of the august National Academy of Sciences. That he had cast doubt on our findings stuck to our conclusions and reports like a lamprey sticks to its host fish, and we came to feel that no matter what we did in defense of our work, it would always be referred to as a site about which "questions" existed.

All this despite a long list of accolades about how precise, how careful, how technically astonishing the excavation had been, as well as the collection of the data and every other technical aspect of the dig. Numerous archaeologists had commented, calling our work "impeccable." Brian Fagan, of the University of California at Santa Barbara, said that the "careful work at Meadowcroft has set a standard." Yet here were a few people, including Vance, carrying on about groundwater's having brought whole or dissolved particles of coal or vitrinized wood into the dating samples, even though no one had ever actually seen such a thing in any of the samples.

There is a very good reason why no one has ever seen coal particles or vitrinized wood brought up through the ground into the samples: neither substance is soluble in water. Even this elementary fact was ignored. As I noted, once raised, the specter of contamination did not die.

But say, for the sake of argument, that somehow the samples were contaminated by some magical vehicle. For a sample that was, say, truly 10,000 years old to appear to be 16,000 years old, it would have had to be contaminated by coal or vitrite in an amount equal to *35 percent* of its weight. More than a third of the volume in each of the thirteen samples taken in Stratum IIa would have to be coal or vitrite. But why would the groundwater have stopped percolating upward exactly and conveniently at the end of the period represented by Stratum IIa? Why wouldn't it have gone upward to contaminate more recent samples? And *mathematically,* the addition of 35 percent by weight of coal or vitrite to create a date of about A.D. 1200 would mean that the sample, if "uncontaminated," would have had to be deposited in the ground some four thousand years in the future.

It is remotely possible that the personnel in four different radiocarbon laboratories could have, upon the rigorous examination of each sample, failed to notice the admixture of 5 percent by weight of one or the other contaminant—but that 5 percent would create an error of as little as five or six hundred years—not six thousand. And to suggest that laboratory personnel could fail to note that a third or more of the sample was a contaminant implies a witless incompetence of astronomical, even unimaginable, dimensions. Only professional naysayers could assert that the samples were contaminated sufficiently to render the early dates so wholly inaccurate. But that is what I was up against. In this regard, it is perhaps worth noting that Tankersley and a colleague, in their zeal to discredit the early Meadowcroft dates, actually contrived a laboratory experiment in which bituminous coal appeared to partially dissolve but only after two hundred hours of immersion in water maintained at 100 degrees Centigrade! Interesting, I suppose—at least to a coal chemist—but most agree that such exercises have no bearing whatsoever on the contamination issue at Meadowcroft—much to Ken's chagrin.

Finally, in 1994, after Haynes's many reiterations of his complaints and the gnat attacks from Dena and Ken and some others, Paul Goldberg and Trina L. Arpin of Boston University stepped in and collected sediment samples from Meadowcroft. Goldberg is the nation's leading scholar and practitioner in the arcane realm of microscopic analysis of sediments, and he made an exhaustive study of undisturbed blocks of sediments at Meadowcroft. This involved cataloguing and analyzing the relationships between the particles of solid materials and the spaces between them, which are called "voids." Indeed, there are many different forms of voids that are characteristic of particular sediments; some of these are irregularly shaped ones called "vughs," some are large, rounded ones called "chambers," and others are long, narrow ones called "channels." Anything that contaminated the sediments at Meadowcroft would have had to pass through the network of voids and would have left unmistakable signs, such as filling the voids with particles of very fine material.

Goldberg and Arpin concluded in a report in the *Journal of Field Archaeology* in 1999, "Most significantly in terms of the Meadowcroft dating controversy, we see no evidence of the effects of groundwater saturation of the sediments, nor was particulate coal material visible in any sample . . . nor do we see evidence of any other mechanisms by which particulate or non-particulate contamination could have been introduced into the sediments in general and into the charcoal samples in particular."

The Goldberg report effectively closed the book on the groundwater-contamination question—after twenty years—though not surprisingly, Haynes said it proved nothing. There has never been any particulate contamination found in any Meadowcroft radiocarbon samples, never any coal seam in the shelter. Furthermore, the earliest inhabitants of the rock-shelter were operating in a mosaic environment that has, beginning in 1975, proved to be wholly consistent with new information about life at the glacier's edge. Even if you average the six deepest dates associated with human artifacts—a procedure that makes no statistical sense at all though it is practiced by some archaeologists—people were in western Pennsylvania at least as early as sometime between 13,955 and 14,555 radiocarbon years ago. Not only that, but the human artifacts from those earliest times no longer exist and, in fact, *never* existed in isolation. Two other sites in the Cross Creek drainage, the Mungai Farm and the Krajacic locality, have both produced distinctive Meadowcroft-style implements, including cores, blades, and a Miller point. So also has Cactus Hill in Virginia. Replication!

So, for now at least, the humans who stopped off at Meadowcroft represent the pioneer population in the upper Ohio River Valley and perhaps the entire Northeast. From their varied tool kit, we know they were hunter-gatherers who opportunistically foraged for a variety of plant and animal foods. They were not specialized hunters of big game, and there are no clear or unambiguous connections between them and the people who produced the Clovis artifacts. Those are now the generally accepted facts. I believe I have made the case.

But the gnats still buzz. Recently, Stuart Fiedel, a previously little-known archaeologist now working for a private salvage-archaeology firm in Virginia, has actually agreed that the Meadowcroft dates are correct but maintains that the context and association of the artifacts and ecofacts are flawed because the stratigraphy of Stratum IIa is hopelessly mixed. Fiedel has no field experience in Paleo-Indian sites or complex late Pleistocene or Holocene sites. He has published one rarely used prehistory textbook but otherwise has no apparent credentials. Now, thirty years after the fact, he feels confident in raising a problem that was somehow overlooked by the hundreds of archaeologists and geologists who visited the site during the excavation. I haven't responded in print to his allegation, though I suggested at a public archaeological meeting that its author would be well advised to reserve some space in the State Home for the Terminally Bewildered. The last I heard, he had written another attack on Meadowcroft and was unsuccessfully shopping it around, trying to find a professional journal that would publish it.

There is but one reason this archaeological farce continues. It is not the script—that is, the data. It is the actors, many of whom have invested so heavily in the canonical view of Clovis primacy that the acknowledgment of a new story—any new story—somehow threatens the integrity of their life's work. Depending on your point of view, this situation is either tragic or comic, but it has *never* been science.

All this time we have been speaking almost entirely about North America, but south of here, beyond a land bridge far narrower than the Bering land bridge, is a huge continent. This too is a place where, recently, the murky question of the first Americans—and of course the Clovis First dogma—has received a stunning blast of light. The view from South America has always shed a somewhat different light on the entire process of the peopling of the New World.

CHAPTER EIGHT

———

ANOTHER ANGLE OF VIEW

I grew up in Youngstown, Ohio, when it held (it may still) the record for the number of car bombings in a year. In fact, according to local lore, car bombing was invented in Youngstown. It was a mob town and, despite several well-intentioned and ongoing reform efforts, still is. As a little kid growing up and going on through high school, I knew and associated with some very hard cases, which probably contributed to my being able to survive the graduate years with The Dark Lord. In any case, such a childhood instills a certain amount of pugnacity in a person, and I have always pretty much responded in kind to bullies and other people who knock the work of my colleagues, teammates, and students.

At times the dogmatic skepticism leveled at Meadowcroft has seemed more like *ad hominem* harassment than science, more like abuse than a search for the truth. But the abuse I took was nothing compared to what my "colleagues" have handed out to a friend of mine, Tom Dillehay, an archaeologist from the University of Kentucky in Lexington who had the audacity to announce not only a pre-Clovis find, but one from South America.

Tom has been accused of virtually every lapse an archaeologist can make; in fact, he has been slandered and libeled by some colleagues here in America who went so far as to accuse him of faking evidence. But by finding pre-Clovis human habitation six thousand miles from the Bering land

Tom Dillehay.

bridge and by failing to buy into the view that it was Clovis hunters who carried All Things to the benighted regions of Central and South America, he unwittingly brought into the open the final raging, incoherent moans of the last of the Clovis First diehards. Judging by the obloquy thrown his way, one would be forgiven for thinking that American archaeologists, as a group of actual people developing a body of knowledge, may harbor just a teensy-weensy gringo-style bias against South America. European archaeologists think that the American preoccupation of these past seventy-odd years with Clovis Man is typically American in its lack of sophistication and headstrong provincialism. Through the years, Latin American archaeology has played an important if often (in North America) overlooked role in our understanding of who the first Americans might have been and when they arrived. Today, Dillehay's site in South America is one of the few stanchions on which the undisputable pre-Clovis presence of humans in the New World rests.

Curiosity about when people might have arrived in Latin America was minimal in the eighteenth and early nineteenth centuries, largely because travelers, antiquarians, and later people who could call themselves archaeologists tended to be preoccupied with the fantastic architectural remains of the great civilizations of Peru and Central America. One exception was a Danish botanist, Wilhelm Peter Lund, who in the 1830s devoted himself to unraveling the history of mankind in Brazil. He explored hundreds of caves, eventually coming across rock paintings of "primitive" animals and also fossil bones, the remains of extinct cold-weather creatures nonetheless found there in the tropics. He came to the conclusion that there had been a great cataclysm—earthquakes followed by a gigantic tidal wave, the melting of the poles, and other global changes, not to mention the Flood— that had put an end to the antediluvian world and its creatures.

Once the planet had calmed down and the waters had risen and sub- sided, God set about the great re-creation of life, leaving some creatures extinct and, of course, introducing mankind. In all, the ante- and the post- diluvian worlds must have taken about five or six thousand years each, so the earth was 12,000 years old. Lund also concluded that humans had lived in Brazil for a very long time and that they must have arrived from the Old World. For reasons that probably had nothing to do with his paleontologi- cal efforts, Lund, who was greatly admired in Brazil and Europe as a botanist, eventually went mad and died tormented by imaginary snakes and army ants.

Little else was said or done about the origins of humans in Latin Amer- ica until the late nineteenth century. The nations of South America did not develop as vigorous a tradition of government-funded science as the United States, and such marginal fields as archaeology and paleontology tended to be underfunded in the universities. Much of the actual archaeological work in South America in these centuries was carried out by foreigners, chiefly Europeans. As we saw, the German Max Uhle carried out sophisticated chronological studies of much more recent cultures than the late Pleis- tocene in Peru and elsewhere and thereby helped to put South American archaeology—and archaeology in general—on a firmer methodological footing.

THE MAD ARGENTINE

In the last quarter of the nineteenth century, there emerged on the South American scene a man whom Vine Deloria, Jr., would find acceptable if not downright heroic. This was the Argentine Florentino Ameghino, a onetime schoolteacher and self-taught geologist, anthropologist, and paleontologist, who, on his twenty-first birthday in 1875, presented the Argentine Scientific Society with the fossil bones of a human that he had found on the pampa. Pressing on with his researches, he later traveled to Europe, where he announced that not only was humanity very old in South America, but it had arisen there and spread to the rest of the world.

His rationale was that he had found human remains from the Tertiary era (the period before the Pleistocene), and since no other Tertiary human remains had been reported from anywhere else, the Tertiary Man from the southern half of South America was obviously the first. He proposed, in chronological order, first a nonhuman progenitor, *Homunculus patagonicus,* then some prehominids called *Tetraprohomo,* followed by various species of *Homo,* and ending up with *Homo pampaeus.* According to his argument, *Homo pampaeus* had migrated north across the recently uplifted isthmus of Panama into North America and from there across the Bering land bridge to Asia, where one branch had become the Mongols and another branch had continued across an unidentified land bridge to Europe, where it had become the white man.

In 1910, Ameghino described his elaborate taxonomy to an international conference of Americanists, and it caught the baleful eye of none other than the Smithsonian's redoubtable Aleš Hrdlička, who made a special trip south to point out the absurdity of *Homo pampaeus* (and all his imagined predecessors stretching back into the Miocene). One of his tactics was, as usual, to cast doubt on the attribution of Ameghino's "fossil-bearing" terrain as Tertiary. In 1912, Hrdlička and Holmes published *Early Man in South America,* which demolished Ameghino's thesis in an academic version of a mob hit. Poor old Florentino didn't have a chance.

It did not take North Americans to bring doubt and scorn down on Ameghino's notions. His own countrymen—including a zoologist at the University of La Plata, Carlos Bruch—were highly skeptical as well. Bruch pointed out that Ameghino's protohuman femur was in fact that of a carnivorous mammal and that one of his primitive human skulls was, if looked at from the proper angle, that of a modern human. Many of the bones Ameghino pegged as early on the human scale were those of monkeys, and the stone tools he found (mostly irregularly chipped cobbles) were of modern manufacture, or not tools at all.

Nonetheless, the notion of Tertiary Man in South America breathed on, if fitfully. As late as 1934, a paleontologist at the Buenos Aires natural history museum claimed on the basis of a couple of molars found near the Atlantic Ocean in Miramar and a piece of jaw found elsewhere that there had been a South American creature, *Homo chapadmalensis,* that was far older than any such human species in Europe.

South Americans then tired of the entire area of prehistoric archaeology before the great Peruvian and other Latin American civilizations, and dropped it for a few years. No one heard any more of Tertiary Man in South America. Of course, by this time Clovis Man had come to light from Blackwater Draw in Arizona, and soon enough it had become largely unarguable, at least in the United States, that he had descended upon South America with overpowering speed. As the prevailing theory went, some battalions from the greater Clovis force must have charged across the isthmus at Panama and blitzed yet another continent in a matter of centuries, or maybe just decades. In a calendrical trice, all the big mammals of South America were said to have been slaughtered or made extinct. And the only proof was that small but—significantly—*fluted* points were scattered here and there across the continent, even as far south as Tierra del Fuego. Q.E.D., right?

A HINT OF IMPERIALISM

Most archaeologists in South America are not especially uncomfortable with the idea that humans probably arrived in the New World from Asia via the Bering land bridge, which is to say they reached North America first and only then migrated into South America. But a rapid-fire blitzkrieg by Clovis hunters seemed a bit too much like a familiar story in Latin America: Yankee imperialism.

By the late 1950s, Latin American archaeology was faced with the same partisan climate as existed in North America: those who swore by the Clovis First school of thought and those who, for various reasons, sought predecessors to Clovis. Danièle Lavallée, a French archaeologist with more than thirty-five years of work in South America, has pointed out that some in the conservative camp "have insinuated that less rigor is displayed in excavation methods and that there is less fuss over the validity of data, especially absolute dates, in South America and Europe. This argument," she adds with a nearly audible sigh, "borders on arrogance." And as she points out in her recent book, *The First South Americans,* the conservatives of the North have long had the weight of evidence on their side—dozens of Clovis sites and hundreds of carbon-14 dates—while those who envision earlier arrivals have a mere handful of sites, some of which have only a few or even just one carbon-14 date to go on. The story, then, is not unlike that in the United States: many sites alleged to be pre-Clovis are greeted with great skepticism, especially from those north of Mexico.

Perhaps the most merciless of the skeptics has been Thomas Lynch, once of Cornell University and now of the Brazos County Museum of east Texas. Lynch spent much of his professional life working in South America and commenting on the work of others there. In 1972, he found some skeletal remains in a northern Peruvian cave that were thought to date to 10,500 B.P. This was duly announced with the proper fanfare, although subsequent work showed that the radiocarbon date was far too old and that the stratigraphy had been significantly disturbed. Burned by the criticism that arose over his error, he became a relentless and highly influential critic of all such early dates, finding disturbed stratigraphy and other flaws everywhere he looked. He has been joined from time to time by the familiar bête noire of northern pre-Clovis claims, Vance Haynes, who, as noted earlier, also became a Clovis First stalwart after being similarly burned. It is said that converts to a religion are the most zealous, and accordingly these two converts have done their best to make mincemeat of much of the South American archaeology directed at the earliest inhabitants of that continent.

It is important to keep in mind, though, that whatever actually took place in the peopling of South America, it happened in a place much different from North America. In South America, very different effects derived from the glacier's advance to its maximum some 18,000 to 20,000 years ago, and the subsequent climatic changes as it receded had very different effects. Here was a very different stage for life from the one up north.

GLACIAL SOUTH AMERICA

The route from North to South America was straightforward, even at the time of the glacial maximum, and it hardly presented a problem for migratory people or other animals. The isthmus of Panama was a far wider thoroughfare than it is now because the waters of the sea were far lower. What glaciers existed were confined to the Andean cordillera and specifically to the mountains of Peru and then, south beyond a largely ice-free region, along the southernmost part of the chain and Patagonia down to Tierra del Fuego. At about 14,000 years B.P., the glaciers began to recede, and by 10,000 B.P. they had melted to the present configuration of snowcapped peaks. The effects were profound, except, oddly enough, in the great Amazon rain forest—a densely packed forest of stunning diversity of plant and animal species and a nearly debilitating humidity. Before widespread clearing for cattle raising and agriculture began in the twentieth century, it stretched for mile after mile after mile, a huge green carpet drained by thousands and thousands of streams and rivers, all tributaries to the huge Amazon River. Here and there are pockets, like islands, of drier savanna lands or areas of grass and sparsely sprinkled trees—the sort of environment where today in Africa you see lions and gazelles.

Until quite recently, paleoecologists felt that at the end of the Pleistocene, the picture was the opposite, something like a photographic negative, with large areas of savanna and pockets of rain forest. Today, up-to-date paleoecological studies have shown that the forest covered much the same area as today, meaning that it has long been more resistant to relatively minor climatic changes than previously expected. But most other parts of the continent were subject to fairly rapid change brought on by the sudden melting of what comparatively little glacial ice there was, combined with a bout of volcanic action that struck the western side of the continent and the flooding of the coasts as sea levels rose. (This was, of course, quite different from in the north, where, as we saw, what had been a busy mosaic of habitats gave way, especially west of the Mississippi, to a large area of relatively uniform and comparatively species-poor prairie.) Such changes would have caused displacements of whatever humans and animals were present and brought about major changes in the way people went about the business of making a living. Even without local or regional upheavals, though, the continent was already a place of vast ecological diversity.

As the ice melted back to its present state in the mountains, for example, a new realm opened up for both animals and humans to exploit. The now ice-free highlands in the Andes and elsewhere offered opportunities for species and summoned physiological changes in human groups, such as much larger lungs and new foraging strategies, just as the frozen wastes of the Arctic favor circulatory systems more conserving of heat. The biggest game animals at such heights were llamas and their relatives—hardly big game in any Pleistocene sense. Hunters no doubt chased down mammals of various sizes and species, using various means depending on the prey and the nature of the habitat. The bolo surely did not originate in the close quarters of the rain forest. And surely Clovis Man, that turbocharged hunter with the big, beautiful spear points, the fearless killer of giants, would almost surely have expired from frustration in a tropical rain forest. There the longest straight shot he could achieve would have been less than a first down in football, and his sun-dappled prey would have disappeared in the shadows while overhead the monkeys and parrots screeched and squawked in cosmic derision.

Logic aside, what is the modern archaeological evidence for Clovis-style and pre-Clovis people in South America?

THE NEED FOR TIME

A great deal of prehistoric archaeological work has been done in South America in the latter part of the twentieth century. Large numbers of sites have been excavated, and it has become clear that by about 11,000 years ago, people had made their way to most parts of the South American continent and had developed a variety of ways of making a living in response to the variety of landscapes they found themselves in.

That they could have accomplished this all in two hundred or even five hundred years strains credulity. This seemingly impossibly short time to travel some ten thousand miles has been a point of contention ever since the 1930s, thanks to Junius Bird, an archaeologist at the American Mu-

Junius Bird.

seum of Natural History in New York (some think he was the actual prototype of Indiana Jones, though Bird was far more mild-mannered in real life). In the late thirties, he found so-called fish-tail fluted points, along with some big mammal bones, sealed off by a rock spall in Fell's Cave in Tierra del Fuego. He assumed these points were some 5,500 years old, but when, after World War II, carbon dating put them at more than 10,000 years B.P., a few people began to question the speed of the Clovis migration. Tierra del Fuego seemed an awfully long way for Clovis Man to go in something like a thousand years, but the points were indeed fluted. And then, essentially burying the questioners, Paul Martin's Clovis blitzkrieg theory came along shortly thereafter—indeed, in the nick of time.

Today we know that at the time Clovis points appeared in North America, people in South America were already practicing many lifeways. Some chiefly hunted camelids (guanacos and llamas) in the Andean highlands, while others chased horses and other herbivores on the pampas and savannas of Argentina. Others still lived chiefly on shellfish and other ma-

Fish-tail projectile points from South America,
ca. 11,000 to 10,000 B.P.

rine foods along the coasts, as shell middens commonly found there indicate. Most people typically lived in small bands, which hunted small game
and occasionally larger animals and depended as well on what plants could
be gathered in their neighborhood. Some people evidently did actively hunt
the Pleistocene megafauna, but it is highly unlikely that they could have
survived only on those efforts without bagging smaller game and spending
much time gathering fruit, nuts, and other plant foods.

The chances are that most such people were merely opportunistic
when it came to the large Pleistocene fauna, killing a mastodon only once
it got stuck or disabled, for example. The spectacularly rapid environmental changes that were under way from about 14,000 years ago until about
10,000 years ago were sufficient to doom most of the Pleistocene fauna—

an extinction event that took a bit longer in the south than in North America for reasons that remain to be explained fully. Horses, for example, plied the pampas after they were extinct in North America. The difference in timing, however, is essentially unimportant.

The peopling of South America has emerged as far more complex, perhaps the result of several if not many separate *entradas* through Central America. By 11,000 to 10,000 years ago, the tradition of fluted points called fish-tail points became widespread throughout the continent. These points bear a considerable resemblance to one another wherever they are found. They typically encouraged the Clovis First model until it became clear that they were preceded in most places by a host of other, localized lithic (and nonlithic) traditions. It is quite possible that by the time these points came into fashion, people who had made their lonely way into the far reaches of the continent in relatively small bands were now living in larger and more numerous bands and were therefore more in touch with one another. In such circumstances, a tradition such as fluting could have passed from group to group very quickly.

The first main question here—essentially forced on archaeologists in South America—is whether or not Clovis people came bursting through the isthmus at Panama and descended on South America with the same speed and lethality with which they supposedly overran North America. In an insight that is also relevant to North America, current work suggests that it was the technology—the idea of the fluted point—that traveled quickly, not the people. It now seems reasonable to suppose that Clovis points struck the fancy of people for some reason, perhaps religious, and the technique of making them spread across the country to people who were already there. The other critical question is whether or not people were indeed there before Clovis. We will review the many attempts to find pre-Clovis evidence before we get to Tom Dillehay, who was the one able to say "Bingo!"

THEORY FIRST?

Sherlock Holmes could look at a perfect stranger and from one insignificant feature or two spin a convincing description of the stranger's profession, his past, and even his character. Detectives in fiction can do that, but it is rare that scientists can develop a viable theory on the basis of a single datum. More often than not, successful theories arise as a result of many facts coming to light that need a new explanation. But in the history of archaeology, many practitioners develop a theory and then set out to find the data to support it. Ameghino, of Tertiary Man notoriety, was one such person; impelled by what was more of a dream than the desire for an explanation, he managed to find supporting evidence anywhere, even in the bones of monkeys. It seems silly to us now, but dreams still do inspire archaeological theories, and some dreamers can then persuade themselves that the evidence is supportive.

And sometimes, as well, logic can lead one astray. In the early days of archaeology in Europe, as the finds delineating the Stone Age occurred, it was perfectly logical to assume that the different styles of toolmaking were a natural evolutionary progression from crude ones to more sophisticated ones—representing the move from savagery to increasing degrees of cultural refinement. It would be taken for granted for a long time that any crude tool was older than a more sophisticated one. This is in a sense much the same as saying that, given the availability of electric tools, no one in the twenty-first century will ever have made or used a manual screwdriver.

In this way, some archaeologists, impelled by the dream of an extremely ancient peopling of the New World, can be easily persuaded that a broken cobble was clearly a unifacial tool and the work of humans that predated the sophisticates known as Clovis. Even such eminent scholars as Louis Leakey could persuade themselves that rocks broken by natural forces (ecofacts) were unifacial tools (i.e., artifacts). The Tom Lynches and Vance Hayneses have done the field a service in pointing this out when it actually is the case.

In South American archaeology in the latter part of the twentieth century, many such mistakes were the work, ironically, of North American archaeologists. One, the maverick Scotty MacNeish, we have already met. As long ago as 1976, Scotty devised his own scenario: at some point—maybe 50,000 years ago, maybe even 70,000—humans came across the Bering land bridge and began a slow advance southward, reaching South America by 20,000 years ago. Their tool kit was simple: crudely worked cobbles and very simple unifacial and bifacial implements derived from the ancient chopper/chopping tool tradition of Asia. During what Scotty called Stage 2, they developed better, more sophisticated tools of stone and bone points. Thereafter, some 15,000 years ago in South America and earlier in the north, they came up with spiffy bifacial points and all the rest of the big-game hunter's tool kit. That there are practically no physical remains of any of the earlier artifacts is no surprise, Scotty said. It simply reflects the very small size of the populations in question and the ample time elapsed that has permitted geological forces to cover up what few artifacts were left behind.

However plausible or implausible that might seem, even Scotty knew that it is difficult to prove the existence of something by the fact of its absence. Over the decades, he assiduously looked for signs that his scenario had in fact occurred. His theory was based on at least one excavation that showed to his satisfaction two or more pre-Clovis stages in the peopling of South America. This was at Pikimachay Cave high in the foothills of the Andes in southern Peru, where he worked in the late sixties into the early seventies. He came across layers that dated between 6,000 and 9,000 years B.P. and, below those, several deeper layers that had been sealed off by a huge rockfall from the cave's ceiling, perhaps the result of an earthquake. Just below the rockfall he found strata that included fossil bones of sloth, horse, and camelids, along with bifaced tools and scrapers. A bone from these layers yielded one date of 14,200 B.P. Below them he found four more layers with the remains of big sloths, a big carnivore, horses, and camelids along with hammerstones, choppers, and other fairly crude implements. There was no charcoal in these layers, but MacNeish obtained two radio-carbon dates from the sloth bones in the neighborhood of 20,000 years B.P., with a large potential variation. From this, MacNeish assumed that small bands of hunters had used the cave from 25,000 to 15,000 years ago when out looking for prey.

Unfortunately, while virtually all archaeologists agree that the tools in the 14,000-year-old layers are indeed tools, most of them question the validity of the single date, and most believe that the "tools" from the earlier levels are simply not artifacts at all. They are generally made from the same volcanic tuff of which the cave itself consists, a very poor material for shaping into a cutting edge. More than likely they fell from the walls on their own. Some, such as Danièle Lavallée, hold out a wan hope that the

14,000 B.P. level might be legitimate. If so, it is the earliest occupation known in South America. I myself find the lithics unconvincing in this regard and the stratigraphy not well enough delineated.

MORE THEORY FIRST

Two other North Americans who have long held out for a pre-Clovis habitation of South America are a married couple, Ruth Gruhn and Alan Bryan, both on the faculty at the University of Calgary. Far less audacious but certainly as persistent as MacNeish, this couple has long stood among the most optimistic that pre-Clovis—and certainly non-Clovis—people reached South America long ago, perhaps as long ago as 20,000 or more years. They almost certainly will be vindicated in spite of the long and unbroken string of failed pre-Clovis sites they have dug. Bryan suggests that the early migrants to South America needed to adapt to a variety of diverse environments—forest, open land, and so forth—and therefore most likely used a simple tool kit of unifacial flakes and simple core tools that could be

Alan Bryan and Ruth Gruhn.

used to make other tools from wood, bone, fiber, and skins. Projectile points used in hunting big game would rarely be found in this scenario, and this has indeed been the case. At some point, some of the migrants would have taken up hunting large animals in the arid savanna regions, using stone projectile points such as those called El Jobo points, which are fairly common along the northern coast. Some time later yet, the notion of fluting arose, probably diffused throughout the south from North America.

This scenario is plausible enough, but regrettably, in decades of excavation in both North and South America, the couple has never found much by way of solid evidence that anything prior to the El Jobo points really existed. Many archaeologists have found what appeared to be the early unifacial tools that are part of Bryan's scenario, but they have almost entirely been found in open ground, without an archaeological context, stratigraphy, dating, or even a certainty that they are artifacts rather than ecofacts. Perhaps Bryan's most important find came when he reexcavated what had once been an ancient, spring-fed water hole in Venezuela called Taima Taima.

The site had been dug earlier—in 1962—by the Venezuelan archaeologist José Cruxent, who had produced carbon-14 dates of 14,000 to 12,000 years ago for some fossil animals. The dates had immediately been attacked on technical grounds, and other results at the site seemed confused, so in 1976 Bryan and Gruhn reinvestigated the site to clarify matters. In a layer of gray sand that lay sealed off below a sterile layer, they found the bones of horse, glyptodont, and a young mastodon lying on its left side, some of its parts still articulated, others missing. A couple of ribs showed markings that could have resulted from butchering. Various stone tools were found in the same layer, along with the remains of branches thought to have come from the animal's stomach. But most important, there was a fragment of a lanceolate bifacial point identified as El Jobo lying in the mastodon's pelvic cavity.

In all, Bryan obtained nineteen carbon-14 dates from the bones, the branches, and charcoal from the gray sand. With one exception, they all fell between 14,800 and 12,800 years B.P., making this what Bryan called "one of the best dated kill-sites in America." He hypothesized that the hunter had thrust his spear into the anus of the mastodon, which had expired from internal bleeding. One has to wonder if a wounded mastodon would allow a hunter anywhere near his rectum, let alone in it! Tom Lynch and others were quick to hypothesize that the association of the bones and the stone tools was merely accidental, the result of sinking through water-saturated soils. This was, after all, a spring-fed water hole. Something similar had been noted in a nearby site dug by José Cruxent in the sixties. Critics asked where the tip of the projectile point was, thus insinuating that the broken point had to have sunk through the mud into the pelvis. But the point and the pelvis, along with the other remains and tools, were sealed in by a layer of clay above them that dates to about 10,000 B.P. Even the ever-suspicious Dena Dincauze conceded that both the point and the bones had to have arrived at their final resting place before 10,000 B.P. Supporters of the site have gone on to point out that had this been found in North America and dated to sometime before 11,000 B.P., no one would have questioned the context; many kill sites of mammoths and mastodons were at water holes. If the context is valid—and several Latin American archaeologists, including the Colombian Gerardo Ardila, find no problem with it—the dates still might not be. These could be resolved by revisiting the bones and artifacts and subjecting them to AMS dating, but for now the site remains controversial at best.

THE PEDRA FURADA CONTROVERSY

Another highly touted site of pre-Clovis habitation is a massive and dramatic sandstone rockshelter in the semiarid thorn forest in the state of Piaui in northeast Brazil, an area where some two hundred rockshelters have been found. Known as Pedra Furada, the rockshelter in question is 30 feet across and 60 feet deep, with the roof looming about 260 feet above the floor, which itself is more than 60 feet above the valley floor. First discovered in 1973, it was excavated beginning in 1978 by Niède Guidon of the School for the Advanced Study of Social Sciences in Paris. She and her French, Brazilian, and Italian colleagues found fragments of rock allegedly stained with paint—that is, cave paintings—and what appeared to be hearths and stone tools made of quartz and quartzite in a deep level that yielded some forty-six radiocarbon dates ranging from 46,000 years B.P. to 14,300 B.P. In all, this old layer produced around 560 "tools," some chopping tools and

*The 1993 inspection team visiting
Pedra Furada, Brazil.*

the likes of burins, but mostly what Guidon and her lithic analyst, Fabia Parenti, said were pieces with "blunt points obtained with two, three or four convergent flakings." All this underlay a layer full of indisputable artifacts that yielded dates from 10,400 years B.P. to about 6000 B.P.

The finds were announced with great fanfare, first at a major scientific conference in Orono, Maine, in 1989, then in the scientific press (for example, the British journal *Nature*), and then in the popular press, with an article in *The New York Times* giving readers the impression that Brazil might well have been colonized before North America! No sooner did this pre-Clovis, even pre–North America, balloon go up than the naysayers descended. Curiously to some, traitorously to others, Tom Dillehay and I were among them.

The quartzite tools, we and Dave Meltzer suggested, were almost surely broken rocks that had fallen into the rockshelter from a deposit of quartzite gravels some three hundred feet above. These could have entered

General view of the excavation area at Pedra Furada.

the rockshelter in a number of ways, and moving water could have scattered them across the entire floor. The ancient "fireplaces" appeared to be nothing more than material blown in from nearby forest fires. Guidon replied that the region had been rain forest at the time, fires are hard to start in rain forests, and anyway, how come the charcoal flecks fetched up only in little areas the size of hearths? To which we naysayers said that charcoal might well have covered the entire floor only to be washed away by rains and floods, except for those flecks that were protected by rocks. Besides, we argued, pollen studies of the surround suggest that the area was drier than a rain forest at the time in question, 30,000 years B.P. During our inspection of the site, I observed no convincing evidence of fireplaces, despite protestations to the contrary. And so the arguments went, leaving the ancient level very much in doubt, chiefly because there really is no way to tell if any of the quartzite "tools" really are man-made and not simply rocks broken by falling.

Additional bad news for the pre-Clovis evidence is that because there are no animal bones—which should have been preserved and would be expected if the rockshelter had been a campsite—there are therefore no telltale cut marks on bones that would strongly indicate a human presence. Perhaps more telling, there are no tools made of any nonlocal rock, despite the presence of high-grade raw materials in the general study area.

On the other hand, little doubt exists that humans used the rockshelter at least 11,000 years ago (the upper level) and perhaps somewhat earlier; for example, some valid human artifacts made of chert and other materials that had to have been imported to the shelter were found in the more recent layer. It remains possible, at least to some investigators, that the rock-shelter could have been used far earlier, if not as a campsite, then perhaps as a quarry where nature had helped the toolmaking process along. In any event, all the pre-Clovis evidence at Pedra Furada remains moot, and I seriously doubt that the central issue of the origin of the alleged quartzite artifacts will ever be successfully settled in favor of an ancient human presence.

(Meanwhile, it would be a mistake not to point out, by way of a side-light, that in the Andean highlands as early as 10,000 years ago, the first steps to controlling the growth of certain plants were being taken: wild potatoes native to high altitudes were being moved to lower elevations. Here, then, were some of the first glimmerings of agriculture in this hemisphere—not so much later than such glimmerings as took place in the Near East and China, where modern humans had been for 20,000 and more years.)

MONTE VERDE

All this brings us back to the discovery made by my friend Tom Dillehay, the preeminent flak catcher of pre-Clovis archaeology. In 1976, he was teaching at the Southern University of Chile when a student returned from a site with a large mastodon tooth and some other bones, which he handed over to the university museum. The site itself had been discovered in the mid-1970s when some locals, clearing a path for their oxcarts, had cut back the creek's bank, revealing wood and stone artifacts along with the bones of a mastodon. Markings on the bones caught Dillehay's eye—either they were scratches made by animals trampling on the bones, or they were cut marks made during butchering. To find out which, Dillehay went to the site in 1977 and, in the course of a limited excavation, found more bones with what appeared to be butchering marks, along with clay-lined hearths and stone tools unmistakably made by humans. Assuming that the site might date as far back as 10,000 years, into the late Ice Age, he was startled and—

Vance Haynes crossing Chinchihuapi Creek during the 1997 site visit to Monte Verde.

like me a couple of years earlier—a bit appalled when radiocarbon dates on the charcoal from the hearths, as well as from bone and wooden implements, came back at more than 12,000 years B.P. Of course Tom was well aware of the Clovis Bar and had seen no reason to question it.

Known as Monte Verde, the site is located on the banks of Chinchihuapi Creek, a tributary of the Maullin River in south-central Chile. It lies about thirty-six miles from the Pacific Ocean in a humid, cool forest, and as it is an open-air locality, is a rarity. Or rather, it *was* an open-air site. Sometime not long after it was inhabited, the waters of the creek rose and covered the site, which eventually filled in, becoming a peat-filled bog that inhibited bacterial decay of things that usually disappear from the archaeological record. In this anaerobic coffin, an eclectic array of normally perishable artifacts, as well as many other items, was preserved over the millennia.

When the radiocarbon dates came back in 1977, Dillehay found his career veering in an unintended direction, toward the quest for the first Americans. For the next ten years or so, Dillehay and a team of, in all, sixty professionals from various disciplines excavated Monte Verde, and for fif-

*1997 inspection team examining stratigraphy at Monte
Verde. Tom Dillehay is on the far right.*

teen years thereafter Dillehay wrote up the results of his excavations and
defended both them and himself from an onslaught of skepticism, naysay-
ing, virulent professional innuendo, and out-and-out personal attack. He
has told me, as well as some other colleagues, that if he had to do it all over
again, he wouldn't. It hasn't been worth the agony.

Based on what he found buried and preserved in the boggy ground,

*Ongoing excavations at Monte Verde. In the foreground,
near the creek, they are uncovering residential structures.*

Residential structure remnants from Monte Verde.
These remains date to ca. 12,500–13,000 B.P.

A stake from the foundation of a residential structure at Monte Verde. Tied
around the stake with an overhand knot is a strip of junco (Juncus sp.)
fiber. This construction dates to 12,500–13,000 B.P.

here is what was happening at Monte Verde some 12,500 years ago: At some point about twenty or thirty people built a twenty-foot-long tentlike structure of wood and animal hides on the banks of the creek. They framed the structure with logs and planks that were staked to the ground, making walls of poles covered with animal hides. Using cordage made of local reeds, they tied the hides to the poles, dividing the interior with similar hide-and-pole walls into what appear to be separate living spaces. Each such area had a brazier pit lined with clay. At many hearths, they left some stone tools and spilled seeds, nuts, and berries.

Outside the tentlike structure were two large hearths, apparently used communally, grinding stones, and a store of firewood. At some point, presumably close to the time when the site was abandoned, someone—probably an adolescent—walked across some soft clay that had been brought to the site to reline the firepits. He or she left three footprints in

Human footprint from an occupation
surface at Monte Verde, dating to
12,500–13,000 B.P.

the clay that were subsequently sealed under the anaerobic ooze that covered the site.

Not far off, these people also built a wishbone-shaped structure of wooden uprights set in sand and gravel hardened with animal fat. Here mastodon carcasses were butchered and tools were made. Here also these people brought and perhaps dispensed some eighteen medicinal plants, half of which were local and half of which came either from the seacoast about thirty-six miles away or from the arid mountain lands some forty miles in the opposite direction. These same plants are actually still used by the local people today for lung and skin ailments. Aquatic food plants formed a good deal of these people's diet, and they also ate the meat of mastodons, paleollama, and small creatures like freshwater mollusks. The

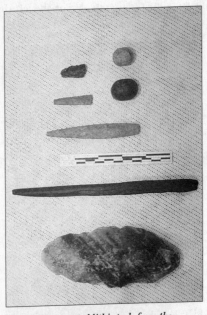

The assorted lithic tools from the MVII occupation at Monte Verde. Top right: two bola stones. Top left and center: El Jobo projectile fragments. Ground slate spear head and a crude quartz biface.

archaeologists even found "chaws" of partly chewed seaweed, nearly perfect molds of the chewer's palate and molars, which they probably sucked on for the high iodine content. In all, the remains of six mastodons were left behind at the site. It seems likely that these beasts were either adventitious kills, perhaps in the nearby boggy areas or scavenged prey of other animals. In addition, wild potato species formed a good deal of the diet, their remains left in the cracks of wooden mortars and food storage pits in the corners of the shelters.

These people also brought salt from the coast a short distance away, pebbles that had been rolled and smoothed in the surf and that they turned

*Remains of a wishbone-shaped foundation
made of clay of a suspected shaman's hut.
Medicinal plant remains were found in and
around this structure, which dates to
12,500–13,000 B.P.*

into chopping tools, and bitumen for fastening stone tools to wooden hafts. From bone, they made digging tools and gouges; from wood, digging sticks and spear shafts. Except for a handful of bifacially flaked stone projectile points and chopping tools, as well as some grooved sling stones and grinding stones, most of the stone tools they used were extremely simple—chiefly pebbles that were only slightly modified—by, say, splitting or knocking off a few flakes with ivory batons.

Clearly the Monte Verdeans were engaged in a multitude of tasks involved in gaining a living from the variety of resources in the numerous ecological zones both nearby and distant. They had situated themselves on prime real estate, a day's walk or two from both the coast and the foothills of the mountains, each with its own array of useful resources. They knew what they were doing, which means they probably were in the area for some time, not just passing through. Some of the hearths and living spaces in the living tent even suggest a certain specialization in the accomplishing of chores: one hearth and its surrounding living space in the tent were characterized by cutting tools made of quartz and fruits and tubers from brackish estuaries; another living space appeared to be a specialized area for working hides. It appears that at least some of the group remained at the site year-round or most of the year.

The Monte Verdeans were probably a group of incipient colonizers in the region, moving in at a time when the glaciers were rapidly receding and the immediate area of the Maullin River was a cool, temperate wetland forest circled by a variety of other habitats and ecological zones. And there they pursued a lifeway far more sophisticated and sedentary than what anybody had expected for such early inhabitants of the hemisphere.

To many who read about this, it just did not seem right. The dates were alarming, of course. It meant that people had been living in what appears to be something like a village, something certainly more socially complex than a band of wandering hunters and gatherers, 10,000 miles south of the Bering land bridge more than a thousand years before Clovis Man had reached Arizona. There was enough trouble already, what with Junius Bird's people being in Fell's Cave in Tierra del Fuego only a couple of hundred years *after* Clovis people appeared in North America. This meant that serious archaeologists had to swallow the idea of proliferating bands of hunters and their families trotting south ten or twenty miles a day, charg-

Biface from the earliest occupation at Monte Verde.
This specimen may date to 33,000 B.P.

ing through deserts and tangled forests, pausing for fleeting moments to mow down the big mammals that got in the way, bolting down hundreds of pounds of meat, racing over mountain passes, splashing through rivers, breast-feeding babies on the run, leapfrogging whole regions, desperately seeking . . . what? Some mystical, mythical destination that they knew lay south?

But aside from the awkward—actually, *impossible*—dates at Monte Verde, the artifacts were all wrong. Some bifaces, a lot of primitive unifaces, and all that other junk. More than one commentator asked, "What planet did these people come from?" The question reflected awe in some and skepticism in others. The Monte Verdeans simply did not meet the expectations of those who were locked into a Clovis-inspired theory of the peopling of the hemisphere. (Remember the role of expectations in this entire unfolding story, starting with the unlikelihood that the Indians could have piled up dirt into grand mounds.)

In 1979, Junius Bird himself, still at the American Museum of Natural History in New York, visited Monte Verde—as it turned out, just when the crew was excavating a sterile level—and pronounced the site void of human artifacts. Soon enough all the scavengers jumped on the still living but bleeding carcass, though most of them had not visited the site. Indeed, to this day, Tom Lynch declares that the wood and bone "artifacts" are doubtful, as are the hearths and remains of the dwellings, and that the bi-facial stone artifacts are intrusive, having slipped down through the muck into the level in question from some more recent habitation. He and others further claimed that the association of remains, artifacts, and hearths with the dated materials was uncertain. In other words, virtually everything was wrong with the excavation and the analysis of its materials. Lynch even sniffed on more than one occasion that Dillehay was not really an archaeologist but "an ethnographer."

On the other hand, Tom had asked me to evaluate the perishable artifacts—the cords used to tie the posts together and so forth—which I did at Lexington, Kentucky, at the university, and, in my mind, there was no question about them. Nor could I find anything about the excavation to squawk about. After all, this was a "wet" site and I had worked at one, the Windover Bog in Florida, which is probably the most important and carefully excavated wet site in eastern North America. My late wife, Rhonda Andrews, several of my students, and I had analyzed all the textiles, basketry, cordage, and wood from that site.

Even Vance Haynes, that grinch of North American archaeology, was quoted in 1992 as saying that it was "pretty hard to overlook the evidence from Monte Verde." Haynes noted that the bifacial projectile point at Monte Verde was very similar to the ones found at Taima Taima in Venezuela.

So what was really going on? Was this really the holy grail? Or was it just another flash in the pan?

___

FIREWORKS

AND THE PALEO-POLICE

For years before and after Aleš Hrdlička suggested to the Colorado Museum's Jesse Figgins that he would be wise to summon a panel of blue-ribbon scholars (meaning, at that time, mostly easterners) the next time he found a human artifact in association with mammoth bones, site visits by luminaries had been seen as a way of verifying an investigator's assertions. It had begun as far back as Brixham Cave and, shortly afterward, in Abbeville, France, when the English scientists unanimously certified the work of the amateur Boucher. In recommending what would have amounted to a permanent committee, Hrdlička said, "I believe that in some such way only can we arrive at conclusions that will command the confidence of every worker."

In 1989, Vance Haynes wrote the following to Dave Meltzer at SMU: "The implications of Monte Verde for American archaeology are so important that I think a panel of objective conservatives should be formed and funded by NSF [the National Science Foundation] to visit the site, examine it, take samples, etc. If a positive consensus results we can then accept the interpretation and formulate new hypotheses for the peopling of the New World. If not, Monte Verde will have to be relegated to the bin of possible pre-Clovis sites awaiting further data." I would be remiss if I did not point out that by the oxymoron "objective conservatives," Haynes meant himself and the Clovis First disciples.

In the early days of the twentieth century, site visits could resolve certain kinds of problems that arose from the lack of widely agreed upon field techniques, the status of finds made by amateurs, and the difficulties of determining age solely on the evidence provided by the geology, associated fauna, and a few other features of the site. By the time of Monte Verde, however, some of these problems were better resolved in other ways. In particular, age determinations were mostly a matter of laboratory analysis, and such dating is no longer anything a site visitor can reasonably comment on except by attacking the excavator's assessment of the stratigraphy from which the carbon-dated samples arose or by finding possible sources of contaminants that the excavator somehow overlooked. As a result, a site visit today really is not in a position to confirm a pre-Clovis site, only to find reasons to reject such an interpretation. Also, in the old days there weren't so many archaeologists or so many specialists involved, and people could generally agree on who were the elite, most distinguished, and wisest arbiters in the field—people like Hrdlička himself or Kidder, who early on pronounced Folsom Man an Ice Age figure. I myself thought that Haynes's proposed visit to Monte Verde was ridiculous. Who among the sophisticated, highly trained, and competent people in the field (or those who thought they were sophisticated, highly trained, and competent) would take the word of a bunch of other archaeologists for whom they might have only modest regard despite their luminous credentials? Nonetheless, the archaeological site visit was born again with every hope that it would settle the matter once and for all.

It took what might seem a long time to pull off the site visit to Monte Verde, considering the site's potent challenge to the dogma of the day. Dillehay had issued an invitation in 1989, which had sparked Haynes's letter to Meltzer, but it took almost another four years before the three of them had prepared a formal proposal to fund the visit. Finding a cross section that would satisfy most willing believers, skeptics, and those on the fence was harder than it at first had seemed. In 1991, the Dallas Museum of Natural History assumed responsibility for the trip and obtained funding from members of its board and the National Geographic Society. This also took a lot of time. Finally, by January 1997, the pantheon of archaeostars had been selected and the Great Chilean Site Visit was under way—first stop Lexington, Kentucky, where Dillehay was a faculty member of the University of Kentucky and where many of the Monte Verde artifacts were housed.

The delegation of course included Meltzer and Haynes, along with Donald Grayson of the University of Washington, Alex Barker of the Dallas Museum of Natural History, Dena Dincauze of the University of Massachusetts (she who had denigrated so much of my stuff at Meadowcroft), Robson Bonnichsen of Oregon State University, and Dennis Stanford, the ever-puckish head of anthropology at the Smithsonian. Also there were three Latin American scholars—Gerardo Ardila of Colombia and Francisco Mena and Lautaro Núñez of Chile—and me. It was not configured as a panel of pre-Clovis skeptics or, conversely, pre-Clovis enthusiasts; rather, it was, as designed, a mixed bag reflecting a range of views. To me, Vance Haynes and Dena Dincauze were skeptical to the point of being closed-minded. I was not actually an official member of the panel since I was obviously biased by having worked on the Monte Verde perishables, but I was invited along to comment on those artifacts. At this time, Meadowcroft was still under a cloud of doubt thanks largely to the continuing nibbling at the edges by Haynes, Dincauze, and some small fry. Monte Verde was now where the excitement lay, and however skeptical the profession was about site visits, the results of this one could have an enormous impact. Certainly the press would eat all the drama up however it was decided. Of course, if Monte Verde checked out, as I knew it should, Meadowcroft would not be hanging out there alone. Replicability!

The avowed purpose of the visit was threefold: (1) to evaluate the controversial (in age) "artifacts" of stone, wood, bone, and other materials and assure both the panel and therefore the world that they were indeed artifacts; (2) to observe the sediments and stratigraphy and make sure that, among other things, the artifacts had not intruded into the old strata; and (3) to ascertain that there was no contamination or other problems that could have confounded the radiocarbon samples.

At the University of Kentucky, where many of the Monte Verde artifacts were archived—especially the lithic material, but also some bone and soft-tissue items—formal presentations were made by Dillehay, me (on the perishables), and two others. The panel examined the material at hand. Then it was off to Chile. Bonnichsen could not make that part of the trip.

We spent a day at the Universidad Austral de Chile at Valdivia, where the remaining artifacts from the site (including the celebrated footprint) were housed and heard a synthesis of the stratigraphy from the university's Mario Pino, a longtime colleague and friend of Tom's. By this time, it was obvious to almost all that the alleged artifacts from Monte Verde housed in Lexington and Valdivia were not only truly man-made but profoundly different from Clovis artifacts. The site visit would be almost anticlimactic. The second day was taken up with travel to the site with stops along the way to examine the local geology of the area. The third and final day was spent at and around the site.

Since the excavation, the main occupation area of Monte Verde had been destroyed by the construction of logging roads and by stream meander, but we were able to inspect a number of stratigraphic sections within and immediately adjacent to the original site. Among other features, we all had a good look at the layer of peat that had covered the archaeological site, which had itself been covered by two distinct layers of sand and gravels. Nothing, we were able to assure ourselves, could have intruded through the layer of peat into the artifact-rich late Pleistocene strata in question. There was nowhere to derive any intrusive items, as there are no overlying later deposits. No one found any source of contamination.

The final report delivered by the panel in the pages of *American Antiquity* in 1997 says, in the typically neutral language of such bulletins, that "all participants assembled at the end of this last day of the site visit to discuss their responses to what they had seen and heard over the course of the preceding week." This is true. We all did assemble—first in a local saloon appropriately called La Caverna.

THE SHOWDOWN AT LA CAVERNA

One of the sponsors of our trip, the Dallas Museum of Natural History, insisted on a group discussion with the hope of achieving a final Brixham- or Folsom-like consensus about Monte Verde. I was skeptical for a variety of reasons beyond my general suspicions about the value of site visits by archaeostars. First of all, there were our two longtime and demonstrably implacable skeptics, Vance Haynes and Dena Dincauze. In addition, we included several very cautious scholars such as Don Grayson, who was largely uncommitted, and Dave Meltzer, who leaned toward a pro–Monte Verde opinion but was remarkably close-mouthed, perhaps with an eye toward not overtly offending his friend and sometime mentor Vance Haynes. Even if Grayson and Meltzer threw in their lot with the pre-Clovis lobby, I did not expect Haynes or Dincauze to follow suit.

I confidently expected that we would see some fireworks. Throughout the previous days of the Monte Verde visit, Dillehay had clearly shown that he would brook no nonsense. He was wired for battle. On one occasion while we were looking at Monte Verde artifacts housed at Valdivia, for example, Haynes questioned the identification of an obviously worked piece of wood as a lance.

"How many wooden lances have you ever seen?" Dillehay asked acidly.

"None," Vance said, but he offered lamely that he had once seen an ancient digging stick.

"Not good enough," Tom said, shutting off the conversation. It was becoming perfectly clear that whatever Haynes's geoarchaeological expertise, it was based on open sites in the arid lands of the American West, and even in the desert, open sites are hard on perishable artifacts. On the other hand, caves and rockshelters in the West are among the best sites for preserving perishable artifacts, but Haynes has rarely worked in them. Monte Verde was a wet site, a place where water can provide thousands of years of anaerobic protection for implements that even in the dry lands of desert open sites will eventually rot away. Haynes simply had very little experience with wood or other perishable artifacts and was even suspicious of stone tools unlike the familiar Clovis type.

On another occasion, Haynes viewed the celebrated and *obviously* anthropogenic Monte Verde footprint and inquired how Dillehay knew it was a human footprint. To this query, Tom could only return a leaden stare. God only knows what else Vance thought it might be. In all fairness, the footprint was not as pristine and obvious as it was when it was first excavated and photographed, but most agreed that even in its deteriorated state, it *was* an impression of a human foot.

It should be noted that both before and after the trip, Haynes was unimpressed by *any* artifact or, indeed, any other indication of a human presence at Monte Verde, the sole exception being *six* stone tools that he reluctantly admitted had been made by human hands. Nothing better reflects his Clovis-germinated stone-tool bias. An even more telling remark reflects the limits to which he would go to dismiss evidence. When confronted with the knotted cordage from Monte Verde, some of which had actually been found *tied* to carbon-dated, 12,500-to-13,000-year-old wooden stakes, he asked whether or not the string might be of more recent age than the stakes. Such a notion was so far-fetched as to be absurd. Was he suggesting that some more recent native had stumbled across an ancient piece of wood somehow preserved above the peat for 13,000 years and for some reason had tied a piece of string around it? Tom and I could only shake our heads.

Back in the late Middle Ages in Europe, a Franciscan scholar at Oxford named William of Occam enunciated a rule of logical thinking that has become known as the Law of Occam's Razor. It guides scientists to this day as a rule of thumb for looking at hypotheses and the data that support them. Essentially, it says that the simplest hypothesis that fits all the known facts is likely to be the right hypothesis. In the nearly manic need to protect a lifelong investment in one hypothesis, Clovis Firsters such as Vance Haynes now seemed prepared to violate that old and useful law, inventing complexities that make Rube Goldberg machines look like the Sharper Image catalog.

We arrived at La Caverna, a small, dark cantina where we sat at long tables, oblivious to any locals who might have been present in the gloom. Tom and I immediately "ordered up"—or "looned down" in archaeological vernacular—as did most of the others, in preparation for the discussion. From the outset, Tom was again on the offensive, and I was in complete sympathy with him. Long before this site visit, as well as during its first days, people had been raising issues about his work at Monte Verde that were either irrelevant, unreasonable, or even plain ignorant. Yet his career, or at least the result of some two decades of it, rested to some degree on the outcome of this very visit. To my mind at least, he had little alternative to attack mode. It is a shame that progress in this field has to be made *at the expense of* someone else's life work or reputation, but if skeptics set themselves up for such a fall by closing their minds, they can really have no complaint. Indeed, I believe firmly that to change one's mind based on new evidence is more the sign of a true scientist than to hold out eternally, making more and more convoluted arguments in an attempt to discredit solid evidence. That kind of intransigence is a one-way ticket to the dustbin of history. Does anyone remember the names of the geologists who savaged an Austrian meteorologist named Alfred Wegener for his absurd notion of continental drift?

As the meeting at La Caverna got under way, Tom bluntly said that Vance Haynes knew essentially nothing about wet sites or their contexts, the obvious implication being that Haynes was too unfamiliar with such sites to comment or be even a decent skeptic. In response to a question by Dincauze, Tom retorted by asking, "What have you done for the past twenty years?" His implication was also perfectly clear: that she, too, knew next to nothing about the kind of site she had just examined or about multidisciplinary research in general.

Tempers flared again and again. Meltzer and Alex Barker, the Dallas Museum representative, tried valiantly to keep the peace, especially since these acrimonious proceedings were being observed by representatives of the National Geographic Society, another trip sponsor. But peace was not about to prevail. At one point I was answering a query (on what, I forget) from Vance Haynes, and Dena Dincauze interrupted. I said pointedly and not very politely, "I'm not addressing you." Meltzer and Barker continued their attempts to calm us down into some semblance of collegiality.

Then, suddenly and in a sense parenthetically, the talk turned to Meadowcroft, and Haynes told me and the assembled multitude that if only I would date just one seed or one nut from the deepest levels at Meadowcroft, he might be led to believe in the antiquity of the site.

That was it. I burst out in derisive laughter. Over the years, in scientific paper after scientific paper, Haynes had asked for yet another date, yet another study, raising yet other picayune and fanciful questions about Meadowcroft, most of which had been answered long before he asked them—not just in the original excavation procedures but in report after report. Up until this time in Monte Verde, I had complied. But here we were, thousands of miles from Meadowcroft, looking into Monte Verde, and he was going on about nuts and seeds! He explained that in his opinion nuts and seeds are easier to pretreat for the removal of contaminants than charcoal is. This is a contention that Bob Stuckenrath, the last director of the Smithsonian and the University of Pittsburgh radiocarbon labs, found laughable. At this point, I knew that by Haynes's tortured reasoning, if I took a seed from Stratum IIa at Meadowcroft and the date came back just as old as the 16,000-year-old date from charcoal taken from a hearth, Haynes would say it had to have been tainted by some soluble contaminant—yet to be identified, of course. And if it came out *younger* than my older dates, Haynes would deem the dates discredited, although it is well known that seeds can migrate between horizons quite easily. If he really felt the need for carbon dating of anything else besides the charcoal of hearths, we had provided just such a date on a fragment of birch bark from an ancient basket: 19,000 B.P., with a large plus or minus of 2,500, putting it easily into the 16,000 B.P. range.

All this was running through my mind, along with the pent-up annoyance and frustration I had felt over the years—like what Tom was going through as well—and, after all these years, I felt only what I can describe as contempt.

"Horseshit," I said constructively. I told Vance Haynes there and then that never would I accede to any request he made for further testing of the Meadowcroft site because if I did he would simply ask for something else in a never-ending spiral of problems. I explained that the matter of Meadowcroft's antiquity was settled as far as most other professionals and I were concerned, and that if any remaining skeptics did not believe it, I could not care less. I then stormed out of the bar with Tom to cool off outside in the parking lot.

Later we rejoined an obviously quieter and more subdued group. To my utter disbelief, a consensus was beginning to heave into sight. Barker had gone around the table asking each participant for an opinion. We left La Caverna for another establishment, where we all had dinner. Tom and I wound up sitting at one end of the very long table. We were joined only by a *National Geographic* photographer. The rest of the party sat at the opposite end. Never mind the "historic" consensus on the age of Monte Verde; it was obvious that we were pariahs, considered badly behaved, overly aggressive, all that. For all his negativity, Vance Haynes is mild and generally soft-spoken. How *could* Tom and I be so hard on old Vance? More than a year later, one of the participants told me that ever since that night, some of the participants have thought of Tom and me as "the bad guys."

By the next morning, the soon-to-be-celebrated consensus had crystallized. Once the site visit ended and the archaeostars went home, the drafting committee (which included Haynes and Dincauze) began writing up the results for *American Antiquity*. Even as it came out in print, Haynes had begun to voice doubts to various colleagues; now he was suggesting a wondrous new array of hypothetical events that could have contaminated the site in some previously unperceived way, including—believe it or not—a volcanic eruption. In January 2000, he voiced his doubts publicly in *National Geographic*. I could hardly fail to notice that this was just what he had done with regard to Meadowcroft: agreeing at first, then recanting and throwing doubts around. I have been told by several Paleo-Indian scholars that Dincauze has said that she was "coerced" into consensus by Tom's and my bullying and boorishness. If not putting up with horseshit is boorishness, then I proudly accept the compliment.

FIREWORKS IN SANTA FE

By 1999, the second huge volume of Dillehay's report had been published by the Smithsonian Institution Press, and despite the original consensus of the paleo-police (by now reneged on by Haynes and Dincauze), controversy continued. I had, in fact, expected no less. Unlike the ever-optimistic Dave Meltzer and Don Grayson, who firmly believe that site visits by recognized authorities can actually change the trajectory of scientific thought, my view was jaded. I recognize that earlier site visits, as at Folsom, have in fact changed scientific perceptions, and that some "neutrals" were indeed swayed by the report of the Monte Verde visit. But most pre-Clovis critics became even more intransigent and outspoken. Still others who had made up their minds about the reality of pre-Clovis human presence long before the visit questioned the authority of the paleo-police to speak for the profession. They certainly didn't need us to tell them what to believe or to confirm what they already knew. Nor, in fact, did our South American colleagues, who rightfully viewed the predominantly North American–based consensus as too arrogant, too little, and, undoubtedly, too late. In any event, in the fall of 1999, a major meeting was called that would include both archaeologists and amateurs. It was named, suggestively, "Clovis and Beyond," and it was sponsored by what on the surface seemed very strange bedfellows: the Smithsonian and a former Santa Fe gallery owner, Forest Fenn.

Fenn had in earlier times been a self-confessed prolific pot hunter, claiming that he hunted pots only on private land and that the Indian religious objects he sold in his gallery in Santa Fe were legitimately his as a result of sales to him by individual Indians. This was a legally murky area decades ago, and federal laws are far tighter now. Fenn eventually sold his gallery and acquired land that contains the ruins of a prehistoric pueblo, which he proceeded to "excavate." Also along the way he acquired an excellent collection of Clovis artifacts, including the so-called Fenn Cache, and has become a trader in such material. When the Smithsonian's Dennis Stanford was asked why he and the institution were collaborating with a man widely perceived to be of the archaeological demimonde, Dennis replied disingenuously that he believed in the notion of rehabilitation.

This great Pro-Am meeting, "Clovis and Beyond," attracted some twelve hundred participants to a large convention center in Santa Fe. The center was clogged with archaeologists, all of whom looked just like the rest of the people in Santa Fe, casually bedecked as they often are in field clothing and turquoise. Flint knappers knapped flint on the terrace in the crisp autumnal air of Santa Fe. Inside, excellent collections of Clovis and pre-Clovis artifacts (including Fenn's), as well as other objects, maps, and books of interest were on display. Controversy seethed during the meeting itself, during which some fifty people delivered papers on the many aspects of the peopling of the Americas.

For one thing, an important late Pleistocene or early Holocene skeleton had recently been taken away from archaeologists by the U.S. Army Corps of Engineers, and several of the archaeologists present in Santa Fe had brought suit against the federal government, seeking its return. This was Kennewick Man, and the plaintiffs were gathering signatures to back their stand. There were also the normal differences of academic opinion on various fine points, such as what had killed the mammoths, that would be aired and typically would remain unresolved.

But the main controversy of the weekend was instigated by a relatively new entry in the world of popular science magazines, *Discovering Archaeology*, an offshoot of the venerable magazine *Scientific American*. That very week, just in time for the meeting in Santa Fe, the magazine published among its colorful, reader-friendly pages a special, highly technical, six-teen-page insert written by Stuart Fiedel, a man whom very few archaeologists had ever heard of. As I mentioned earlier, Fiedel is an archaeologist with a company that engages in cultural resource management (CRM) services, what used to be called salvage archaeology, on contract with highway departments, local governments, federal agencies, and so forth. So far as anyone I have ever spoken to knows, this is the only kind of archaeological work he has done.

Fiedel's report was a wholesale attack on Dillehay's evidence at Monte Verde, from his procedures and protocols to his results. After finding what the Smithsonian Institution Press called copyediting errors in Dillehay's report (which were later corrected on-line and in a just published errata volume) Fiedel insisted that therefore there was no way to truly associate the artifacts Tom found with dated strata. The editors of *Discovering Archaeology* decided to publish his article even though it was far too technical for most of their readers, presumably to stir up a hornet's nest and thereby gain some publicity for their nascent publication. They succeeded. After providing Dillehay and his lithic specialist, Michael Collins of the University of Texas, with a couple of weeks and a few thousand words to respond, they also sent the piece around to several archaeologists, myself included, for comment, giving us a week and a few hundred words apiece to do so. These hasty and brief comments were included in the report.

This procedure was considered by most archaeologists present at the "Clovis and Beyond" meeting to be the sort of thing where a referee would have instantly called "foul." Complex arguments in the social sciences as well as the hard sciences are traditionally, and for very good reasons, carried out, first at least, in the pages of what are called peer-reviewed journals. If I have something to say about an archaeological site, I submit it to an archaeological journal, and the editor, if he is interested, sends it out to other people in the same field (peers) who will point out flaws and ask for them to be repaired, reject it, or (rarely) say it is wonderful as it is.

Nothing like this had happened with Fiedel's report—nor did the reviewers' nearly unanimous condemnation of most of Fiedel's points result in the jettisoning of his report, as it almost surely would have in a scientific publishing context. For all its efforts to bring the excitement of archaeology to a wider public, no one would ever accuse *Discovering Archaeology* of having the kind of editorial judgment appropriate for such a dispute over highly technical matters. (And I would have to say that I can only imagine one basic response from the magazine's typical readers to this great gray blather of technical details: "Huh?") Naturally enough, Vance Haynes and two other adamant Clovis First advocates, Frederick Hadleigh West and Tom Lynch, immediately found unassailable merit in Fiedel's effusion, not even taking umbrage at his thinly disguised inference that some evidence had been faked.

People at the meeting in Santa Fe were abuzz with all of this and naturally enough awaited more lengthy oral responses to Fiedel's report. On the second day, Dillehay took the podium and quietly but forcefully accused Fiedel of having "a limited mental template," thanks to his inexperience with anything as sophisticated and complex as a modern, multidisciplinary excavation, not to mention a wet site such as Monte Verde. He wondered how it was that Fiedel could find such flaws in his work when the eighty or so professional archaeologists and graduate students who had worked on the excavation or the attendant analyses over the years had found nothing of the sort, and he went on to say that Fiedel and other doubters were simply and essentially lost in "fantasy." Dillehay received a standing ovation, which is not the sort of thing that usually occurs at academic meetings.

I followed Dillehay and made my own sarcastic comments about the Old Faith and the doubters still carping about matters at Meadowcroft that had long been settled. I suggested that it was time to ignore altogether "the embittered acolytes of a religion that dies harder than Bruce Willis or Rasputin."

It was not all attack and defend, however. People from numerous fields, including linguistics and molecular genetics, discussed relatively new findings in this field that tended to support the pre-Clovis point of view. Other reports chronicled what appeared to be other pre-Clovis sites. Many of them were given over to the propounding of new pre-Clovis speculations and hypotheses about the timing and routes by which people might have come. And at one point Michael Collins, an old hand at the study of late Pleistocene America, exclaimed, "My God, this is an exciting time. Let's enjoy the fun and get on with the positive aspects of researching this."

His comment reminded me of another I had read earlier by Douglas

Price of the University of Wisconsin at Madison. It was a chapter he wrote called "The View from Europe" in a symposium volume on the peopling of the New World that Dillehay and Meltzer had put together in 1991. Price pointed out that there were considerable similarities to be seen in the peopling of North America (with people heading south into previously uninhabited country) and the peopling of northern Europe, especially Scandinavia, with people moving north into country available once the ice began to recede. The evidence was fairly clear now, he wrote, that these pioneers into Europe's recently deiced lands had not been "mobile, carefree, happy bowmen" as previously thought. Instead, such things as cemeteries of this period found in Denmark suggested that they had, on the contrary, been largely sedentary, both inland and on the coasts, and that marine and plant foods had been far more important in their diets than red meat.

As Price argued, the mammoths and woolly rhinos of the area were already largely extinct by the time northern Europe began to warm up; they were not in any case found in association with human remains or artifacts. The pioneers did wipe out the last populations of aurochs, elk, and reindeer, but only on remote islands of the northern seas. Indeed, the auroch persisted until it was finally rendered extinct in Poland in the nineteenth century. So there was no wholesale slaughter of meat on the hoof in northern Europe to match the supposed blood-drenched blitzkrieg of Clovis Man.

One of the great differences between European and American archaeology of this period is that in northern Europe preservation is better. Thanks to the lay of the land, there are vastly more sites, specifically a large number of lakes, wetlands, and peat bogs (wet sites like Monte Verde) where lithics and perishable artifacts remain more intact. As Price pointed out, in North America there are only a few late Pleistocene sites, and these are mostly temporary camps such as Meadowcroft Rockshelter. We have come up with practically no base camps or settlements, though they almost surely existed, as they did in South America. Price advised that we in the Americas spend a lot more time looking in old wetlands and along old lakeshores.

With exceptional courtesy, Price also mentioned another difference between the two continents' styles of archaeology. In discussing the Hamburgian culture, one of the characteristic tool kits that had moved north in Europe as the glacier receded, he pointed out that there was great uncertainty as to whether it had originated in France or as far east as Ukraine. But, he said, the matter of origins generates a great deal more "heat" in America than in Europe—why, he wasn't sure. Perhaps, he went on, there was more to learn in America about our Ice Age past from cooperation than from acrimonious exchange.

———

THREE-LEGGED STOOLS AND

SKULL WARS

For many of the True Faith, the Clovis Bar was confirmed in the early 1980s by three other lines of evidence arising from linguistics and human biology. Archaeologists will steadfastly and to a person say that if there's no evidence of "it" in the ground, we cannot really believe that "it"—whatever "it" may be—happened. But they are perfectly happy to have people from other disciplines come along with theories, evidence, or even just opinions that confirm their own views. To have three legs on the stool of one's argument is reassuring. Four is even better.

Just at the time in the seventies and eighties when Meadowcroft and Monte Verde had begun challenging the whole fabric of archaeological "truths" about the peopling of the New World, there came along three lines of inquiry: (1) linguistic studies, (2) the study of tooth morphology, and (3) a forensic technique of studying genes that had led to the recently popularized notion that we humans are all the children of a single, original female whom Western science named, with breathtaking originality, Eve. From these various lines of inquiry there arose a nearly euphoric sense of the justness and truth of Clovis First.

LANGUAGE, TEETH, AND GENES

Despite the fact that archaeology and linguistics fall under the academic umbrella of anthropology, at least in the United States, most American archaeologists are not trained in linguistics or are even much aware of how linguists work. Yet for years scholars of the indigenous languages of North and South America had complained that 11,200 years simply wasn't anywhere near enough time for the nine hundred or so separate languages that were present in the New World at the time of Columbus's arrival to arise from one invasion of fifty or a hundred would-be big-game hunters who presumably spoke one tongue. In North America alone there were some three hundred spoken languages deriving from either six or eight different root language stocks called phyla. For example, one such phylum is called Macro-Siouan, and it includes not only the languages of such Plains tribes as Crow, Mandan, Omaha, Winnebago, and Sioux but also the languages of the Mohawks and other Iroquoian tribes of New York State and Canada, as well as the Cherokees, who were from the Carolinas, the Catawbas, the Caddoan tribes, and the Yuchis. By linguistic reckoning— which calculates how long it takes a fundamental root word such as that for "mother" or "sun" to change from the original—it seemed clear that even 15,000 years was insufficient time to account for such remarkable diversity.

One of the North American language phyla includes the ten languages of the Eskimos (Inuits, preferably) and Aleuts in the far north; another includes the thirty-eight languages called Athapaskan—spoken mostly by northern Canadian tribes but including the Apaches, the Navajos, and some California groups. It has long been taken as certain that the Athapaskan-speaking peoples—also called Na-Denes—were relatively late arrivals on the continent, followed yet later by the Inuits and Aleuts. If true, this left an impressive 250 languages spoken by the Indian tribes in the present United States alone. Though nothing compared to the polyglot world of New Guinea, where some 700 languages used to exist, those 250 languages represent a lot of linguistic evolution.

Could some of the linguistic diversity of the Americas, therefore, have developed in Asia? And would that suggest that several different groups of people arrived here at different times? Or was it essentially one group of people that wandered out on the misty steppes of Beringia and wound up populating a hemisphere, with the exception of the late-arriving Na-Denes, Inuits, and Aleuts?

The complaints and suggestions of the linguists fell on archaeological ears that were mostly deaf. Whatever linguistic methods of computation were, they surely did not have the weight of in-the-ground, tangible artifacts that could be excavated, fondled, and dated by radiocarbon analyses. Archaeologists could ignore the theories of linguists as though they were a cloud of gnats flying around their heads. That is, until they found Joseph Greenberg, a linguist who entered the fray in the early 1980s with a different and convenient theory.

Greenberg announced that all the other native languages of the Americas except Na-Dene, Aleut, and Inuit had arisen from a single root language he called Amerind. Part of his reasoning was that all of the Amerind languages—about nine hundred in all—share approximately 280 words, as well as a few grammatical forms. Most notably, and unique among the languages of the world, their first-person pronouns begin with *n* and their second-person pronouns with *m*. This was strong evidence that a single group of people sharing a single language had been the first arrivals—read Clovis—particularly when it was added to evidence arising from other nonarchaeological fields, such as the anatomy of teeth.

All human beings share the same basic dental patterns, but different groups share certain minor, or secondary, dental characteristics. All of us, for example, have thirty-two adult teeth including our first molars, but some groups of people have different numbers of roots on the first molar. In all, human teeth have more than twenty different secondary characteristics. Christy Turner, a biological anthropologist at the University of Arizona, undertook a study of some 200,000 teeth from 9,000 prehistoric American Indians, along with thousands of teeth from Siberia, southern Asia, Africa, and Europe. Based on all the secondary characteristics, it is possible not only to distinguish Asian teeth from African and European teeth but also to separate the Asian teeth into two separate groups. One group, called "Sundadont," is characteristic of teeth from Southeast Asia and begins to show up in the fossil record about 30,000 years ago. From this group the second, known as "Sinodonts," evidently evolved, and they characterize most northern Asians and *all* the native populations of the Western Hemisphere.

One of the key traits of Sinodont teeth, which arose in Asia about 20,000 years ago, is extra ridges on the insides of the upper incisors, giving them a distinctive shovel shape. Sinodonts also possess three roots on the lower first molars, and there is, of course, variation among them. Na-Dene teeth are different from Inuit-Aleut teeth, and both groups' teeth differ from those of the rest of the Indian people of the hemisphere. Seemingly a perfect match for Greenbergian linguistics, paleodentistry added its own approximate time scale as well. And both these promising lines of evidence pointed to a single arrival. The Clovis First archaeologists, the great majority of North American archaeologists at the time, were delighted—even more so when the molecules that make up the genes began to tell the same story.

In the 1980s, the idea of working out the entire genetic code of *Homo sapiens* was a dream that seemed a long way from fruition. What with outbreeding, inbreeding, and natural mutations, human genetics can be pretty messy. But there is another type of DNA found in small organelles within cells called "mitochondria," which are responsible for energy metabolism within the cells. Inherited exclusively from the mother, this DNA mutates naturally five or ten times faster than the DNA found in the cell's nucleus, which is the result of the seemingly haphazard mixing of DNA from both parents. Scientists believed they could clock the changes in mitochondrial DNA, known as mtDNA: on average, every one million years between 2 and 4 percent of mtDNA will have mutated of its own accord.

Soon—to simplify an extremely complex matter a bit—it was found that groups of Indians geographically widely separated nonetheless had nearly identical variations in their mtDNA. This meant that the group ancestral to them all had to have been very small. Q.E.D. So here was evidence for Paul Martin's band of rampaging Clovis hunters. As the biochemists peered more closely, though, what had been thought to be a clear picture became much murkier. Since the variations in mtDNA common to the native people in this hemisphere share only a few characteristics with those found in Asians, the variation clock must have begun to tick once people arrived here, not before. Also, it began to appear that the clock had begun ticking between 21,000 and 42,000 years ago.

LANGUAGE STOCKS AND HAPLOGROUPS

It soon turned out that the more or less single story told by genes, teeth, and language had big problems. The neat biological and linguistic tale that matched the tale of Clovis First began to unravel. According to the evolutionary rates postulated for teeth, the ancestral people of all three distinct groups of native people began to differentiate only some 13,000 years ago. The rates of tooth evolution also suggested that the Inuits *preceded* the Na-Denes to this hemisphere, which flew in the face of all other evidence holding that the Inuits came after the Na-Denes. Furthermore, the 13,000-year-old onset of differentiation suggested by the teeth differs from the genetic evidence, which showed the differentiation as beginning more than 20,000 years ago and the Na-Denes preceding the Inuits. In the meantime, forensic scientists at the Federal Bureau of Investigation, who use mtDNA to "fingerprint" victims and criminals, began finding that reading mitochondrial evidence was more complicated than it at first seemed. The molecular biologists would soon agree, and they had to refine their own techniques.

Meanwhile, Greenberg's nearly pan-Indian root language, Amerind, was coming in for voracious counterattack. Chiefly, it was seen as an oversimplification, disguising important differences and overemphasizing similarities. Students of historical linguistics were—not to put too fine a point on it—outraged (though not speechless with rage; academics are never speechless). A not atypical example was a paper prepared for a 1994 conference on methods of investigating the peopling of the Americas by Ives Goddard of the Smithsonian and Lyle Campbell of Louisiana State University. They referred to Greenberg's treatment of language as "superficial" and his argument as "specious" to an extent even greater "than other types of data used by prehistorians." Greenberg's so-called multilateral comparison of many languages looking for similar-sounding words with similar meanings had nothing whatsoever, they said, to do with the historical way that languages might have come about. For example, the criteria Greenberg established for Amerind also include Finnish. The actual history of languages is far too complicated for that sort of analysis: languages go extinct all the time, some groups of people are multilingual, changes occur at different frequencies, and words from several different languages can converge adventitiously. As for the first-person *n* and second-person *m,* the two historical linguists scoffed that not only is it not a unique pattern in the world (it is used in Swahili), but it is also not all that common in the Americas. As even Greenberg noted and then overlooked, the most common first-person sound in South American native languages is *i.*

Having explained that postulating Amerind as a unitary language was "a vacuous hypothesis," Goddard and Campbell had—at least to their own satisfaction—utterly destroyed the Greenberg analysis. They went on to say that so malleable are languages that historical linguistics cannot of its nature take languages very far back with any sense of confidence. That a multilateral comparison of European languages does show legitimate similarities is no surprise, since most are relatively recent anyway, having split off at most some six thousand years ago. Earlier than that, they said, tracking languages back to common roots is not presently possible. Certainly, tracking languages twice as far back—or farther—is out of the question. According to their analysis, a single root language for most American Indian languages is not ruled out, but neither are several root languages representing several different migrations of people in the deep past.

So almost as soon as all this nonarchaeological evidence appeared to be standing stalwartly behind the comfortable archaeological dogma of Clovis First, the three-legged—indeed, counting Overkill, four-legged—stool was yanked away. It seemed that an equally good case could be made from linguistics, dentition, and genes that there was a long period, maybe 10,000 years or more, during which numerous groups already somewhat different from one another in various ways could have made several separate forays across the Bering land bridge or along its coasts. Indeed, some could have ventured out on the land bridge of Beringia and returned, others could have reached the new continent (not that it would have seemed to be a new continent) and gone back to Asia, and some could have perished without a trace. In any event, by the mid-nineties those archaeologists who needed a one-time arrival sometime shortly before Clovis culture appeared in North America were back on their own, unbuttressed by dental studies, mtDNA, or most linguistic theory.

At this point, traditional linguists were again confronted by another revolutionary in their midst, Johanna Nichols of the University of California at Berkeley. Among other claims, she says she *can* track languages back beyond the 6,000-year cutoff point—in fact, *way* beyond. Somewhat in the tradition of the starship *Enterprise,* she has boldly gone into territory that most other linguists have not dared to explore. Although she is taken more seriously by the linguistic community than Greenberg, not everyone finds her work beyond doubt, and some harrumph that she is altogether wrong. What else is new in the world of social science?

Nichols's method has little to do with the traditional linguist's comparison of words and phonemes to find similarities and therefore relationships. Comparative methods have so far left linguists without their holy grail, a single tree from which all languages have branched over time. Instead they are confronted by some two or three hundred separate trees (what Nichols calls "stocks") that are hard to relate one to another. For example, the so-called Indo-European stock has 144 branch languages, all of which can be traced back about 6,000 years, beyond which is murk. Other stocks have fewer or more member languages; some, such as Korean, Basque, and maybe the language of the Zuni Indians, have only one. How these stocks are related remains enigmatic.

Nichols's strategy is instead to determine the grammatical building blocks (the regularities) within and among language stocks and to map them. One might think of these as the girders and cement blocks, or the infrastructure, upon which a variety of differently adorned buildings can be erected. The building blocks tend to last, she says, while languages based upon them come and go. There are several dozen such building blocks, some of them fairly familiar, such as whether a verb typically goes at the end of a sentence (as in Latin), somewhere in the middle (as often is the case in English), or at the front. Some are quite arcane: for example, what Nichols calls "ergativity," a feature of languages that use special prefixes or suffixes to modify a verb. For example, the tense of an ergative verb may be indicated by a prefix rather than a different form of the verb. Where we say "I shot a deer," a speaker of such a language would say "I (past) shoot a deer." Other languages, such as Chinese and Navajo, use vocal pitch or tone to change the meaning of words. (In Navajo, a tin-eared imitator, trying to say something as straightforward as "Hello," may wind up, thanks to the wrong musical pitch, saying something scatological instead, such as "I fart often," to the hilarity of his or her Navajo listeners.)

Such grammar regularities among different languages suggest ancient affinities, if not from direct relatedness. They could have arisen from coincidences and not from a single ancestral language: for example, a grammatical feature might have been borrowed from a newly arriving but otherwise unrelated group of people and incorporated as a useful construct. After all, people borrow styles in such archaeological markers as ceramics and blue jeans as well. Further, as Nichols argues, it is important to remember that languages and even their subgroupings within a given stock, called families, arise and can go extinct. On average, she finds, one new family of languages occurs in a stock about every four thousand years; this gives her a form of clock that lets her date linguistic "events" far more distantly in the past than was heretofore thought possible.

Another grammatical feature Nichols and others have identified is "a numerical classifier." In English we would say, "I see six clouds shaped something like fish." In many Asian languages one would say, hypothetically, "I see six (bleep) cloud." The bleep would indicate both plural and fish-shaped. A different bleep might indicate plural and round. In mapping languages that use numerical classifiers, Nichols found that they circle the Pacific Ocean, as do languages that put the verb first in a sentence, as well as languages in which the pronouns begin with m and n. Indeed, many of the languages circling the Pacific rim share all three features. Nichols interprets this to mean that there was a great wave of migration beginning in southeastern Asia about 11,000 years ago and spreading south to New Guinea, north through Asia, and from there eastward to North America, where it traveled down the west coast of the New World.

On the other hand, some of the languages of New Guinea share certain features with some of the languages of Australia: in particular, a grammar, called "concord classes," in which verbs and pronouns have to agree with nouns as to gender. Nichols says that this is a very ancient feature, as is ergativity, and languages with both these features are found in Australia, the New Guinea highlands, and the eastern regions of North America. This suggests a much earlier and sustained wave of migration beginning some

50,000 years ago (when the block of land including Australia and New Guinea was first peopled)—which over the millennia could well have put people into the interior of North America long before Clovis—easily by 20,000 to 30,000 years ago.

So, by virtue of what Nichols calls "historical linguistic geography," a field in which she is not only preeminent but essentially alone, one can reasonably imagine several waves of people arriving in the Western Hemisphere over many thousands of years. And this would leave plenty of time for people to have fetched up in such mutually distant places as southern Chile and western Pennsylvania prior to the appearance of the Clovis tool kit.

While the linguists sort these bold innovations out among themselves and in their own manner, my like-minded colleagues such as Tom Dillehay and I naturally rejoice, and all the more so since molecular genetics, always progressing, has now lent yet further credence to the reasonableness of Nichols's scenario. It is our turn to sit on a three-legged stool.

Progress in molecular genetics in the past decade has been spectacularly rapid. Most notably, we now have the human genome spelled out before us, and we have determined at least in a preliminary way how to head off a growing list of human maladies by manipulating individual genes. Less likely to make headlines is the progress scientists have made in assessing the times and places of origin of various groups of human beings by reading mitochondrial DNA, the exclusively male Y chromosome, and other molecular markers. By the early 1990s, it was becoming clear that the molecular genetics of native populations of the Americas (particularly as revealed in mtDNA) was quite a bit more complex than it had at first seemed.

As women spread across the globe in ancient times, their mtDNA was steadily changing due to copying errors and radiation, both of which lead to small mutations in the helical strand in their mitochondria. When populations reached a place and stayed there, these mutations came to be associated with a particular region. For this reason some changes are found only in particular regions or continents. These lineages can be thought of, at least poetically, as the descendants of various daughters of Eve.

According to Theodore Schurr of the Southwest Foundation for Biomedical Research in San Antonio, Texas, several laboratories, his own included, have found four main mtDNA lineages, called haplogroups, among the native populations of the Americas. Conveniently labeled A, B, C, and D, they are also found in most modern populations in Asia. The exception is Siberia, where B is absent. Importantly, the four haplogroups—A, B, C, and D—are never found among Europeans, Africans, or Australians.

The molecular genealogists have also pegged other lineages in the world, such as L, which is almost exclusively African, and H and X, which accounts for about 3 percent of the modern European sample. Today there is a scattering of both L (African) and H (European) in American Indian populations, but so little that it most likely represents intermarriage since Columbus's time. Indeed, throughout recorded history, there has always been considerable intermarriage between Indians and people of both European and African origins, and it would be highly surprising if the H and L lineages were absent. But the other European haplogroup, known as X, is another story. It is found in both Europe and the Indian subcontinent, but nowhere else in Asia nor in the native populations of South America. Instead it is scattered among North American tribes as distant from one another, at least geographically, as the Ojibway of the upper Midwest, the Zuni of the Southwest, and the Bella Coola of the Pacific Northwest.

All this suggests that many different groups arrived on this continent prehistorically. Given the presumed rate of mutation of mtDNA, the A through D haplogroups could have begun arriving as early as 25,000 to 35,000 years ago and the X people between 15,000 and 30,000 years ago. In this regard, it also should be stressed that while the X group no longer exists in Asia, it *may* have once and thus could well be a more parsimonious source of this population in the New World than transatlantic movement. There are also five Y-chromosome groups present in native American populations, and by similar analyses these suggest an earliest arrival of 40,000 to 50,000 years ago. Obviously, all these dates need to be reconciled in some manner; given the rate at which population genetics is advancing, perhaps they will be before long.

By mapping small mutations within haplogroups, it has become possible to see in ever-finer detail human migration patterns from as far back as the dawn of modern humans in Africa. It appears, for example, that once humans left Africa for Eurasia, they took a coastal route across present-day Saudi Arabia, through Iraq and Iran and along the coasts of Pakistan and

India, eventually reaching the island regions of southeast Asia. This may well have been the staging area for subsequent waves of migration into such realms as Australia and New Guinea between 60,000 and 45,000 years ago. (This sounds almost identical to Johanna Nichols's linguistic time map, doesn't it?)

Indeed, in Asia and other Old World regions, it appears that archaeological evidence is beginning to match up in quite wonderful symmetry with both linguistic analyses of the sort Nichols is doing *and* molecular genetics studies. The movement of people into Melanesia and Polynesia, for example, which took place far later than any entry into the Americas, has also been mapped genetically and shown to coincide nicely with both linguistic and archaeological studies.

Although many researchers had believed that it might be the first issue of human dispersal to be solved conclusively by molecular studies, the populating of the New World remains a bit murky genetically as far as timing and the number of waves of immigrants go. Rebecca L. Cann, a professor at the John A. Burns School of Medicine at the University of Hawaii at Manoa, recently reviewed all these types of evidence for the journal *Science*. She wrote that it is still possible for geneticists today to look at the four main haplogroups present in native populations in the Americas and argue for all of the following scenarios: a relatively recent, sustained, continuous migration; a single wave beginning some 45,000 years ago; or many movements separated by thousands of years. These studies also support speculation that some people entered the landmass called Beringia before the glacial maximum, found themselves isolated there by the growing ice, and arrived farther south only after the glaciers began to recede.

Despite all this molecular fingerprinting, plenty of uncertainty remains about who the first Americans were and when they got here. Where once there was what one of my colleagues, Dennis Stanford of the Smithsonian, has called a "boring story," now we are presented with an exhilarating complexity, a wide-open field. As Cann says, the one thing that molecular genetics now confidently *rules out* is the late entry into the Western Hemisphere of only a single group—which is to say, the dispersal story that has served for nearly seventy years as the foundation of Clovis First. It's this simple: no single group of adventurers in those days could have included people of so many different haplogroups. The casting directors of *Star Trek* may have seen the crew of the ship *Enterprise* as a multiethnic affair, but Pleistocene bands were almost surely only extended family groups.

The mtDNA research is becoming increasingly controversial in other realms—some political, some just silly. For example, researchers from Oxford, England, have taken note of the British fascination with matters of lineage and started up a company called Oxford Ancestors, which invites people to send in cells scraped from the inside of the cheek for analysis. For a fee that seems not unreasonable, they will then trace the applicant back to one of the "seven daughters of Eve" who were chief among the distant ancestors of the people of the United Kingdom. The original woman was of course Eve, and all the haplogroups from A to Z descended from her. So Oxford Ancestors enables one to find out if he or she is a "daughter" of Ursula (haplogroup U), who dwelled in Greece 25,000 years ago, or Tara, and so forth.

Though Heaven knows what this practice might do to the House of Lords, it seems harmless enough. The increasingly sophisticated studies of early humans in the New World, however, have had somewhat unexpected and politically tense ramifications. In spite of definitive evidence that all human beings are more genetically alike than two bands of chimpanzees on either side of a hill, some people believe that to look into these minuscule genetic differences is to slide down the slippery slope into Hitlerian racism and eugenics. To counter the idiotic evil of racism, it has become fashionable in some circles to deny that there are any biological differences at all among people, which to my mind is just as idiotic.

The lineages we have been talking about are almost unnoticeable, totally trivial variations among the billions of nucleotides that make up someone's mtDNA or Y chromosome. The differences that do exist, such as skin color, are all simple differences mediated by a handful of genes; essentially, they are only skin deep. Any feature that is truly significant, such as intelligence, musical talent, or, say, athletic ability, is mediated by huge arrays of genes that produce vast numbers of proteins in long and complicated developmental events. Indeed, it is science that will prove—and, in fact, already has—that all humans, whatever their apparent differences, are almost indistinguishably alike genetically.

What makes the tiny differences in one or a handful of related genes important to know is the genetic predispositions of some groups to certain diseases, and of course to deny these differences or impede investigation of them is to shoot oneself in the foot. Cultural differences are another matter altogether. It is fashionable to say that all cultures are adaptive, meaning that they are all intelligent responses to the environment at hand, but it cannot be denied that, in the course of time, some cultures have proven less adaptive than others. I would argue that a culture that opts for ignorance over knowledge is asking for trouble just as certainly as a language that resists growing with the times will soon go extinct—as many have.

Another real-world issue raised by the debate over these genetic matters is whether it is appropriate, moral, or even legal for someone to take DNA samples from some people within a group—say, the Amish in Pennsylvania, the !Kung of the Kalahari Desert, or the Iroquois—or to make genetic profiles of the group *without* its express approval. This raises a whole hornet's nest of issues—such as the right of the individual over the group and vice versa—not to mention the practical dilemma of who is to speak for the group. From there the philosophical and legal questions cascade: Who among a group with an identifiable culture owns that culture? Is a culture to be construed as property, similar to the intellectual property rights of an artist or inventor? Or is a person's (ethnically distinct) genetic material group property?

It is pretty safe to say that no such questions ever occurred to earlier generations of archaeologists who sought enlightenment about the first Americans; however, no archaeologist working in the Americas today can be isolated from such considerations, mostly because of another kind of evidence long pursued: bones.

BONES

The face plastered on the cover of a national newsmagazine never would have appeared there had it not looked so much like the British actor Patrick Stewart and so little like what people think American Indians look like. In fact, the face was an illusion—an illusion within an illusion, surrounded by yet another illusion. First off, it looked like Patrick Stewart only from one angle, and that was the angle in the famous photograph. Turned from the three-quarter view to a full-face shot, its jaw looked much heavier, its face wider, and it presented an altogether different mien from the unmistakably Caucasian, indeed northern European face of the starship *Enterprise*'s second commanding officer, Jean-Luc Picard. That is illusion number one.

Illusion number two arises from the fact that the face was constructed by a statistical method of adding clay in certain thicknesses to the model of a skull. This is a forensic technique that the police use to reconstruct a general idea of the appearance of someone's face after the actual face is long gone, only sometimes leading to an identification. But a slight change in, say, the angle of an eyelid or the turn of the lip in the corner of the mouth, or the presence or absence of facial hair, can make someone look quite different, even unrecognizable. So at best, the face was a plausible but generalized statistical projection of a face no one alive had ever seen.

The third illusion was that the skeleton behind all this was that of a European. That's the way it was reported in the press, so people who looked at the reconstruction kept that preconception in mind. Why else

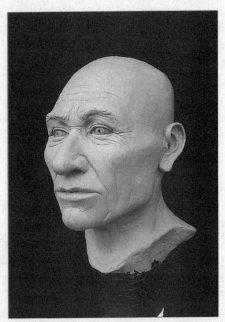

Reconstruction of the Kennewick skull.

would editors of national magazines have selected the one view of the reconstruction that most clearly fit the stereotype of a European? So that uncounted numbers of Americans could persist in the absurd belief that it was a white guy, not an Indian, who got to the Americas first. Even more inappropriately, most people—and even some of the scientists involved in the Kennewick caper—overlooked the astounding diversity of facial features within any strain of humans such as "Caucasian," not to mention the fact that such strains change greatly, feature by feature, over the millennia.

This was Kennewick Man, the nearly complete skeleton found in southern Washington State in July 1996 and the most famous American skeleton ever found. Another error in much of the press coverage was that, at an age of 9,300 years B.P., Kennewick Man represented one of the first Americans. Given his age, he was in fact 2,000-odd years younger than Clovis, and at the time of his discovery, there were already sound reasons to believe that humans had arrived in the Americas more like 20,000 years ago—some ten *millennia* before Kennewick Man met his end. Even so, 9,000-year-old "Patrick" was widely seen as the first here, and a group of Norwegian Americans calling themselves the Asatru Folk Assembly, Aryan loonies from California (where else?), publicly considered suing the U.S. government for the return of the skeleton. Even if this was merely a publicity lark, it worked remarkably well, as they were featured in *The Sunday New York Times Magazine*. They dropped the suit and almost immediately dropped out of sight as well. Of course, many vociferous Indian groups took all of this as yet another gigantic slur on the part of the dominant society, not to mention another salvo in the ongoing scientific assault on their religious beliefs.

Before long a dispute over the proper disposition of the skeleton reached federal court. Under the Native American Graves Preservation and Repatriation Act (NAGPRA) of 1990, human remains that are ancestral to Indian tribes are to be returned to the tribes in question. The Confederated Tribes of the Umatilla Indian Reservation, located some seventy-five miles from the spot where Kennewick Man emerged from an eroding bank of the Columbia River, claimed him as an ancestor. Meanwhile, physical anthropologists and archaeologists, who said he was too old to be directly ancestral to any modern local tribes, wanted to go further than the initial examination (which had led to the Patrick Stewart reconstruction, among other things). The matter ended up in court, but not before the U.S. Army Corps of Engineers, which is in charge of the land where the skeleton was found, destroyed the site in the name of "stabilizing" it.

Throughout all this, Kennewick Man went from being a Caucasian (whatever that is!) to being Caucasoid, an even more nebulous term that includes a lot of people from the subcontinent of India all the way into Europe, not to mention some outlying groups such as the aboriginal dwellers in Japan called the Ainu. Later it seemed he was closer to the Ainu or maybe Polynesians than to anything else—provisionally, of course, and always subject to further analysis. Meanwhile, the skeleton was locked up in a vault in a local university until a federal judge decided between the Umatillas and the archaeologists. That this was a highly sensitive matter goes without saying. That it turned into an appalling mess is also quite evident.

In my opinion, many archaeologists remain at least passively opposed to the provisions of NAGPRA, while some are actually actively opposed. This attitude is clearly part of the background of the bizarre events surrounding Kennewick Man, and the events since his discovery have, if anything, solidified any anti-NAGPRA sentiment that existed.

Kennewick Man's skull was found by college students during hydroplane races on the Columbia River near Kennewick. The police were notified, and they called the coroner, who in turn called a private anthropological consultant, who in due course returned to the site and found a large number of bones that had been associated with the skull. It was soon apparent to the consultant, James Chatters, that this was not a white settler, as he had first thought. There appeared to be a remnant of a stone spear point lodged in his hip, a point that had not been manufactured locally for some four or five thousand years. It also turned out that the man, who had been about five feet nine and maybe forty-five years old when he died, had been a healthy, well-nourished youth but had subsequently suffered various injuries, some of which had been quite debilitating. One of these was a crushing blow to his ribs that had left one arm almost useless. Another was, of course, the spear point in his pelvis, also largely healed. One tough guy, he was also, Chatters was convinced, not a Native American, or at least not like modern Native Americans.

At a press conference, Chatters may or may not have used the word

"Caucasian" to describe his find—most likely he said Caucasoid—but he also said the skeleton resembled nothing as closely as a "premodern European." Within days, the local paper's report had exploded Kennewick Man into national fame, bruiting the notion that Europeans had predated American Indians on this continent.

One of the first things Chatters had done in inspecting the skeleton (which he was allowed to take to his home lab until the Army Corps of Engineers demanded it back) was to send a small finger bone off to the University of California at Riverside to be carbon-dated. The lab there obliged Chatters with the date in a mere seventy-two hours: the skeleton appeared to be 8,400 years old. Later changed to 9,300 years, that date made Kennewick Man one of the handful of truly ancient sets of human remains found in North America, though not the oldest.

Another of these ancient Americans was the Spirit Cave Mummy, which also appeared on the cover of a newsmagazine (*Newsweek* in April 1999). He was discovered as long ago as 1940 in a rockshelter east of Carson City, Nevada, and was thought at the time to have died about 3,000 years ago. Laid to rest in a shallow grave dug into a rockshelter, he had been buried with twined rabbit fur robes and quite sophisticated plaited textiles. Now dated by Riverside to more than 9400 B.P., he is the oldest naturally mummified body in North America, and his remains reside in the Nevada State Museum. When attention was again brought to him, the Northern Paiute tribe claimed him under NAGPRA, and then so did the Fallon Paiute Shoshones.

Back in the late 1960s, when I was doing my dissertation research on prehistoric basketry, I had the opportunity to spend some time at the Nevada State Museum. Although I examined and reanalyzed most of the basketry collection, I did not have the chance to examine the Spirit Cave materials firsthand. Nonetheless, based on the fact that by 1999 I had analyzed or reanalyzed most of the prehistoric basketry in western North America, I was asked by one of the attorneys for the Fallon Paiute if I would be willing to testify that as evidenced by the associated perishables, specifically the plaited mats and the twined robes, the Spirit Cave mummy was part of the population that was ancestral to the tribe. I said I couldn't because according to what I knew he wasn't, but the attorneys asked me to be a consultant anyway.

After studying all of the pertinent technical literature on the Spirit Cave basketry and textile remains produced by my friends and colleagues Kay Fowler of the University of Nevada at Reno, and Amy Dansie, then of the Nevada State Museum, I concluded that, as I had suspected, there was no stylistic connection between the perishable fiber artifact traditions of the Spirit Cave individual and those of the Paiutes. The techniques were in fact distinct. As I later explained to a reporter from *The Washington Post*, based on my analysis "there is no practical possibility that he [i.e., Spirit Cave Man] is the lineal genetic ancestor of any contemporary Great Basin group." Drawing upon this and other evidence, the Bureau of Land Management eventually decided to reject the Paiutes' claim because of their failure to demonstrate affiliation. This is what should have happened with Kennewick Man (and may yet ultimately happen).

The Army Corps of Engineers has subsequently announced its intention to repatriate the remains to the Umatillas, which triggered a lawsuit by eight leading anthropological scholars, led alphabetically by Robson Bonnichsen of Oregon State University—hence the name of the case, *Bonnichsen et al. v. The United States of America*. The *et al.* included Vance Haynes; Dennis Stanford, head of the Smithsonian's anthropology department; D. Gentry Steele of Texas A & M; C. Loring Brace of the University of Michigan; George W. Gill of the University of Wyoming; and two men who probably knew as much about skull types as anyone in the country, Douglas Owsley of the Smithsonian's physical anthropology staff and his mentor, Richard Jantz of the University of Tennessee. These two were in the process of developing the world's largest computer database of ancient human skeletal materials in the world. Basically, this consists of nearly thirty specific measurements of skulls, work first begun by the physical anthropologist William W. Howells back in the thirties and forties. By comparing skulls with these measurements, one can assign a given skull to a particular population, such as Pacific Islanders, since each separate population generally shares certain salient skull shape features. Yet it is of course important to remember that individuals within such a population may have a varying degree of the group's general characteristics.

In any case, the Bonnichsen suit was brought for technical violations by the government of both NAGPRA and of federal laws governing administrative procedure; it sought injunctive relief (the skeleton was now sequestered and off limits to further examination) for harm done to the plaintiffs by the deprivation of their right, as professional anthropologists, to pursue their profession. At least indirectly, the issue of science versus religion hung over the case like a shroud.

Meanwhile, the Interior Department released a report by a panel of scientists that said that Kennewick Man could not be linked either to any modern American Indian tribes or to Europeans. This agreed with Chatters's assessment that he had stood out "from modern American Indians, especially those who occupied Northwestern North America in later prehistory." He was, the panel observed, morphologically closer to the Ainu of Japan or to Polynesians, the latter having arrived in the South Pacific much later than Kennewick Man had patrolled the Columbia River. Joseph Powell, a member of the panel and a physical anthropologist at the University of New Mexico, said that Kennewick Man "fits into an emerging pattern that these earlier American people are not like the modern people of today." Two scenarios are possible, he said, if it turns out that Kennewick Man is in fact not distantly related to American Indians: people from his period in the late Pleistocene were wiped out at some point and left no descendants, or they had features from all over the Pacific rim that have simply changed and diversified over time.

The Indians, on the other hand, stated that *all* humans from earlier times in the New World were ancestral, that Kennewick Man was included, and that to use any invasive procedures such as taking DNA samples from him would be a sacrilege. Indeed, the only nonsacrilegious act would be to reinter his remains as soon as possible.

Incomprehensibly to us scientists, in a move that was crassly political, the former secretary of the interior, Bruce Babbitt, sided with the Umatillas and ordered the Kennewick remains returned despite the lack of *any* tangible indications of affiliation. Indeed, the claim was to be honored based not on hard criteria but rather on the highly questionable grounds of oral tradition or, more simply, a fictive or mythic relationship. Needless to say, this unfortunate ruling was not to be the last word, and the aggrieved scientists continued to battle out the issue in federal court.

Even with the skeleton out of the picture, though, there were still many things that could have been learned about him through studying the site where he had been found. But soon after he was found, the corps passed along the order to stabilize the site, and in a matter of days, it was covered with some forty-five tons of coarse cement blocks and planted with willow trees and hawthorn.

While Kennewick Man lay imprisoned in storage and the millstones of justice ground imperceptibly on, I was invited by the lawyers for the eight archaeologists to visit what remained of the site and arrived there in early March. I spent a day or two locally, talking with the principals involved, and then visited the site, where I was utterly appalled. Over the years I have been directly involved in designing and implementing site stabilization efforts for the Army Corps of Engineers at the Paintsville Lake Reservoir area in Kentucky, the Bluestone Reservoir area of West Virginia, and the Tennessee-Tombigbee Waterway of Mississippi. Because of the precise geoarchaeological protocols I developed at Meadowcroft and expanded and refined in hundreds of other sites here and abroad, over the past fifteen years I have served as an expert witness in *all* of the federal prosecutions of cases involved with the Archaeological Resources Protection Act in which forensic geoarchaeology was needed. In short, I believe I can speak about

"Stabilized" deposits at Kennewick, Washington. The horizontal features are coconut logs added by the Army Corps of Engineers to stabilize a putatively eroding riverbank.

the techniques of stabilizing an archaeological site. And what happened to the Kennewick site was such a travesty that it had to be deliberate destruction.

In the first place, you can tell from looking at it on the ground and in aerial photographs that the riverbanks nearby had not significantly eroded since the discovery; nothing really needed to be done to preserve the site, at least for the short term. Nevertheless the corps dumped coarse, heavy riprap and biodegradable "logs" on the site and then planted willow trees and, more recently, hawthorn, which have long roots that will, of course, destroy the integrity of the layers below, turning any macro- or microstratigraphy into gibberish. If they were convinced that the site might be washed away, which is highly unlikely, they could have built a rock berm around the beach or used brush piles, tires, or even a material known as geofabric to protect against wave action, or even just planted grass—none of which measures would have compromised the site. In addition, they permitted no further useful archaeological work to be done at the site, such as cutting a continuous face across the entire exposed bank or digging trenches away from the river toward the highway. Unless further human remains were found, no such work would have involved any further invoking of NAGPRA. Instead, all microstata, as well as any artifacts or ecofacts, are now forever dumb, voiceless, and irretrievable. In my view, what the corps did was ethically irresponsible, morally bankrupt, and profoundly stupid.

Sadly, like many less celebrated NAGPRA claims, this entire affair has been characterized by a great deal of poor judgment throughout, not to mention a plethora of accusations of incompetence, innuendos about wrongdoing (including alleged thefts of skeletal parts), and, worst of all, a sharp polarization between archaeologists who favor NAGPRA and those who are adamantly opposed to it. Let me be perfectly clear here: I am personally sympathetic to the return of Native American remains to claimants who can demonstrate direct lineal affinity genetically or culturally—that is, through undeniable artifactual continuities, congruent settlement patterns, or indeed any other tangible indications of relatedness. However, I am utterly opposed to the return of unaffiliated material to any claimants whatsoever or to the return of items to claimants based on oral traditions of affiliation unsupported by evidence. Unlike my colleague David Hurst Thomas of the American Museum of Natural History, I feel no need to pay for the sins of my insensitive archaeological or anthropological ancestors—who often did treat Native Americans and their remains in a cavalier or even callous manner—by supporting the return of any remains or artifacts claimed by any Native Americans, simply because it is now seen as the politically correct thing to do. In fact, it is precisely the reverse of the proper course of action. Even in cases of demonstrated affiliation, I strongly encourage claimants to allow the study of skeletal or artifactual remains before they are returned.

It need not have happened this way, and I can say with some confidence that it would not have happened this way in my own state of Pennsylvania. The Pennsylvania Historical and Museum Commission, which oversees the protection and preservation of the archaeological and historical patrimony of the commonwealth, has developed a very positive relationship with resident and formerly resident Native Americans and has encouraged a productive and positive interchange between that community and the state's archaeologists. As a result, the relatively few NAGPRA claims within the state have been generally free of rancor, and, if such a thing is possible, a few potentially contentious situations have actually been—dare I say it—almost humorous.

Eleven years ago, a mine operator expanding his gravel quarry near the shore of Lake Erie encountered a large late Woodland ossuary in which a number of Native Americans had been collectively interred. I was called in as a consultant by the mine owner and the state of Pennsylvania, and I immediately contacted the cultural affairs officer of the closest resident Native American group, the Seneca Nation, in nearby New York. I inquired whether the tribe was interested in these remains and whether it would like to send an observer to the planned excavations. In return I was asked about the circumstances of the mass burial and was ultimately told in no uncertain terms, "Senecas don't practice secondary burial in mass graves. These remains you discovered are probably Erie. We killed those guys, and we don't want their bones." They did allow that if we insisted, they would take them for reburial, but they did not object to their study, asking only that proper and respectful protocols be observed.

Similarly, in a more recent case, the Senecas asked for the return of remains found in a solitary disturbed burial in a house construction project, but only *after* they had been fully studied. The Senecas clearly believe it is both useful and appropriate to know more about their ancestors or others who lived in their ancestral territories, and both the tribe and the archaeological community have benefited by the knowledge generated by this reasonable attitude.

However, in the case of Kennewick Man, *nobody* involved locally acted properly, in my opinion. Some of the archaeologists went off the mark with their exuberant Europeanoid claims, inflaming the Native Americans, who, not surprisingly, made a wholly unsupportable claim of cultural and biological affiliation. At that remove in time, there is simply no reasonable way to make such a claim. The NAGPRA law is very vague on this, allowing claims on religious and traditional grounds rather than any actual information. While the eight anthropologists' suit was on other grounds, NAGPRA is almost certain to fail a constitutional challenge someday down the pike, on the basis of the First Amendment clause about the establishment of religion. Indeed, if it were not Native Americans claiming religious reasons for not allowing scientific investigation but, say, Southern Baptists or Muslims, there would not be the slightest hesitancy to throw the claims out as absurdly unconstitutional. In the case of Kennewick Man, the government bent over backward to accommodate the claim of the Umatillas for reasons that were chiefly political and/or politically correct. To my mind, destruction of the site by the corps is comparable to the blowing up of the Buddhist statues in Afghanistan by the Taliban fanatics. In all, a huge and bitter legacy has now been inherited by all sides to this dispute.

What light has all this controversy shed so far on the question of who the first Americans were and how and when they got here? That Kennewick Man looks practically nothing like any contemporary Indian people is not, on the whole, a very great surprise. None among the handful of skeletal remains from this time period looks much like contemporary Indians either; they tend to look more like southern Asians, it seems. This fits fairly well with what has been surmised from linguistics and mtDNA analysis about the origins of the people who settled the Western Hemisphere—that people in southern Asia spread out south and north as long as 40,000 years ago or more and probably arrived in the Americas at various times over thousands of years. As Owsley and Jantz have pointed out, this Pacific affinity among our oldest skeletons is a pretty good match for the mtDNA haplogroup B, which is common in the Pacific and southern North America, but not in northeastern Siberia or northwestern North America. If Kennewick Man's remains are ever returned for further scientific investigation, it would be quite a stunning surprise if he did not turn out to be one of the four common Asian and Native American haplogroups.

In fact, Kennewick Man's chief value *might* have been what we could have learned about how he lived his life from artifacts and ecofacts in the site where he was found. Was he interred by companions, or did he die alone? Was he a fisherman? If so, and it seems he may have been, how did he fish? Did he spear salmon, net them, or pluck them out of the water with his bare hands? Was it salmon-spawning season when he died? Of course all of these questions have been rendered unanswerable now.

Given their extreme rarity in the Americas, it is unwise to make too much of any single skeleton or other human remains from this period. Not only are there great diversity and complexity in the human anatomy—the differences often shading imperceptibly from one type to another—but there are also individuals who simply don't fit the type even though they are members of it. After all, the National Basketball Association now has a ballplayer from the People's Republic of China who is seven feet six, scarcely your typical Chinese. Furthermore, the skull is exceptionally malleable in evolutionary terms and capable of changing greatly over generations, much less thousands of years. For example, native skeletons from some two or three millennia after Kennewick Man show resemblances to today's native populations. So far, all that the older skeletons tell us for sure converges with what the linguists and the molecular biologists tell us: that more than one group of people showed up here a long time ago and populated the entire hemisphere. This too is what the archaeological record now shows with considerable clarity. After more than a half century, the questions of who they were, when they got here, and how remain wide open. Indeed, we are living in one of the most dynamic periods in the history of New World archaeology.

CHAPTER ELEVEN

WHO ARE THOSE GUYS?

In the movie *Butch Cassidy and the Sundance Kid,* Butch and Sundance are relentlessly pursued across Utah by a determined white-hatted lawman, Joe Lefors, and his Native American scout, the improbably named Lord Baltimore. Watching their persistent pursuers track them in the dark, by lantern light, across sandstone slickrock, Butch and Sundance repeatedly turn to each other impressed but perplexed and ask each other, "Who *are* those guys?" Who, indeed? Although they suspect the identity of their stalkers, they don't really know the answer. In reverse, the same is likely to remain true here: we stalkers of the first Americans do not know yet who "those guys" we seek really are.

Although it would be reasonable to suppose that I have some well-defined ideas about who the people who first entered the New World were, I don't. I don't have an exact, or even inexact, scenario in my large head about how people first arrived on the continent. Certainly I don't know exactly who they were, precisely when they arrived, or even how many times they came and then sallied forth to make a life—or more accurately, lives—for themselves. What I do know firsthand is that some of those guys were here in western Pennsylvania hanging out in a large rockshelter above a quiet creek sometime around 16,000 years ago. More important, I believe I know what their presence does and doesn't imply about the first colonizers of the New World.

People sometimes accuse me of being obsessed with the details of excavation, rather than the meaning to be derived from it. A while back, my friend and longtime colleague David Madsen of the Utah Geological Survey told me that a newspaper reporter had been asking about me, and he had told her I was the kind of archaeologist who spends more time on "field minutiae" than on the interpretations of excavations. I told Dave that I took that as a compliment.

Right now, thanks to developments over the past couple of decades, the number of things we don't know for sure about the initial peopling of this hemisphere exceeds what we do know. Those unknowns will perhaps be resolved one day by the many subfields we have talked about thus far—glacial geology, genetics, linguistics, and so forth—but the real answers about who those guys were will have to come from the ground. Only the discovery of actual artifacts or human remains that are solidly dated and found in unexceptionable circumstances will provide us with the resolution we seek. And this means that the data *must* be retrieved in an appropriately resolute manner—which is why I took Madsen's comment as a compliment.

In our pursuit of the initial colonists of this hemisphere, we have concentrated on the record of those who made it or succeeded, as is only natural. We like winners. But almost surely in those days, there were also losers—failed colonists from doomed colonizations who arrived on the edge of the continent or even penetrated well into it and then, for one reason or another, simply didn't survive. We know from both population genetics and ethnographic analogues that the first successful colonists would have had to arrive in a band of at least fifty people. Otherwise, the population would have dwindled from accidents, illness, age-based attrition, and ultimately a scarcity of mates.

No matter if only one or a half dozen of these groups entered the New World, the overall population size was *very* small and would remain so for a long time. Moreover, dispersed as they would soon be over a vast landscape, their tracks and traces would be—and in fact, are—very hard to find. As Tom Dillehay, Dave Meltzer, and many others have pointed out, those pioneers are virtually invisible, archaeologically speaking. Paul Martin and Vance Haynes, of course, use this invisibility to suggest that no one was here before Clovis and that only with Clovis's lethal points is there a widely detectable and unmistakable indication of human presence.

I suggest a much more likely alternative. Recently, the eminent British archaeologist and Paleolithic specialist Clive Gamble visited Meadowcroft in the course of making a film about the dispersal of anatomically modern humans around the world. In a discussion about the numerical scarcity of pre-Clovis sites such as Meadowcroft and Monte Verde, he reminded me about an article he and some colleagues had written several years before on the initial colonization of northern Europe toward the end of the Pleistocene, as the great Scandinavian ice sheet retreated. In that article, Gamble and company stressed that it had taken nearly four thousand years for humans to spread north only eight hundred miles into a region they already knew existed. So much for blitzkrieg, Clovis-style dashes across the landscape of some unknown continent.

More important, however, was the nature of the evidence of the initial penetration of the northern third of the European continent. The earliest sites were few, small, widely dispersed, and virtually invisible, and Gamble ascribed them to what he called the "Pioneer Phase" of colonization, which by its very nature was highly ephemeral. For several thousand years, this would remain the case, until populations began to increase significantly, sites became larger and more common, and the threshold of visibility had been crossed. At this point, humans would have passed on to what Gamble called the "Residential Phase" of colonization. Standing as we were at Meadowcroft, one of literally only a handful of early New World sites, we heard Gamble's point loud and clear. Sites such as Meadowcroft and Monte Verde represent the Pioneer Phase in the peopling of the New World, while the Clovis horizon marked the threshold of visibility and the initiation of the Residential Phase.

But what exactly *is* the Clovis horizon? Clovis experts, especially the traditionalists, think they know the answer to this. Not simply a distinctive technological suite, Clovis is to them also a sociopolitical and, presumably, a genetic and linguistic entity as well. They consider Clovis people first and foremost hunters of big game, and their trademark fluted points are eloquent testimony to their skills.

Most people in the field, though, no longer think that is true. We now know that the diagnostic fluting of Clovis and later Folsom points conveyed no particular advantage in the hafting of stone points onto wooden or ivory shafts, nor in facilitating the penetration of such shafts into the resistant hides of thick-skinned megafauna. Why, then, are they "suddenly" everywhere or at least seem to be? Often found unused in special caches, Clovis points may in fact represent, if not luxury items, then perhaps something quite different. As Dave Meltzer muses, they could have played a crucial role not in hunting but in social bonding between far-flung groups—serving, perhaps, like a secret handshake.

Whatever the hallmark fluted points may represent, for now Clovis is more than ever an enigma, another of the great unknowns. Where it came from, what it was all about, and what happened to it after its brief stint on the earth are all open questions. My guess is that Clovis points and other lithic technologies will not, in the long run, provide the answer to who the first Americans were or when and how they got here. The lithic record alone will not and cannot fully explicate the successful colonization of this hemisphere. Most of what the first colonizers made and used in their daily life was perishable—constructed of wood, leather, bone, and plant fiber— and most of it has not survived. Where it is present at places such as Monte Verde, or in dry caves or permafrost, it tells us far more about the first colonists than any Clovis point or, indeed, any other modified rock ever will.

The rarity of perishable artifacts, coupled with the scarcity of early sites, means that when such sites are found they *must* be excavated with exquisite precision and monomaniacal attention to detail. Such sites and their contents need to be managed with the care one provides for one's most sacred objects. Anything less, and these extremely rare sites will be ruined, their evidence left ambiguous and their precious insights forever lost.

Although, in truth, I am not bereft of opinions about the identity of the pioneers, I did take Madsen's comment as a compliment. Some others in my field have developed quite elaborate ideas about the great adventure of peopling the New World; what follows are "answers" several authorities have put forward in the last few years, some staggering in their precision, others astounding in their boldness.

NENANA IN THE TANANA,
THEN THE WORLD?

———

One story goes like this: About 11,800 years ago, some people were living in central Alaska in the Tanana River valley, which leads into the upper Yukon River basin. As we know from the existence of Arctic ground squirrels there, it was steppelike in those days, and some of its inhabitants, whom we call the Nenana after the neighboring valley, probably explored the Yukon plateau fairly far south in the warm summer months, eating plants, fish, waterfowl, and big game along the way. Each summer they extended their base camp a bit farther southward, noting that the great ice sheet that stood a mile high at its edge was retreating. Once out of the mountains, they would have seen the vast welcoming plains of Canada stretching away to the horizon. This pioneering band might well have rushed back to the Tanana Valley to tell the others about these wondrous lands and then come back the following summer along with not only the rest of their band but a couple of other bands, too, who were eager for a new and better world. "It is very likely," wrote the author of this model, "that there were people whose curiosity and quest for knowledge of the beyond would urge them ever southward."

Then one of the bands' leaders decided he would go headlong to the south as far as he could go, and at summer's end, he and his followers found themselves on the shores of Lake Peace in Alberta. Later on, back in Alaska, these people made tools from the gigantic bones they had occasionally found lying about in the gravel outwashes of cold-running rivers. Although they had never seen the creature that had left its bones lying around, just south of Lake Peace they saw what they could imagine was its spoor—huge tracks together with enormous piles of dung. Adrenaline must have rushed, and they surely would have pressed onward.

The time was now 11,700 years ago, and the band had reached Boone Lake near Grand Prairie in Alberta. Among the poplar trees, they spotted their first mammoths, a herd of gigantic beasts unlike anything they had ever seen. For a while they watched; then they attacked. They managed to wound a young mammoth, only to have the enraged matriarch charge them. When they hurled their small, light spears at the matriarch, they bounced off, so the hunters fled for their lives.

Before too many days passed, the band of hunters learned that the more they attacked the mammoth herds, the more wary the herds became, and soon enough they realized they needed heavier arms—bigger spear points with longer shafts. One of the hunters got the bright idea to make it easier to mount bigger spear points on longitudinally notched foreshafts. At first he experimented, removing a longitudinal flake from each side of the nearly completed big bifacial spear point. After perhaps days of breaking almost completed points, nicking his thumbs and fingers, and turning the air blue with late Pleistocene invective while the women kept the little children out of earshot, he succeeded.

Voilà—Clovis Man.

A few years later, he and his obedient followers, now highly skilled hunters, arrived in a winter camp near Wilsall, Montana. In all, it had taken six years for the band to travel from the upper Tanana Valley to what archaeologists call the Anzick site—a distance of some 3,500 miles, an easy march if they made about four miles a day from May to October each year. There at the Anzick site, the band leader's infant son drowned and was buried at the base of a small rock cliff with offerings of stone and bone implements. Summoned onward by the now-mythological promised land of the south, they went on to populate the entire hemisphere in a few hundred years, bands proliferating, splitting off, pushing on, and leaving caches of their fluted points behind, perhaps as markers of their passing, perhaps as offerings, or perhaps as a useful munitions dump in case they had to return.

Then trouble began. The world became drier, with year after year of drought. The water tables dropped, big game desperately gathered around the remaining water holes and fell easy prey to the hunters. Then, to make matters worse, the world turned bitterly cold during a period that lasted a thousand years, called the Younger Dryas. Winter freezes meant even less water for game. They perished, the remnants of once-great herds finally done in by the hunters. Among the big herds, only bison remained. Then, a good while later, some of these Clovis people, perhaps on the hunt somewhere in the Great Basin, ran into others, people who had arrived on the west coast via a coastal route.

This explanation of the peopling of the Americas sprang from the mind of none other than Vance Haynes in the year 2001. It is supported, he says, by several circumstances: Nenana folk were in the Tanana Valley by about 11,700 B.P., when a warming trend occurred, creating an ice-free route through the two glaciers by 11,600 B.P., and Clovis folk were in Montana and central Texas by 11,550 B.P. Vance's hypothesis, as recounted above, is the only one of the few now floating about that simply cannot possibly be true. It is based, first and foremost, on the existence of the Nenana folk in the Tanana Valley in 11,700 B.P.

Given the long-held notion that people arrived in this hemisphere via the Bering land bridge, it is not at all surprising that archaeologists have looked on both sides of the Bering Strait for evidence of these people. With the discovery of the Clovis culture in the 1930s, it made sense to seek the remains of people who predated Clovis, people whose technology might have evolved into the unique fluted points of Clovis. Though not for a lack of trying, no one could find such remains. Instead, they found a variety of sites with microblades, the kind that can be stuck several at a time into notches in bone or wood foreshafts to make a composite javelin or dart point. Admittedly, eastern Siberia and western Alaska comprise an enormous amount of real estate, and hundreds of sites may well have gone unnoticed. But over the decades no one found any stone artifacts that might have evolved into Clovis—until the 1970s, when intensive excavation began in a place called Dry Creek in the Nenana River valley.

There Roger Powers, an expert in Russian prehistory, found the usual microblades, but in a stratum below he came across a number of older artifacts, notably some small, thin, triangular bifacial points and some teardrop-shaped points. Two other sites nearby bearing similar points— Walker Road and Moose Creek—soon came to light, and the three sites together served as type sites, which are the basis for recognizing the Nenana complex. The Nenana complex is defined entirely by lithic material, there being few or no organic tool remains. In all, the complex consists of points, knives, scrapers, perforators, hammers, anvils, and so forth. Radiocarbon dates came in averaging 11,300 B.P. and ranging from 11,800 to 11,000 B.P.

In other Nenana sites discovered later, such as one in the Tanana River valley, it became clear that these people had enjoyed a diet of cranes, ducks, swans, geese, beaver, squirrel, bison, caribou, and maybe even elk. Broken mammoth bones were also found, but it is not clear that mammoths actually lived there among the Nenana people or that they hunted and ate them. The bones could simply have been the results of prior deaths, as Haynes suggests in his scenario. In any event, by 10,500 B.P., about the time Folsom points made their appearance in the American Southwest, the Nenana complex, with its bifacial spear points, was abruptly replaced by the bearers of the Denali culture, people who made not bifacial points but true microblades. So abrupt was the change that some scholars, including archaeologist E. James Dixon of the University of Alaska, believe that the Nenana people were displaced—basically run off—by another group. It may be, Dixon says, that interior Alaska was "a region repeatedly reoccupied by different cultural groups."

The age of the Nenana complex has since been reassessed and is now thought to be 11,300 to 11,000 B.P., too late to be ancestral to Clovis. Vance Haynes seems to have missed that development, or perhaps simply ignored it or dismissed it out of hand. For decades Vance has appeared to be scientific and eminently reasonable by repeatedly calling for multiple working hypotheses. Unfortunately, for Vance himself there is but one working hypothesis, and it no longer adds up.

The sad fact is that the evidence is not going to make any difference to Vance, a man who, as one of his colleagues said, is now an example of someone whose mind has snapped shut, never to open again. With the exception of a handful of Haynes spear-carriers, the field has now clearly tilted toward the camp that believes in a pre-Clovis presence. Some like to argue whether this is what should be called a "paradigm shift" or not. Others question whether there ever was a paradigm (Clovis First) that needed shifting once the problems with it became too embarrassing to be ignored, or if it all happened differently from the way it is supposed to according to the philosopher of science Thomas Kuhn, who invented all the paradigm stuff. Frankly, such discussions don't make much difference, nor do they contribute much to the search for the first Americans. You can fit a lot of abstractions along with a host of angels on the head of a pin, and the rest of the world is going to yawn and turn on the ball game on TV.

The handful of people in the field who still can't accept a pre-Clovis presence in the Western Hemisphere remind me of a bumper sticker that had a brief run in the late seventies and the eighties. It said STOP CONTINENTAL DRIFT. In fairness, there are also some who just wish there were more pre-Clovis sites. For these people, the fact that there have been *any* questions raised about Monte Verde and Meadowcroft makes them doubt the overwhelming evidence. They would love to have replicability before them, or more pre-Clovis sites. Happily, now there are.

REPLICABILITY

Replicability was not one of the necessary criteria formulated by that ultimate hardnose, Aleš Hrdlička, or anyone else in America or abroad until

Excavations at Cactus Hill, Virginia.

Artifact mapping at Cactus Hill.

relatively recently. What the Clovis First fanatics didn't seem to notice was that, with all the replicability of Clovis sites, there were a lot of other post-Clovis sites, and some contemporary ones as well, showing an enormous variety of lithic styles, that all argued eloquently for behavioral diversity, bespeaking far more arrivals in this hemisphere than a single (and late) group. This is true not only in South America, where the various material cultures show no affinity whatsoever with Clovis, but also in North Amer-

Profile of sand dune deposits at Cactus Hill.

Mike Johnson, project director of the ASV Cactus Hill Excavations, retrieving a C-14 sample.

Clovis point from Cactus Hill.

ica. The search for pre-Clovis has provided a great deal of incentive throughout the seventy-odd years since the finds at Blackwater Draw, motivating such people as Scotty MacNeish, Ruth Gruhn, and Alan Bryan, never mind their failure to find the grail. But now it is in hand—this grail called pre-Clovis sites—and more of them will no doubt turn up as the years go by. Undoubtedly, such finds will produce as many questions as answers, which is one reason why people still study to be archaeologists.

Several sites are under investigation that appear to be as old as, if not older than, Meadowcroft. One of these is called Cactus Hill, located on the shore of the Nottoway River, which meanders slowly across the coastal plain of Virginia into Albemarle Sound on the North Carolina coast. The site is located in a six-foot-deep, sequentially migrating sand dune and has been simultaneously excavated by two different teams, one directed by Joseph McAvoy of the Nottaway River Survey, under a grant from the National Geographic Society, the other by Michael Johnson of the Archaeological Society of Virginia. If this sounds like having two wives in one kitchen, that is exactly the situation. The two teams barely speak to each other. Even so, the two men did manage to combine their efforts in one of several reports issued from the site, the last being an article in *National Geographic* in 2000.

The first three feet down in the dunes contain historic- to Clovis-era material, but four inches below that, in an unmistakably separate and

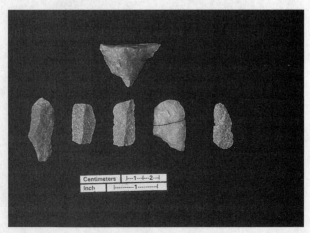

Pre-Clovis artifacts from Cactus Hill.

*General view of Saltville, Virginia. Pleistocene faunal
remains have been recovered here, some in association with
archaeological material of late Pleistocene age.*

older horizon, are a hearth and a charcoal concentration beneath an array
of stone tools. This hearth is dated to 15,070 ± 70 B.P. and the carbon beneath the tool cluster to 16,670 ± 730 B.P. The pre-Clovis flaked-stone
items are mostly blades made from quartzite cores collected elsewhere and
made at the site by flaking the cores with soft stone hammers. Also represented are a couple of lanceolate, unfluted, bifacial points that could have
been projectile points or hafted knives. Like the tools at Meadowcroft,
these appear to have been the work of people who were foraging for a variety of faunal and floral food resources.

Another such site is reported from Saltville, Virginia, which is located
in southwestern Virginia just north of the North Carolina–Tennessee border. Today this is classic Appalachia, a country of snakelike creeks and hills
and also, incidentally, the home in nearby Poor Valley of the A. P. Carter
family, who popularized real country music in the twenties and are still
heard from in the persons of June Carter Cash and her husband, Johnny. In
the Saltville Valley, investigations of fossiliferous deposits of Quaternary
age have been ongoing for some twenty years. Recently Jerry McDonald of
the Virginia Museum of Natural History came across, resting on top of
bedrock, a five-thousand-year-long sequence of sediments dating back to
between 13,000 and 14,510 years B.P.

*Excavations at Saltville. The bone bed
has yielded modified bone artifacts
and stone tools in excess of 13,000 B.P.*

*Excavations at Saltville. The excavator is working in a mid-
den deposit associated with the edge of a Pleistocene-age pond.*

Modified bone tool from Saltville. This artifact may be a
pressure flaker used for stone tool production.

In a layer nearest the bedrock are the remains of a mastodon that may
have been butchered and burned, which, if true, makes it one of the very
few mastodons known to have been eaten by people. Associated with the
mastodon's remains are two choppers or wedges of sandstone, a piece of
bone deliberately grooved by a person, a heavily modified and extensively
used bone tool, and some flakes made of nonlocal chert. Evidently, the bone
tool is from a musk ox tibia and was directly dated to 14,510 ± 80 B.P.

Bone scraping tool from Saltville, made from a long bone of a
musk ox (Bootherium bombifrons), *dating to ca. 14,500 B.P.*

Ongoing excavations at Topper, South Carolina. The deposits shown span the entire Holocene and late Pleistocene.

Archaeologists excavating Ice Age deposits at Topper.

*Archaeologists examining the deep
stratigraphy at Topper. The upper
units span the Holocene, while the
lower are from the late Ice Age.*

Above the mastodon layer are two more layers that apparently represent two separate occupational interludes. One includes a column of weathered pieces of bedrock that seem to be man-made, for what purpose no one knows, and below that are some lithic materials and fragments of aquatic life—fish, bivalves, and the like—along with twigs that date to nearly 14,000 years ago. Again, this appears to have been the tool kit and the "table scraps" of some generalized foragers taking seasonal advantage of the place.

Another pre-Clovis site, called Topper, is located on the Savannah River in South Carolina, on the border with Georgia. At the meeting in Santa Fe in 1999, Al Goodyear of the University of South Carolina described this site, pointing out that at one stage of excavations there, he had reached what was evidently a Clovis-era layer and had gone no farther, as-

Burin fragments from Topper.

suming, as so many colleagues did, that that was as early as human habitation went. But recent reports had impelled him to look a bit farther down on a high Pleistocene terrace above the river, which was associated with an outcrop of chert and a quarry site.

The site consists of one layer of sand about four and a half feet thick, underlain by another distinct layer of sand about another three feet thick, underlain in turn by yet another distinct layer of claylike sand. In the upper layer are artifacts that date from Clovis times to the period of European contact. While in the bottom layer, Goodyear found an enigmatic assemblage of stone flakes, burins, microblades, and microblade cores, but no bifaces. Some of the chert used was nonlocal, meaning someone had brought it there, and there appear to be several distinct rock-chipping stations. This lithic suite, as it is called, dates back to at least 15,000 to 16,000 years ago, based on optically stimulated luminescence (OSL) dates obtained from the sands.

PROLIFERATING POSSIBILITIES

Serious questions remain about Topper, Saltville, and Cactus Hill, and these sites will indeed benefit from continuing investigation and confirmation. Yet with such sites coming to the fore and Meadowcroft and Monte Verde already securely established as pre-Clovis, except in the minds of fanatics, the days of Clovis First are finally over and the old questions can arise, fresh and wonderful to behold. Who are those guys? How did they get here? When? Scenarios for pre-Clovis migration abound, ranging from the conservative to the freebooting. Brian Fagan, an indefatigable chronicler of American archaeology in both textbooks and popular books, as well as a professor of anthropology at the University of California at Santa Barbara and an early and vocal supporter of Meadowcroft, expresses a cautious view in his latest college-level textbook on world prehistory. He assumes that most human activity on the continent dates from sometime after 20,000 years ago and that practically no one lived in Siberia before 18,000 years ago, neither of which are unreasonable suggestions based on a conservative interpretation of available data. Similarly, few people lived in frigid Beringia during the glacial maximum, but then, about 12,700 B.C. or 14,650 years ago, the temperatures in the far north rose rapidly and people began heading across the land bridge and south. Once under way, they ranged far and wide.

Computer modeling, Fagan says, suggests that if people took the "least-cost" approach to all this pioneering—meaning that they took the least arduous routes into the unknown places that would provide them with food and good stone for tools—they would have needed only two millennia to settle the New World from polar bear land to penguinville. But this is a linear approach, and the sites of early human habitation do not necessarily obey linear rules. Indeed, they do not appear to be linear at all but rather are scattered thinly over huge regions, which suggests that people leapfrogged their way into the New World, settling some areas and ignoring others. Then, he suggests, Clovis people came along and filled in the blanks on the map. For by 11,400 years ago, North America entered into the Younger Dryas, the cold snap mentioned earlier, which could have caused wetter and more favorable game conditions on the Great Plains and in the Southwest and allowed Clovis folk to flourish, spread out, and adapt to a wide range of environments, its artifacts diversifying by what he calls "stylistic drift."

As Fagan says, this picture is "still little more than a theoretical scenario," and indeed it leaves many questions unanswered. First of all, why would hunters and gatherers, who always live a relatively parlous life, go racing past a perfectly well stocked habitat and leave behind the possibility of an occasional reunion with relatives and old friends during which information could be exchanged and mating arranged? Why would people who knew, for example, how to hunt larger or smaller herbivores "leapfrog" into a coastal area where they had to learn how to fish? And if the Clovis culture spread out from some good times on the plains in 11,200 B.P., why are there more Clovis sites in the Southeast of the present United States than in the West, and perhaps older ones to boot? And finally, where did the people at Meadowcroft in 16,000 B.P. leapfrog from?

Perhaps the biggest problem I have with Fagan's otherwise quite plausible scenario is that he still has the initial percolation of humans into the New World pegged at about 14,000 B.P., which gives them only about 1,500 years to reach Monte Verde and another 1,300 years to populate the rest of the hemisphere. Despite the fact that this is a much longer time than Martin or Haynes allows for the penetration of the hemisphere, it is still, at least in my mind, too short to provide enough time to adjust and adapt to the 8,000 miles of mountains, rain forests, plains, and deserts with their ever-changing array of potential game and plant food resources. Remember, each new habitat offers not only potentially novel plant and animal foods but also new medicinal and/or poisonous plants at each step. One false bite and you're dead or hallucinating for a week. More seriously, Fagan's allotted colonization interval seems too short to account for the great diversity in technology and lifestyles that seem to be well established by 11,000 years ago, and further, his numbers seem too brief in comparison to the documented colonization rates for either interior Australia or Northern Europe during deglaciation. But, of course, all this may be simply chronological hairsplitting.

Generally speaking, I think Fagan and I would both agree that people tend to proceed slowly and with a bit of caution into new territory, especially people such as most hunters and gatherers, who live by hard-won traditions. Another way of looking at this is called the return rate. According to this view, a group in a given hunting-and-gathering area is not likely simply to leave for new territory until the price is right—meaning that their territory is sufficiently depleted or altered that the cost of making a living there appears to be higher than the costs and dangers of trying someplace new where the old techniques, the old lore, may not be applicable.

To oversimplify, guys who are used to sticking little spears in dying mammoths in some swamp are not likely to be able to reap an immediate harvest of meat from monkeys running around in the canopy of a rain forest. And the New World was made up of lots of huge and different ecosystems that had to be mastered if the continents were to be filled with humans. As we have seen and as Gamble has suggested, that process simply had to take a lot more than a few centuries or even a few millennia. The rapidity with which we today adopt whole new technologies can confuse us about the deep past and make us forget how slowly traditional human societies change. As a caveat here, of course, it is worth pointing out that there are still cattle ranchers in the American West who are doing things on the range exactly as their great-grandfathers did, and for no other reason than that that is what their great-grandfathers did.

THE LATE PLEISTOCENE YACHT CLUB

The big problem presented by the existence of pre-Clovis sites is that, for all anyone can tell, the ice-free corridor between the Cordilleran and Laurentian glaciers was open around early Clovis time, but it had been shut for several thousand years before that. The only likely solution is that they must have come by boat. You could presumably leave coastal Asia, say the islands north of Japan, which at the height of the glaciers were mostly connected, and paddle along the warm Japanese current north to Beringia, east to Alaska, and down the western coast of North America. But where would you put in along the west coast of North America when it was covered out to the edge of the continental shelf with the Cordilleran glacier? Happily, it now turns out that the Cordilleran glacier was never in total command of the coast. There were what scientists call "refugia" along the way, ice-free spots that sailors would think of as safe harbors where they could gather themselves, kill a few seals or whatever, and then be on their way.

In this manner, paddling or maybe even sailing along by means of skin or woven plant fiber sails, people could have whisked down the coast in fairly short order. The idea of a coastal route was promulgated as early as 1960, even before the problems with the Clovis model and the ice-free corridor arose. From several angles, the notion is quite appealing. For one, the Clovis point, affixed to a bone shaft that in turn is affixed to a wooden shaft, is very similar to the Inuit harpoon. Couldn't the Clovis configuration have arisen from people who hunted fish and marine mammals with harpoonlike weapons along the food-rich shores of the continent? That may be getting pretty speculative, but it is a fact that people got to Australia at least 40,000 years ago, and they could have gotten there *only* by some sort of watercraft over open water. Why would such maritime folk have decided to go only south?

With the Nenana culture evidently out of contention as a Clovis precursor, E. James Dixon, who has spent much of his professional career as an archaeologist poking into sites in Alaska, has recently become a champion of the coastal route. Initial colonization, Dixon says, could have taken place around 13,500 years ago by people moving down the west coast of the continent in small boats, presumably made of hides. Human remains have been found on one of the Channel Islands of California, Santa Rosa. There parts of a female skeleton were discovered a few years back and have been redated to between 11,100 and 11,500 years ago. Far to the south, on the Peruvian coast, two archaeological sites have recently come to light— Quebrada Tacahuay and Quebrada Jaguay—replete with the remains of fish and other marine animals. Clearly, some people had made an adaptation to a coastal, marine way of life only a few centuries after the time of the first Clovis hunters.

According to the coastal theory, people could have traversed the entire length of the New World in about a thousand years, moving inland from there and eventually populating every place east to the Atlantic coasts. One would not reasonably expect to find a lot of archaeological sites along the coasts much older than those already found for the very good reason that the coast of pre-Clovis times is almost entirely underwater now due to the melting of the glaciers, which began about 14,000 years ago and continued for several thousand years before the ice and sea levels reached their present configuration. But even in three hundred feet of murky waters and the muck and goo of the continental shelf, all is not lost.

In the 1990s, two Canadians—Daryl Fedje of Parks Canada and Heiner Josenhans of Canada's geological survey—used high-resolution sonar to complete a detailed bathymetric map of the landscape about 170 feet deep in Juan Pérez Sound, about a half mile off the Queen Charlotte Islands of British Columbia. Below them was a land of onetime river valleys, floodplains, and ancient lakes. The Canadians dredged up huge quantities of muck and found a stump of a pine tree and other woody remains that dated via carbon-14 to some 12,000 years B.P. Elsewhere they found the shells of plentiful shellfish dating from the same era. In other words, here was a place that would have been habitable by herbivores and predators, including human predators, even before the ice had retreated far to the north. In a burst of amazing good luck given the nature of their task, they also spotted in some dredged-up goo a triangular, flaked blade of dark basalt about four inches in length. Clearly it is an artifact, and the associated sediment has been subsequently dated to about 10,000 years ago.

Proponents of a coastal route for the First Americans were, of course, overjoyed. Although none of the evidence put people in actual boats proceeding down the coast before 12,500 years ago, at which point some were living a bit inland at Monte Verde, it confirmed that such a route had been possible, even plausible, to some minds. Added to this came what some might claim as another kind of evidence—the mitochondrial DNA from North American brown bears.

It had evidently long been thought that the four genetically distinct populations of brown bears in North America originated in four separate invasions of the continent. But researchers from Oxford University, studying brown bears frozen in the permafrost for 36,000 years, found that all four genetic strains were present, suggesting a single invasion some 36,000 years ago. The Oxford scientist in charge, Alan Cooper, noted that bears and humans have much the same ecological requirements and that brown

Fanciful portrayal of Solutreans en route to the New World.

bears, significantly, migrated down the coast of Alaska, not through any ice-free corridor. "Humans," Cooper is reported to have said, "might have done the same thing."

I doubt that brown bear ecology has ever before been offered to further a major archaeological theory, and coastal proponents are not likely to make too much of Cooper's speculation. Still, it is nice to know. Even less likely to be taken seriously is another maritime theory for the peopling of the continent that comes to us via the Smithsonian Institution, the former home of that ferocious doubter of a century ago, Aleš Hrdlička. There, the head of the anthropology department, Dennis Stanford, along with Bruce Bradley, an archaeological consultant and acclaimed lithic specialist from the Southwest, have proposed an Atlantic crossing for the progenitors of Clovis Man.

A number of phenomena that have come to light in the last fifty years or so have brought them to this astonishing hypothesis. As early as the 1950s and early 1960s, it was realized that Clovis sites were most common in the southeastern portion of the United States. Although he was not taken very seriously at the time, back then an archaeologist named R. J. Mason proposed that it was probably in the Southeast that the characteristic Clovis technology had arisen. As we have seen, the best guess now about Clovis technology is that it itself was what traveled so widely, not the people who used it. In other words, once it came into being—and it may well have been invented in the Southeast—it was exported from group to group very quickly, and as it moved throughout the hemisphere, it changed to one degree or another by virtue of either local requirements or Brian Fagan's technological drift.

At about the same time as Mason's notion, others noted that if they weren't fluted, Clovis points would look quite a lot like the points made by people who lived from about 25,000 to 18,000 years ago along the coast of southern France, Portugal, and Spain—the Solutreans. These people seem to have arrived in Europe, perhaps from Asia, with an entirely new and unprecedented means of making stone points: pressure-flaking. By pressing a piece of bone or wood against the surface of the flint, they flaked off slivers across the tool, much as those other master flint knappers—the makers of Clovis and Folsom points—did. They made exquisitely chipped points in the shape of laurel and willow leaves, some with a stem on the base for attaching the point to a shaft. While very well made, the Solutrean points are not quite as exquisite as Clovis points. Could they somehow have been the precursor of Clovis?

Back then, however, the Solutrean connection seemed particularly unlikely since there was such a long hiatus between the most recent date for the Solutreans (18,000 years ago) and the oldest date for human habitation in North America (11,200). But that hiatus has now been narrowed down, perhaps to the vanishing point, by the finds at Monte Verde, Meadowcroft, Topper, Saltville, and Cactus Hill. So Dennis and Bruce reframed the Solutrean connection, postulating that near the end of their time on the Iberian peninsula, the Solutrean folk took to the sea in some sort of boat and headed north, skirting the glacial ice in places like Greenland, then south, fetching up somewhere near the Carolinas and, within give or take a few thousand years, coming up with fluting. Dennis, who has a gift of gab something like that of Jesse Jackson, likes to say, "Iberians, not Siberians."

The day back in 1999 that Dennis broached this to a bunch of us he had invited to the Smithsonian, most present wondered what drug Dennis was on that day. There are some people, such as Larry Straus of the University of New Mexico, a longtime specialist on Solutrean lithics, who say—not to put too fine a point on it—that Dennis and Bruce are nuts. Straus says that despite a few "superficial" similarities, the lithic technologies of Solutrean and Clovis folk are profoundly different. Additionally, the truly diagnostic Solutrean "signature" forms—the leaf-shaped, shouldered, and stemmed points—don't show up at all in Clovis sites, and while Solutreans made lanceolate bifaces shaped vaguely like Clovis points, they never fluted them. Others point out that the Solutreans lived as far east in Europe as the Rhône River, but never managed to get across it; it seems unlikely that people who couldn't get across a river would have taken to sea. In his own defense, Dennis will tell you that nothing about his idea is impossible and that he just wants to make sure that archaeologists don't overlook any possibilities now that the Clovis First model is dead, that that "boring story" need no longer be told, and that the peopling-of-America question is wide open. Fair enough, I suppose, especially since the technology to build blue-water boats with sails almost certainly existed in the upper Paleolithic, and, as Dennis's wife, Peggy Jodry, rightfully points out, archaeologists have all too often ignored water travel.

The trouble with coastal routes across either the Pacific or the Atlantic is that at present there is basically no evidence at all that either actually happened. A single point found in the water off British Columbia with a single date of 10,000 B.P. is hardly something to bet the mortgage on. In fact, as David Madsen has pointed out in a forthcoming book, *Entering America,* the Pacific coastal route, which is the one taken as a serious idea, has come about not from actual evidence, but chiefly as a "default" alternative necessary since the Clovis First model has been discredited. But there are yet other significant problems with the coastal theory in terms of its timing.

First of all, even if the maritime pioneers got to the west coast of the present-day United States by, say, 13,500 years B.P., it seems unlikely that they could have reached western Pennsylvania by that same time or earlier. They would have had to march east across the Rocky Mountains, the Great Plains, and the Mississippi Valley, a distance of some 2,500 miles. Another problem with the coastal theory is that it accounts only for pioneers accustomed to coastal foraging and essentially one entry. On the other hand, genetic evidence, for starters, makes it now appear likely that there were multiple entries. Some might well have been people from a coastal, maritime tradition, but others probably started off as inland people. As Madsen points out, "It is likely that the colonization of the Americas involved continuous contact between donor populations and immigrant populations, since the probability of a single small group surviving is very low."

One suggestion that arises from time to time is that people came straight across the ocean. Although he does not take that idea very seriously, Dennis Stanford notes that people have in fact proven that you could float across the Atlantic without much effort. Thor Heyerdahl, who made a career out of confusing possibility with history, suggested that people from Easter Island could easily have floated over to the South American coast. Of course, even if evidence existed that they had done so (and it doesn't), it would have had nothing to do with the earliest settlement of the Americas. The settlement of Easter Island and the rest of the South Pacific islands and archipelagos took place within the last few millennia, not anywhere near time as deep as Clovis. Madsen dismisses all the notions of what might be called oceanic drift: "It is conceivably possible that a lost boat-load of seafarers could have washed up on the shores of the New World, albeit very unlikely, but the presence of continuous trans-oceanic exchange at this time depth will have to be demonstrated before these colonization scenarios can be taken seriously."

PRE-MAX

Yet another hypothesis has recently been put forth for consideration by David Madsen and a variety of colleagues. Let us at least assume that, one way or another, the first Americans came from Asia. We can also guess with some confidence that at the glacial maximum, beginning about 20,000 years ago, Siberia was not only an awful place but for all intents and purposes, an uninhabitable one. This even applies for people who had bone needles and could sew skins together into tailored fur suits, and the same is to be said for Beringia and the better part of Alaska. People had moved into subarctic Siberia when it was warmer, between about 30,000 and 20,000 years ago, with most of the known sites dating from 24,000 to 20,000 B.P., just before the last glacial maximum (or LGM). There they developed the techniques to make a living in cold desert-steppe landscape. After that period, traces of people are not found; they all appear to have moved south again when the far north became uninhabitable. No one in his right mind would have gone there then, and people who did would likely have perished without a trace.

So suppose people began to move across Beringia starting about 24,000 years ago, tracking the mammoths and other creatures big and small they were used to hunting. What would have awaited them on the American side? Ice. And lots of it. Starting about 30,000 years ago, the Laurentide glacier extended across the northern Canadian plains and heaved up against the Canadian Rockies. In other words, there was no ice-free corridor through that part of the continent until after 11,000 B.P.

But it seems there was indeed one ice-free way to go south, along the north–south lowlands that lie between the interiors of Alaska and the Yukon and the unglaciated valleys of the Cordillera in the Pacific Northwest. Up until about 20,000 years ago, these valleys may well have remained habitable, even as the Cordilleran ice sheet began to coalesce out of many separate montane glaciers. Timing is, of course, everything: if the valleys were still passable by about 20,000 B.P., the colonization of the

Americas could have begun about that time or earlier. But if the valleys were impassable by about 22,000 B.P., a pre-LGM entry seems less likely.

This pre-LGM entry also depends on the speed with which hunters and gatherers could be expected to expand into uninhabited space. Many mathematically elegant models have been devised to determine such migration rates: they include population growth rates as well as diffusion rates and figures for such arcane matters as optimal foraging theory and estimates of edible biomass in the neighborhood. A couple of early models agreed that foragers could have expanded from Alaska to Tierra del Fuego, some ten thousand miles, in a thousand years; another said it would have taken two thousand years max to fill both continents. That's about ten miles a year, which hardly seems excessive when thought of as actual distance traversed each year, even when these new Americans would be passing through many different ecosystems, each with its own climate conditions, prey animals, and so forth. Presumably, people newly adapted to the subarctic conditions of Siberia 24,000 years ago could have sustained the same migratory rate across Beringia and into Alaska, especially given the fact that the same conditions (weather, animals, etc.) prevailed throughout the region. Little new would have had to be learned.

But as David Madsen points out, if people had started traveling from Lake Baikal 24,000 years ago, headed, however inadvertently, for the New World, moving at ten miles a year would have brought them to Denver, Colorado, by the year 23,450 B.P. Even with a low-end birthrate, they would have marched to Denver by 22,900 B.P. And of course, there is no archaeological evidence to suggest that people were in Denver that early. If people got here that early, there should be a recurrent pattern of sites with carbon dates ranging between, say, 22,000 and 12,000 years ago. So what happened?

Madsen is not about to buy the quick-march-to-Denver scenario. In fact, he suggests it as a way of casting doubt on *all* the blitz-through-the-Americas migration models. Instead, he suggests the possibility that archaeologists simply may not be seeing many pre-Clovis sites for the same reasons noted by Gamble: they are the sites of pioneering people, both insubstantial and few and far between. For example, had it not been for the lucky break of anaerobic preservation under the peat in Monte Verde, the only artifacts that would exist there for archaeologists to look at would have been a handful of broken rocks, only a few of which were clearly shaped by the hand of man. Much of the Monte Verde tool kit was, of course, made from perishable materials, and it is highly likely that the major portion of the tool kit of early Americans is much the same—invisible by virtue of no longer existing. Also, as noted earlier, finds of rocks that appeared to be fashioned into choppers and hand axes and that were assumed to be ancient as often as not turned out to be the products of more recent Indian people. The flip side could also be true: hastily described sites could be seen as having modern Indian material that is in fact Paleolithic in origin. There are, in short, many ways that we might be blind to pre-Clovis, pre-LGM sites.

Of course, this is pretty weak tea for an archaeologist to suggest, and Madsen says that overlooking sites may well play a small part. What is needed as a matter of theory here is something that would explain why candidate pre-Clovis sites are quantitatively so rare. It may well have to do not so much with archaeologists' general myopia but with the fact that their minds are still clouded somewhat by one aspect of the old story: the notion that a group of people arrived at some point in what was a land of plenty, pumped out babies at an astonishing rate, and spread across the landscape faster than an invasion of dandelions. This notion of blitzkrieg migration is an inheritance from the mathematical models of migration that were "tweaked," Madsen says, in order to make sense out of theories that bring humans to these shores later rather than earlier. Part of *this* presupposition is another—that the New World was a grand cornucopia, a world where all the major food groups were present and easily harvested, begging to be mowed down, offering themselves up for the good of the newcomers in the manner of modern Indian tribes' most cherished stories.

It might not have been *that* welcoming a place in those days—as Madsen says, not exactly the Garden of Eden or Paul Martin's Clovisia the Beautiful. For one thing, short-faced bears would have been around before the glacial maximum and might well have eaten a whole lot of pioneers. The first Americans may not have made out like overkilling Clovis bandits; instead they may pretty much have huddled in familiar ground, hunting familiar animals and collecting familiar plants for long, long periods of time, even as they experienced lower birthrates and a lot more mortality—especially, but not only, child mortality. In a situation in which a band of people—essentially a large extended family—found that its membership was likely to be depleted every now and then by disease, accident, or large predator, the likelihood of their setting off happily (or even unhappily) for points totally unknown, far away from other potential mates, would seem unlikely. Just because they did not have computers yet doesn't mean that these people were stupid.

Most models of forager migration rates are of necessity based on ethnographic information derived from, at the earliest, the nineteenth century on into today, a period when most hunter-gatherers surely have faced a different world than the first Americans did. Today, there are no saber-toothed cats and no gigantic predatory bears that can run as fast as a horse. The bands and tribes studied in modern times by anthropologists and others have had thousands of years to work out a way of life based on the ecosystems in which they find themselves, not to mention the benefit of metal tools and trinkets supplied by neighboring sedentary folk, missionaries, traders, and curious anthropologists. For pioneers arriving from generations of living in subarctic conditions, most of the New World would have been staggeringly new, and probably bewilderingly so at first.

Looking at all this from another angle, if early folk with Siberian lifestyles were in such an all-fired rush to get to Tierra del Fuego, why weren't early anatomically modern folk in a similar rush to populate Europe and Asia once they left Africa, or to fill up Australia at a rate of ten miles per year once they got there from southeastern Asia? Evidently it took more than 13,000 years for anatomical moderns to fill Europe from its southeastern margins, and this is also about the rate at which Australia filled up. It seems that in Australia, once people got there by boat, there was a period of some 30,000 years when the population size remained nearly stationary, growing very slowly. The result is relatively few Aussie archaeological sites dating to before the Holocene—just as in the New World.

This, then, is what Madsen calls the Pre–Late Glacial Maximum hypothesis. Like all the others, it is filled with ifs and maybes. It has the advantage of according with such nonarchaeological insights as Nichols's linguistics, which suggest that people arrived in the New World in plenty of time to have moved eastward across North America and to reach Meadowcroft. Nor does it necessarily *preclude* arrivals via other routes in later times. Currently, there are five certain pre-Clovis sites in the Americas, and there may be as many as twelve in all. Except for Cactus Hill and Meadowcroft, where the tool kits are similarly manufactured though of different materials, all these pre-Clovis sites and candidate sites manifest very different technologies from one another (as well as from Clovis). So we do not have what archaeologists would call a Pre-Clovis culture: we have a number of pre-Clovis cultures, none of which appears to be the parent technology of Clovis or even a distant relative. So at present we still have no idea where Clovis and its fluted points came from; this remains a worthy question for today's and tomorrow's archaeologists.

Indeed, all the old questions remain unanswered: who, when, and how. But the very existence of such a high level of cultural variability in pre-Clovis times, and for that matter in Clovis times as well, strongly suggests that there were multiple incursions into this hemisphere by people who were probably diverse genetically, using the ice-free corridor when it was available, the less formidable coastal route, *and* one of the other routes before the last glacial maximum as well as after it. Multiple routes would, of course, accord with both the linguistic and genetic evidence that several groups migrated here several times over the millennia.

A WHOLE NEW WORLD

Today, the study of the early peopling of the New World is vibrant and alive with possibilities. The questions with which we began this book and this chapter—who were those guys, when did they get here, and how?—remain without definitive answers. What we can say is that we have peeled back a lot of layers of ignorance over the past century or so. At the very least, we now know better who those guys weren't: they were neither the lost tribes of Israel nor the Atlanteans, they weren't Neanderthal-like, and they didn't get here only a few thousand years ago. They weren't a single band of anyone, much less a band of fifty or a hundred turbocharged hunters.

Today there are multiple routes to explore, multiple times to pin down, multiple groups of people who were potentially those early pioneers. Whereas a hundred years ago the archaeologist's quiver had very few arrows, today an expanding host of new disciplines and subdisciplines is brought to bear on the old questions, each in turn raising new questions to the answers, which then raise even more questions. Are we getting close to answering the basic questions of who, when, and how? Who knows? It is not at all impossible that some students who are now undergraduates in college, thinking about a career in archaeology, or maybe some kids in high school, thinking mostly about the opposite gender, will become famous for having found the unmistakable traces of the very first Americans. If so, I hope it will be one of my students, although I would not wish on any of them the kind of vituperative and pestiferous melee that I have dealt with over the past three decades. Perhaps now that the Clovis curtain has been pulled down and its only remaining proponents are considered extremists, the field of early-man studies can go forth more in the European manner proposed by Doug Price—without such acrimony, but instead with a cooperative spirit.

I would not count on that. And lest everyone start feeling all warm and fuzzy, there is another *big* problem to which I have alluded here and there in this account and that still plagues most studies of the peopling of the Americas, especially the North American studies. It is embodied in the question "Who are those *guys*?" as well as in the phrase I let slip just a paragraph back—"early-*man* studies."

It is all very well to establish where the first Americans came from and how they got here and when, but a far more important question in the long run is surely this: How did they go about the business of living and succeeding in a new land? For a century in New World studies and more than twice as long in the Old World, the lifestyles question has been focused on what males did. There are several reasons for this gender myopia. First, up until recently it was mostly males doing the archaeology. Second, the archaeological record, by nature, has preserved stone tools, the traditional province of males—or so we would like to believe—at the expense of more perishable items, the likely realm of females, and it has strongly shaped our interpretational biases to this very day. If we have ignored the role of females despite the best efforts of a whole recent cadre of feminist archaeologists, what of children and old people of either sex? In the Clovis scenarios, they are largely ignored, except to be imagined as something of a drag, slowing down the great intercontinental bloodbath.

This gender bias is changing, slowly perhaps, but fast enough that a new view is inevitable, and this is not necessarily only because more women are involved in archaeology, though that certainly is a great part of it. (After all, the answers you get often depend on the questions you ask.)

The new view, though, is also a result of the facts. As early as the 1960s, the late Walter Taylor noted that in his excavations in a series of dry caves in Coahuila in the 1940s, finished perishable fiber artifacts were four times more common than artifacts of wood and *twenty* times more common than stone tools. This same ratio has been found again and again in hundreds of dry caves, rockshelters, and other contexts where conditions favored the preservation of *all* of a group's technology. Much the same ratios of fiber, wood, and stone artifacts are found in hunter-gatherer societies of more recent times, even in Arctic and sub-Arctic settings.

And for the archaeologist who attends to this common aspect of the hunting-gathering life, an entirely new picture emerges. At least as far back as the late Pleistocene, there is plenty of evidence that people were making things out of plant fiber, weaving it into baskets, cordage, nets, sandals, and textiles in both the Old World and the Americas. The oldest such arti-

Artist's reconstruction of late Ice Age net hunter emphasizing plant fiber–based technology and the role of women in Ice Age economies.

fact known so far from North America is the piece of basketry found at Meadowcroft dating between about 12,800 and 11,300 years ago. There is also a far older Meadowcroft perishable that is between 19,000 and 17,000 years old, a single element of what appears to be intentionally cut birchlike bark similar in shape to the strips later employed in Meadowcroft plaiting. If this single strip is indeed what we think it is, it is not only the oldest piece of perishable technology in the hemisphere, but it makes a pre–late glacial maximum arrival practically a certainty.

Elsewhere throughout the Americas, from Clovis-era sites and those that are younger, sophisticated fiber artifacts have turned up in quantity. Little doubt can remain that such artifacts were an important part of the armamentarium of the first Americans. Cross-cultural studies of hunter-gatherers and other tribal people suggest that the making of fiber artifacts—textiles, basketry, nets, and so forth—is associated with both sexes. Among the Hopi, women make baskets and men do the weaving, but other

Cache of Clovis points and assorted
tools from the Anzick site, Montana.

evidence suggests that in pre-market societies, basketry, and weaving in particular, is normally the labor of women. So we may take the presence of such materials in an archaeological site as signs of the presence there of the women of the band—a presence which has almost universally been overlooked. The existence of this "soft" technology—as Bob Bettinger of the University of California, Davis, calls it—has profound implications for our understanding of these people's behavior and even social organization. The presence of such artifacts dating back into the late Pleistocene and before suggests that perhaps the ability to make use of plant fibers in order to produce useful objects was one of the first major steps in the development of modern humanity as we understand it.

Even without such wide-ranging speculation, the existence in the late Pleistocene of the kind of knots needed to make nets, what are called sheet bends or weaver's knots, is highly suggestive. Hunting with nets is a communal affair. It takes relatively less expertise to succeed and is a lot less dangerous than confrontational hunting of the sort accomplished with spears and javelins. As a result, net hunting uses the entire group—women, children, and geezers, as well as the hunting-age men. Ethnographic studies have shown that it takes a long time for a young adult male to become

Funeral of Clovis First.

truly proficient as a hunter; only after ten or fifteen years, between the ages of twenty-five and thirty, do men in several South American tribes today learn enough to reach their maximum hunting efficiency. On the other hand, net hunting permits virtually all hands to help garner much-needed protein without putting women and children at risk. Netting also suggests large harvests of meat in a short period of time, which in turn would permit large gatherings, feasts, ceremonialism, dancing . . . a heightened camaraderie. By keeping perishable artifacts and the role of women in mind, we are able to present a less testosterone-infused and ultimately more likely alternative to the Clovis big-game model.

THE GREAT ADVENTURE

Someone once wrote that the movement of humans into the New World would be the last great continental-scale colonizing effort of our species until we quit this planet for another. Whoever those first colonists were and whenever they got here, imagine the adrenaline rush of realizing you were embarked on a trip into country where no one had ever been before. (Would the first Americans have known that was what they were doing? Probably they would have realized it before too long—after all, they would not have seen any thin columns of smoke rising on the horizon ahead.) After a while, it would dawn on you that you and the members of your group were strangers in a very strange land, all alone in this place with its exotic plants and animals and its utterly new landforms.

That is the kind of rush that most of us will never experience, and indeed, most of the details of that ancient, dangerous, arduous adventure will remain unknown—lost, forever fragmentary, a matter of guesswork based on small, adventitious clusters of evidence that have long lain mute in the ground and remain, to a greater or lesser degree, enigmatic. But that such things, these dim tracks and artifacts of so distant a past, can still speak to us, however haltingly, and that they still have so much more to say . . . that is the great adventure available to us.

AFTERWORD

As this book goes to press, it is worth noting that the Kennewick issue remains unresolved and as contentious as ever. A hearing was held in federal appeals court in Portland, Oregon, on June 19–20, 2001. Attendees included not only all but one of the aggrieved plaintiffs in *Bonnichsen et al. v. the United States of America,* representatives of the claimant tribes, the Army Corps of Engineers, and the Department of the Interior, but also interested third parties such as the Society for American Archaeology, the press, various Native American activists, and yours truly. The presiding magistrate, John Jelderks, valiantly attempted to unravel what Paleo-Indian scholar Brad Lepper has called the "Gordian knot controversy." He very diligently explored the opposing positions on a variety of issues, the most basic of which were the appropriateness of Bruce Babbitt's decision to repatriate the Kennewick remains and, more fundamentally, the reality of the alleged cultural affiliation between Kennewick and the claimant tribes.

Jelderks made it clear—at least to this not very impartial spectator—that he was not very sympathetic to the government's position and yet at the same time he took exception to some of the scientists' positions as well. Given the notoriety and gravity of the case, as well as the fact that the outcome will almost surely be appealed to the U.S. Supreme Court, Jelderks warned that his decision would be carefully considered and not delivered any time soon. This prophecy has proven accurate.

Whatever the outcome, I can only reiterate that the Kennewick remains will probably not fundamentally alter our understanding of the chronology of the peopling of the New World, no matter what the final disposition is.

On another, still-unfolding, front—and to my mind, a far more exciting one—are the continuing excavations at the Gault site. Gault is a very large and deeply stratified open site covering more than thirty acres on the Edwards Plateau of central Texas. To date, it has yielded abundant archaeological evidence of human occupation extending back to at least Clovis times, ca. 11,200 years ago, as well as tantalizing hints of even older occupations. Though collectors have plundered Gault's Archaic and more recent horizons for more than eighty years (often with the active collaboration and encouragement of past landowners), the deeper, older deposits have largely escaped despoliation.

In 1990, David Olmstead, an amateur archaeologist, recovered in a deep excavation two Clovis points associated with elaborately incised stones, which were brought to the attention of the University of Texas at Austin in 1991. University of Texas archaeologists ultimately confirmed the existence of a deeply buried Clovis component at Gault, which in turn led to extensive professional excavations by scholars from a variety of aca-

Mike Collins, director of
the excavations of Gault.

demic institutions and the Texas Archaeological Society. The work there has gone on under the overall supervision and coordination of Mike Collins (he of Monte Verde fame) and the auspices of the Texas Archaeological Research Laboratory.

At the time of writing, not only have the archaeologists on the Gault excavations team identified and explored later Paleo-Indian manifestations like Folsom and Midland but, perhaps most significantly, they've recovered almost 500,000 pieces of worked stone, as well as bone, ivory, and animal teeth, attributable to Clovis times. Gault is the largest collection of Clovis materials from any one site in North America, and according to Collins's estimates, it may even have yielded half of all the Clovis material found in stratified context in *all* of North America!

This density of material is by no means reflective of the pattern of a few artifacts left by a handful of highly mobile mammoth hunters, as predicted by the Clovis Firsters. Instead, it clearly indicates the presence of a large and perhaps even semisedentary population exploiting not just—or even mainly—mammoths, but rather a great diversity of local resources, which at any other later time in the site's history would be synonymous with a generalized Archaic lifestyle. As Collins speculates, Paleo-Indians were probably drawn to Gault for the same reasons as their Archaic "successors," namely that the location of Gault at an ecotonal boundary or frontier between ecological zones provided a richly diverse and abundant supply of broad-spectrum resources for hunter-gatherers at all time periods.

*Ongoing excavations in the Clovis horizon
at the Gault site.*

About 27.5 inches below the Clovis occupation there are flakes that are most likely of pre-Clovis ascription. While this is certainly worth noting, it is the sheer size of Gault's Clovis occupation that in both Collins's view and my own seriously undermines the traditional view of Clovis First. Gault is no overnight campsite for a small band of highly mobile Clovis elephant killers. Nor for that matter are Shoop in Pennsylvania, Thunderbird and Williamson in Virginia, or Carson-Conn-Short in Tennessee. No, these are very large Clovis base camps reflective not of ephemeral populations thinly spread across the landscape, populations who got here "yesterday" in Ice Age terms, but unambiguous evidence of the residential phase of colonization by groups who may have first ventured here 5,000 or even 10,000 years earlier. Indeed, large sites like Gault *are* the visible evidence of Gamble's residential phase of colonization.

As Collins said in Santa Fe, this *is* an exciting time to be an archaeologist. Places like Gault and others yet to be discovered ensure that the great adventure can only continue.

BIBLIOGRAPHY

A NOTE ON SOURCES

What follows are the main sources used in the process of compiling this book. A number of sources were helpful throughout, and they are listed first under the head "General." The rest are listed chapter by chapter. A complete bibliography of the entire subject of the early peopling of the New World, including technical reports, reviews, books, and popular accounts, would go on for more pages than taken up by this entire book and would serve little purpose in this context.

I am told that I sometimes seem a bit contentious about the work that has gone on these past several decades at Meadowcroft Rockshelter, so, by way of providing readers with a chance to pursue my claims for this site further, I have included as complete a list of Meadowcroft publications and papers as I could compile as of this writing. They include not only works produced directly under my supervision or with my collaboration and participation, but also a limited number of popular treatments produced by journalists.—J.M.A.

GENERAL

Carlisle, R. C., ed. "Americans Before Columbus: Ice-Age Origins." *Ethnology Monographs,* vol. 12. Pittsburgh: Department of Anthropology, University of Pittsburgh, 1988.

Daniel, G. *A Hundred and Fifty Years of Archaeology.* Cambridge, Mass.: Harvard University Press, 1976.

Dillehay, T. D., and D. J. Meltzer. *The First Americans: Search and Research.* Boca Raton, Fla.: CRC Press, 1991.

Fagan, B. M. *The Great Journey: The Peopling of Ancient America.* New York: Thames and Hudson, 1987.

———. *Ancient North America: The Archaeology of a Continent.* New York: Thames and Hudson, 1995.

Meltzer, D. J. *Search for the First Americans.* Washington, D.C.: Smithsonian Books, 1993.

Willey, G. R., and J. A. Sabloff. *A History of American Archaeology,* 3d ed. New York: W. H. Freeman and Company, 1993.

OVERTURE: NOT FOR THE TIMID OF HEART

Deloria, V., Jr. *Red Earth, White Lies: Native Americans and the Myth of Scientific Fact.* New York: Scribner, 1995.

CHAPTER ONE: GLIMPSES THROUGH THE LOOKING GLASS

Driver, H. E., ed. *The Americas on the Eve of Discovery.* Englewood Cliffs, N.J.: Prentice-Hall, 1964.

Grayson, Donald K. *The Establishment of Human Antiquity.* New York: Academic Press, 1983.

———. "Americans Before Columbus: Perspectives on the Archaeology of the First Americans." In "Americans Before Columbus: Ice-Age Origins," edited by R. C. Carlisle, 107–123. *Ethnology Monographs,* vol. 12. Pittsburgh: Department of Anthropology, University of Pittsburgh, 1988.

———. "Nineteenth-Century Explanations of Pleistocene Extinctions: A Review and Analysis." In *Quaternary Extinctions: A Prehistoric Revolution,* edited by P. S. Martin and R. G. Klein, 5–39. Tucson: University of Arizona Press, 1984.

Henige, D. *Numbers from Nowhere: The American Indian Contact Population Debate.* Norman: University of Oklahoma Press, 1998.

Honour, H. *The European Vision of America.* Cleveland: Cleveland Museum of Art, 1975.

Lehner, E., and J. Lehner. *How They Saw the World.* New York: Tudor Publishing Company, 1966.

Rouse, I. *The Tainos: Rise and Decline of the People Who Greeted Columbus.* New Haven, Conn.: Yale University Press, 1992.

Settipane, G. A. *Columbus and the New World: Medical Implications.* Providence, R.I.: Oceanside Publications, 1995.

Silverberg, R. *The Mound Builders.* Athens: Ohio University Press, 1970.

CHAPTER TWO: THE GLACIER'S EDGE

Flint, R. F. *Glacial and Quaternary Geology.* New York: John Wiley and Sons, 1971.

Officer, C., and J. Page. *Tales of the Earth.* New York: Oxford University Press, 1993.

Sibrava, V., D. Q. Bowen, and G. M. Richmond. *Quaternary Glaciations in the Northern Hemisphere.* Oxford: Pergamon Press, 1986.

Sugden, D. E., and B. S. John. *Glaciers and Landscape.* London: Edward Arnold, 1997.

Wright, H. E., J. E. Kutzbach, T. Webb III, W. F. Ruddiman, F. A. Street-Perrott, and P. J. Bartlein. *Global Climates Since the Last Glacial Maximum*. Minneapolis: University of Minnesota Press, 1993.

CHAPTER THREE: CHARISMATIC MEGAFAUNA

Ainsworth, C. "Love That Fat." *New Scientist,* September 16, 2000.

Geist, V. "Periglacial Ecology, Large Mammals, and Their Significance to Human Biology." In *Ice Age People of North America,* edited by R. Bonnichsen and K. L. Turnmire, 79–84. Corvallis: Center for the Study of the First Americans, Oregon State University Press, 1999.

Kurtén, B. *Before the Indians.* New York: Columbia University Press, 1988.

CHAPTER FOUR: GOOD-BYE, GLACIAL MAN; HELLO, CLOVIS

Boldurian, A. T., and J. L. Cotter. *Clovis Revisited: New Perspectives on Paleoindian Adaptations from Blackwater Draw, New Mexico.* Philadelphia: University Museum, University of Pennsylvania, 1999.

Meltzer, D. J. "The Antiquity of Man and the Development of American Archaeology." In *Advances in Archaeological Method and Theory,* vol. 6, edited by M. B. Schiffer, 1–51. New York: Academic Press, 1983.

———. "The Discovery of Deep Time: A History of Views on the Peopling of the Americas." In *Method and Theory for Investigating the Peopling of the Americas,* edited by R. Bonnichsen and D. G. Steele, 7–26. Corvallis: Center for the Study of the First Americans, Oregon State University Press, 1994.

———. "On 'Paradigms' and 'Paradigm Bias' in Controversies Over Human Antiquity in America." In *The First Americans: Search and Research,* edited by T. Dillehay and D. Meltzer, 13–49. Boca Raton: CRC Press, 1991.

Stegner, Wallace. *Beyond the Hundredth Meridien.* Lincoln: University of Nebraska Press, 1953.

Van Riper, A. B. *Men and Mammoths: Victorian Science and the Discovery of Human Prehistory.* Chicago: University of Chicago Press, 1993.

CHAPTER FIVE: TIMING IS EVERYTHING

Grayson, D. K. "Nineteenth-Century Explanations of Pleistocene Extinctions: A Review and Analysis." In *Quaternary Extinctions: A Prehistoric Revolution,* edited by P. S. Martin and R. G. Klein, 5–39. Tucson: University of Arizona Press. 1984.

Klein, R. G. *The Human Career: Human Biological and Cultural Origins.* 2d ed. Chicago: University of Chicago Press, 1999.

Martin, P. S. "Pleistocene Overkill." *Natural History* 76, 10 (1967): 32–38.

———, and R. G. Klein, eds. *Quaternary Extinctions: A Prehistoric Revolution.* Tucson: University of Arizona Press, 1984.

Mead, J. I., and D. J. Meltzer. *Environments and Extinction: Man in Late Glacial America.* Orono: Center for the Study of Early Man, University of Maine, 1985.

Meltzer, D. J., and J. I. Mead. "Dating Late Pleistocene Extinctions: Theoretical Issues, Analytical Bias, and Substantive Results." In *Environments and Extinctions: Man in Late Glacial North America,* edited by J. I. Mead and D. J. Meltzer, 145–173. Orono: Center for the Study of Early Man, University of Maine, 1985.

CHAPTER SIX: THE PRE-CLOVIS QUEST

Haynes, C. V., and G. A. Agogino. "Geochronology of Sandia Cave." In *Smithsonian Contributions to Anthropology* no. 32. Washington, D.C.: Smithsonian Institution Press, 1986.

Hibben, F. C. *The Lost Americans.* New York: T. Y. Crowell Company, 1946.

McGowan, K., and J. A. Hester, Jr. *Early Man in the New World.* Garden City, N.Y.: Doubleday and Company, 1962.

Preston, D. "The Mystery of Sandia Cave." *The New Yorker,* June 12, 1995, 66–83.

CHAPTER SEVEN: MELEE OVER MEADOWCROFT

Adovasio, J. M., J. Donahue, R. C. Carlisle, K. Cushman, R. Stuckenrath, and P. Wiegman. "Meadowcroft Rockshelter and the Pleistocene/Holocene Transition in Southwestern Pennsylvania." In *Contributions in Quaternary Vertebrate Paleontology: A Volume in Memorial to John E. Guilday,* edited by H. H. Genoways and M. R. Dawson, *Carnegie Museum of Natural History Special Publication* no. 8, 347–369. Pittsburgh: Carnegie Museum of Natural History, 1984.

Adovasio, J. M., J. Donahue, and R. Stuckenrath. "The Meadowcroft Rockshelter Radiocarbon Chronology 1975–1990." *American Antiquity* 55, 2 (1990): 348–354.

Dincauze, D. F. "The Meadowcroft Papers." In *Quarterly Review of Archaeology* 2 (1981): 3–4.

Donahue, J., and J. M. Adovasio. "Evolution of Sandstone Rockshelters in Eastern North America: A Geoarchaeological Perspective." In *Archaeological Geology of North America: Centennial Special,* vol. 4, edited by N. P. Lasca and J. Donahue. Boulder, Colo.: Geological Society of America, 1990.

Goldberg, P., and T. L. Arpin. "Micromorphological Analysis of Sediments from Meadowcroft Rockshelter, Pennsylvania: Implications for Radiocarbon Dating." *Journal of Field Archaeology* 26, 3 (1999): 325–342.

Guilday, J. E., and P. W. Parmalee. "Vertebrate Faunal Remains from Meadowcroft Rockshelter, Washington County, Pennsylvania: Summary and Interpretation." In *Meadowcroft: Collected Papers on the Archaeology of Meadowcroft Rockshelter and the Cross Creek Drainage,* edited by R. C. Carlisle and J. M. Adovasio (1984): 163–174. Paper presented at the symposium "The Meadowcroft Rockshelter Rolling Thunder Review: Last Act." 47th Annual Meeting of the Society for American Archaeology, Minneapolis, Minnesota, April 14–17, 1982.

Volman, K. C. "Paleoenvironmental Implications of Botanical Data from Meadowcroft Rockshelter, Pennsylvania." Ph.D. dissertation, Graduate College of Texas A&M University, 1981.

CHAPTER EIGHT: ANOTHER ANGLE OF VIEW

Adovasio, J. M., and D. R. Pedler. "Monte Verde and the Antiquity of Humankind in the Americas." *Antiquity* 71, 273 (1997): 573–580.

Dillehay, T. D. *Monte Verde: A Late Pleistocene Settlement in Chile,* vol. 1, *The Paleoenvironmental Context.* Washington, D.C.: Smithsonian Institution Press, 1989.

———. *Monte Verde: A Late Pleistocene Settlement in Chile,* vol. 2, *The Archaeological Context.* Washington, D.C.: Smithsonian Institution Press, 1997.

———. *Monte Verde: A Late Pleistocene Settlement in Chile,* vol. 2, *The Archaeological Context and Interpretation, Errata.* Washington, D.C.: Smithsonian Institution Press, 2002.

———. *The Settlement of the Americas.* New York: Basic Books, 2000.

Lavallée, D. *The First South Americans: The Peopling of a Continent from the Earliest Evidence to High Culture.* Translated by P. G. Bahn. Salt Lake City: University of Utah Press, 2000.

Meltzer, D. J., J. M. Adovasio, and T. D. Dillehay. "On a Pleistocene Human Occupation at Pedra Furada, Brazil." *Antiquity* 68, 261 (1994): 695–714.

Meltzer, D. J., D. K. Grayson, G. Ardila, A. W. Barker, D. F. Dincauze, C. V. Haynes, F. Mena, L. Núñez, and D. J. Stanford. "On the Pleistocene Antiquity of Monte Verde, Southern Chile." *American Antiquity* 62, 4 (1997): 659–663.

CHAPTER NINE: FIREWORKS AND THE PALEO-POLICE

Meltzer, D. J., D. K. Grayson, G. Ardila, A. W. Barker, D. F. Dincauze, C. V. Haynes, F. Mena, L. Núñez, and D. J. Stanford. "On the Pleistocene Antiquity of Monte Verde, Southern Chile." *American Antiquity* 62, 4 (1997): 659–663.

CHAPTER TEN: THREE-LEGGED STOOLS AND SKULL WARS

Begley, S., and A. Murr. "The First Americans." *Newsweek,* April 26, 1999, 50–58.

Cann, R. L. "Genetic Clues to Dispersal in Human Populations: Retracing the Past from the Present." *Science* 291, 5509 (2001): 1742–1748.

Chatters, J. C. "The Recovery and First Analysis of an Early Holocene Human Skeleton from Kennewick, Washington." *American Antiquity* 65, 2 (2000): 291–316.

Downey, R. *Riddle of the Bones: Politics, Science, Race, and the Story of Kennewick Man.* New York: Copernicus, 2000.

Feder, K. L. *The Past in Perspective: An Introduction to Prehistory,* 2d ed. Mountain View, Calif.: Mayfield Publishing Company, 2000.

Goddard, I., and L. Campbell. "The History and Classification of Indian Languages: What Are the Implications for the People of the Americas?" In *Method and Theory for Investigating the Peopling of the Americas,* edited by R. Bonnichsen and D. G. Steele, 189–208. Corvallis: Center for the Study of the First Americans, Oregon State University Press, 1994.

Nichols, J. *Linguistic Diversity and the Peopling of the Americas.* Berkeley: University of California Press, 1995.

Schurr, T. G. "Genetic Diversity in Siberians and Native Americans Suggests an Early Migration to the New World." In *Entering America: Northeast Asia and Beringia Before the Last Glacial Maximum,* edited by D. B. Madsen. Salt Lake City: University of Utah Press, 2002.

Smith, D. G., R. S. Malhi, J. Eshleman, J. G. Lorenz, and F. A. Kaestle. "Distribution of mtDNA Haplogroup X Among Native North Americans. *American Journal of Physical Anthropology* 110, 3 (1999): 271–284.

CHAPTER ELEVEN: WHO ARE THOSE GUYS?

Dixon, J. E. *Quest for the Origins of the First Americans.* Albuquerque: University of New Mexico Press, 1993.

Fagan, B. M. *People of the Earth: An Introduction to World Prehistory,* 10th ed. Upper Saddle River, N.J.: Prentice Hall, 2001.

Haynes, C. V., Jr. "Clovis, Pre-Clovis, Climate Change, and Extinctions." Manuscript for review, on file, Mercyhurst College, 2001.

Housley, R. A., C. S. Gamble, M. Street, and P. Pettitt. "Radiocarbon Evidence for the Lateglacial Human Recolonisation of Northern Europe." *Proceedings of the Prehistoric Society* 63 (1997): 25–54.

Madsen, D. B., ed. *Entering America: Northeast Asia and Beringia Before the Last Glacial Maximum.* Salt Lake City: University of Utah Press, 2002.

AFTERWORD

Collins, Michael B. "The Gault Site, Texas, and Clovis Research." *Athena Review* 3, 2 (2002).

MEADOWCROFT PUBLICATIONS

Adovasio, J. M. "The AENA Compilation of Fluted Points in Eastern North America: A Perspective from Meadowcroft Rockshelter." In *Archaeology of Eastern North America: Fluted Point Survey,* vol. 11, edited by R. M. Gramly, 6–11. Buffalo, New York: Buffalo Museum of Science, 1983.

———. "The Appearance of Cultigens in the Upper Ohio Valley: A View from Meadowcroft Rockshelter." Paper presented at the 45th Annual Meeting of the Society for American Archaeology, Philadelphia, Pennsylvania, May 1–3, 1980.

———. "Early Human Populations in the Upper Ohio Valley: A View from Meadowcroft Rockshelter." Paper presented at the First Discovery of America Conference on Ohio's Earliest Inhabitants, Ohio Archaeological Council, Columbus, Ohio, 1992.

———. "Meadowcroft Rockshelter." In *The Oxford Companion to Archaeology,* edited by B. M. Fagan, 415–416. Oxford: Oxford University Press, 1996.

———. "Meadowcroft Rockshelter: A 16,000-Year Chronicle." Paper presented at the Annual Meeting of the American Anthropological Association, San Francisco, 1975.

———. "Meadowcroft Rockshelter and the Peopling of the New World." Paper presented at the Quaternary Land-Sea Migration Bridges and Human Occupation of Submerged Coastlines Symposium, Scripps Institute of Oceanography, La Jolla, California, 1981.

———. "The Miller Complex." In *Archaeology of Prehistoric North America: An Encyclopedia,* edited by G. Gibbon, 524–526. New York: Garland Press, 1998.

———. "Multidisciplinary Research in the Northeast: One View from Meadowcroft Rockshelter." *Pennsylvania Archaeologist* 53, 3–4 (1982): 57–68.

———. "The Ones That Will Not Go Away: A Biased View of Pre-Clovis Populations in the New World." Paper presented at Stalking the Mammoth Hunters: From Kostenki to Clovis Plenary Session, 55th Annual Meeting of the Society for American Archaeology, Las Vegas, Nevada, 1990.

———. "The Ones That Will Not Go Away: A Biased View of Pre-Clovis Populations in the New World." In *From Kostenki to Clovis: Upper Paleolithic-Paleo-Indian Adaptations,* edited by O. Soffer and N. D. Praslov, 199–218. New York: Plenum Press, 1993.

———. "Perishable Artifacts, Paleoindians, and Dying Paradigms." Paper presented at the Clovis and Beyond—Peopling of the Americas Conference, Santa Fe, New Mexico, 1999.

———. "Pre-Clovis Populations in the New World." Paper presented at the Soviet-American Archaeological Field Symposium, U.S.S.R., 1989.

Adovasio, J. M., and R. L. Andrews. "The Origins of Perishable Production East of the Rockies." Paper presented at Symposium 31: Perishable Fiber Industries from Eastern North America; Conservation, Analysis, and Interpretation, 49th Annual Meeting of the Society for American Archaeology, Portland, Oregon, April 11–14, 1984.

Adovasio, J. M., and A. T. Boldurian. "Who Are Those Guys? An Examination of the Pre-Clovis Flintworking Complex from Meadowcroft Rockshelter and the Cross Creek Drainage." Paper presented at the 51st Annual Meeting of the Society for American Archaeology, New Orleans, Louisiana, 1986.

———. "Who Are Those Guys? Some Biased Thoughts on the Initial Peopling of the New World." Paper presented at the Americans Before Columbus: Ice Age Origins Symposium in Honor of T. Dale Stewart, Smithsonian Institution, Washington, D.C., 1987.

Adovasio, J. M., A. T. Boldurian, and R. C. Carlisle. "Archaeological Research Activities of the University of Pittsburgh in 1984." *Current Research in the Pleistocene* 2 (1985): 3–5.

———. "Who Are Those Guys?: Early Human Populations in Eastern North America." Paper presented at "Mammoths, Mastodons, and Human Interactions," A National Symposium on Late Pleistocene Archaeological Interpretations, sponsored by Baylor University and the Cooper Foundation of Waco, Texas, 1987.

———. "Who Are Those Guys?: Some Biased Thoughts on the Initial Peopling of the New World." In *Americans Before Columbus: Ice-Age Origins,* edited by R. C. Carlisle, 45–61. *Ethnology Monographs,* vol. 12. Pittsburgh: Department of Anthropology, University of Pittsburgh, Pennsylvania, 1988.

Adovasio, J. M., and R. C. Carlisle. "Un Campamento de Cazadores Indios Durante 20.000 Años." *Investigación y Ciencia* 94 (1984): 80–85.

———. "An Indian Hunters' Camp for 20,000 Years." *Scientific American* 250, 5 (1984): 130–136.

———. "An Indian Hunters' Camp for 20,000 Years." In *Historical Geology: Interpretations and Applications,* edited by J. M. Poort and R. C. Carlson. New York: Macmillan Publishing Company, 1984.

———. "The Meadowcroft Rockshelter." *Science* 239, 4841 (1988): 713–714.

———. "The Meadowcroft Rockshelter Radiocarbon Chronology: Some Facts and Fictions." Paper presented at the 53rd Annual Meeting of the Society for American Archaeology, Phoenix, Arizona, April 27–May 1, 1988.

———. "Pennsylvania Pioneers." *Natural History* 95, 12 (1986): 20–27.

Adovasio, J. M., R. C. Carlisle, K. A. Cushman, J. Donahue, J. E. Guilday, W. C. Johnson, K. Lord, P. W. Parmalee, R. Stuckenrath, and P. Wiegman. "Paleoenvironmental Reconstruction at Meadowcroft Rockshelter, Washington County, Pennsylvania." In *Environments and Extinctions: Man in Late Glacial North America,* edited by J. I. Mead and D. J. Meltzer, 73–110. Orono, Maine: Center for the Study of Early Man, 1985.

Adovasio, J. M., R. C. Carlisle, J. Donahue, K. A. Cushman, and R. Stuckenrath. "Meadowcroft Rockshelter: Paleoenvironment and Archaeology." Paper presented at the Ninth Biennial Meeting of the American Quaternary Association, University of Illinois, Champaign-Urbana, Illinois, 1986.

Adovasio, J. M., D. C. Dirkmaat, and D. Pedler. "Monte Verde, Meadowcroft, and the Initial Colonization of the Americas." Paper presented at the Dual Congress 1998, International Association for the Study of Human Paleontology and International Association of Human Biologists, Sun City, South Africa, 1998.

Adovasio, J. M., and J. Donahue. "Geoarchaeological Investigations in Pennsylvania: One View of the State of the Art." Paper presented at the 59th Annual Meeting of the Society for Pennsylvania Archaeology, Pittsburgh, Pennsylvania, 1988.

Adovasio, J. M., J. Donahue, R. C. Carlisle, K. Cushman, R. Stuckenrath, and P. Wiegman. "Meadowcroft Rockshelter and the Pleistocene/Holocene Transition in Southwestern Pennsylvania." In *Contributions in Quaternary Vertebrate Paleontology: A Volume in Memorial to John E. Guilday,* edited by H. H. Genoways and M. R. Dawson, 347–369. *Carnegie Museum of Natural History Special Publication* no. 8. Pittsburgh: Carnegie Museum of Natural History, 1984.

Adovasio, J. M., J. Donahue, R. C. Carlisle, J. D. Gunn, and R. Stuckenrath. "Meadowcroft Rockshelter." In *National Geographic Society Research Reports,* vol. 17, edited by J. S. Lea, N. L. Pwars, and W. Swanson, pp. 95–111. Washington, D.C.: National Geographic Society, 1984.

Adovasio, J. M., J. Donahue, K. Cushman, R. C. Carlisle, R. Stuckenrath, J. D. Gunn, and W. C. Johnson. "Evidence from Meadowcroft Rockshelter." In *Early Man in the New World,* edited by R. Shutler, Jr., 163–190. Beverly Hills, Calif.: Sage Publications, 1983.

———. "The Meadowcroft Rockshelter: New Evidence for Late Pleistocene Man's Presence in the New World." Paper presented at the 25th Annual Fall Workshop of the Michigan Archaeological Society, Monroe, Michigan, 1981.

Adovasio, J. M., J. Donahue, K. Cushman, and J. D. Gunn. "Data Recovery, Multidisciplinary Research and Paleoenvironmental Reconstruction in the Northeast: A View from Meadowcroft Rockshelter, Washington County, Pennsylvania." Paper presented at the Annual Meeting of the Society for Pennsylvania Archaeology, 1980.

Adovasio, J. M., J. Donahue, J. E. Guilday, R. Stuckenrath, J. D. Gunn, and W. C. Johnson. "Meadowcroft Rockshelter and the Peopling of the New World." In *Quaternary Coastlines and Marine Archaeology: Towards the Prehistory of Land Bridges and Continental Shelves,* edited by P. M. Masters and N. C. Flemming, 413–439. New York: Academic Press, 1983.

Adovasio, J. M., J. Donahue, J. D. Gunn, and R. Stuckenrath. "The Meadowcroft Papers: A Response to Dincauze." *The Quarterly Review of Archaeology,* September 1981, 14–15.

Adovasio, J. M., J. Donahue, J. Gunn, and R. Stuckenrath, with J. Herbstritt and W. C. Johnson. "The Meadowcroft Rockshelter/Cross Creek Archaeological Project: Retrospect 1982." In *Meadowcroft: Collected Papers on the Archaeology of Meadowcroft Rockshelter and the Cross Creek Drainage,* edited by R. C. Carlisle and J. M. Adovasio (1984): 257–268. Paper presented at the symposium The Meadowcroft Rockshelter Rolling Thunder Review: Last Act, 47th Annual Meeting of the Society for American Archaeology, Minneapolis, Minnesota, April 14–17, 1982.

Adovasio, J. M., J. Donahue and R. Stuckenrath. "The Meadowcroft Rockshelter Radiocarbon Chronology 1975–1988: Some Ruminations." Paper presented at the 53rd Annual Meeting of the Society for American Archaeology, Phoenix, Arizona, 1988.

——. "The Meadowcroft Rockshelter Radiocarbon Chronology 1975–1990." *American Antiquity* 55, 2 (1990): 348–354.

——. "Never Say Never Again: Some Thoughts on Could Have and Might Have Beens." *American Antiquity* 57, 2 (1992): 327–331.

Adovasio, J. M., J. Donahue, R. Stuckenrath, and R. C. Carlisle. "The Meadowcroft Rockshelter Radiocarbon Chronology 1975–1989: Some Ruminations." Paper presented at the First World Summit Conference on the Peopling of the Americas, University of Maine, Orono, Maine, 1989.

Adovasio, J. M., R. Fryman, A. Quinn, and D. Dirkmaat. "The Archaic West of the Allegheny Mountains: A View from the Cross Creek Drainage, Washington County, Pennsylvania." Paper presented at the symposium The Archaic Period in Pennsylvania, 65th Annual Meeting of the Society for Pennsylvania Archaeology, Pittsburgh, Pennsylvania, 1994.

Adovasio, J. M., R. Fryman, A. G. Quinn, D. C. Dirkmaat, and D. R. Pedler. "The Archaic of the Upper Ohio Valley: A View from Meadowcroft Rockshelter." Paper presented at the symposium Hunter-Gatherers into Horticulturalists: The Archaic Prehistory of the Ohio Area, Ohio Archaeological Council, Cleveland, Ohio, 1995.

——. "The Archaic of the Upper Ohio Valley: A View from Meadowcroft Rockshelter." In *Archaic Transitions in Ohio and Kentucky Prehistory,* edited by O. H. Prufer, S. E. Peddle, and R. S. Meindl. Kent, Ohio: Kent State University Press, 2002.

——. "The Archaic West of the Allegheny Mountains: A View from the Cross Creek Drainage, Washington County, Pennsylvania." In *The Archaic Period in Pennsylvania: Hunter-Gatherers of the Early and Middle Holocene Period,* edited by P. A. Raber, P. E. Miller, and S. M. Neusius. *Recent Research in Pennsylvania Archaeology* 1 (1998): 1–28.

Adovasio, J. M., R. Fryman, A. G. Quinn, and D. R. Pedler. "The Appearance of Cultigens and the Early and Middle Woodland Periods in Southwestern Pennsylvania." Paper presented at the 68th Annual Meeting of the Society for Pennsylvania Archaeology, Wilkes-Barre, Pennsylvania, 1997.

——. "The Appearance of Cultigens and the Early and Middle Woodland Periods in Southwestern Pennsylvania." In *The Early and Middle Woodland Periods in Pennsylvania,* edited by P. A. Raber. *Recent Research in Pennsylvania Archaeology* no. 3. Harrisburg, Pa.: Pennsylvania Historic and Museum Commission, 2002.

Adovasio, J. M., R. Fryman, A. G. Quinn, D. R. Pedler, and S. Prescott. "The Appearance of Cultigens and the Early Woodland Period in Southwestern Pennsylvania." Paper presented at the 63rd Annual Meeting of the Society for American Archaeology, Seattle, Washington, 1998.

Adovasio, J. M., J. D. Gunn, J. Donahue, and R. Stuckenrath. "Excavations at Meadowcroft Rockshelter: 1973–1974: A Progress Report." Paper presented at the Annual Meeting of the Society for American Archaeology, Dallas, Texas, 1975.

——. "Excavations at Meadowcroft Rockshelter: 1973–1974: A Progress Report." *Pennsylvania Archaeologist* 45, 3 (1975): 1–30.

———. "Excavations at Meadowcroft Rockshelter: 1973–1976: A Progress Report." Paper presented at the Annual Meeting of the Southeastern Archaeological Conference, Tuscaloosa, Alabama, 1976.

———. "Meadowcroft Rockshelter." Paper presented at the Annual Meeting of the Southwestern Anthropological Association, San Diego, California, 1977.

———. "Meadowcroft Rockshelter: Evidence for Human Occupation Back to 16,000 B.P." Paper presented at the 11th Annual Meeting of the Geological Society of America, Denver, Colorado, 1976.

———. "Meadowcroft Rockshelter: Retrospect 1975." Paper presented at the 41st Annual Meeting of the Society for American Archaeology, St. Louis, Missouri, 1976.

———. "Meadowcroft Rockshelter: Retrospect 1976." Paper presented at the Annual Meeting of the Eastern States Archaeological Federation, Richmond, Virginia, 1976.

———. "Meadowcroft Rockshelter: Retrospect 1976." *Pennsylvania Archaeologist* 47, 2–3 (1977): 1–93.

———. "Meadowcroft Rockshelter: Retrospect 1977." Paper presented at the Annual Meeting of the American Anthropological Association, Houston, Texas, 1977.

———. "Meadowcroft Rockshelter, 1977: An Overview." *American Antiquity* 43, 4 (1978): 632–651.

———. "Meadowcroft Rockshelter: Retrospect 1978." Paper presented at the 44th Annual Meeting of the Society of American Archaeology, Vancouver, British Columbia, 1979.

———. "Progress Report on the Meadowcroft Rockshelter—A 16,000-Year Chronicle." In *Amerinds and Their Paleoenvironments in Northeastern North America,* edited by W. S. Newman and B. Salwen, 137–159. *Annals of the New York Academy of Sciences,* vol. 288. New York: New York Academy of Sciences, 1977.

Adovasio, J. M., J. D. Gunn, J. Donahue, R. Stuckenrath, J. Guilday, and K. Lord. "Meadowcroft Rockshelter." In *Early Man in America: From a Circum-Pacific Perspective,* edited by A. L. Bryan, 140–180. *Occasional Papers No 1 of the Department of Anthropology, University of Alberta.* Edmonton, Alberta: Archaeological Researches International, 1978.

———. "Meadowcroft Rockshelter 1973–1977: A Synopsis." In *Peopling of the New World,* edited by J. E. Erickson, R. E. Taylor, and R. Berger, 97–133. *Anthropological Papers,* vol. 23. Los Altos, Calif.: Ballena Press, 1982.

Adovasio, J. M., J. D. Gunn, J. Donahue, R. Stuckenrath, J. Guilday, K. Lord, and K. Volman. "Meadowcroft Rockshelter—Retrospect 1977: Part 1." *North American Archaeologist* 1, 1 (1979–1980): 3–44.

———. "Meadowcroft Rockshelter—Retrospect 1977: Part 2." *North American Archaeologist* 1, 2 (1979–1980): 99–137.

Adovasio, J. M., J. D. Gunn, J. Donahue, R. Stuckenrath, J. E. Guilday, and K. Volman. "Yes Virginia, It Really Is That Old: A Reply to Haynes and Mead." *American Antiquity* 45, 3 (1980): 588–595.

Adovasio, J. M., D. C. Hyland, and O. Soffer. "Perishable Fiber Artifacts and the First Americans: New Implications." Paper prepared for inclusion in *New Directions in First American Studies,* edited by B. T. Lepper. Corvallis: Center for the Study of the First Americans, Oregon State University Press, 2000.

Adovasio, J. M., D. C. Hyland, O. Soffer, and J. S. Illingworth. "Perishable Technology and Late Pleistocene/Early Holocene Adaptations in the Americas." Paper presented at the 66th Annual Meeting of the Society for American Archaeology, New Orleans, Louisiana, 2001.

Adovasio, J. M., and W. C. Johnson. "The Appearance of Cultigens in the Upper Ohio Valley: A View from Meadowcroft Rockshelter." *Pennsylvania Archaeologist* 51, 1–2 (1981): 63–80.

Adovasio, J. M., and D. R. Pedler. "A Long View of Deep Time at Meadowcroft Rockshelter." Paper presented at the symposium Current Archaeological Research in Pennsylvania and Related Areas, 65th Annual Meeting of the Society for American Archaeology, Philadelphia, Pennsylvania, 2000.

———. "Pioneer Populations in the New World: The View from Meadowcroft Rockshelter." Paper presented at the XIII International Congress of Prehistoric and Protohistoric Sciences, Forlì, Italy, 1996.

———. "Pre-Clovis Sites and Their Implications for Human Occupation Before the Last Glacial Maximum." Paper presented at the 66th Annual Meeting of the Society for American Archaeology, New Orleans, Louisiana, 2001.

———. "The Stratigraphy and Chronology of Meadowcroft Rockshelter (36WH297)." Paper presented at the North Asia/North America Connections Workshop, National Museum of Natural History, Smithsonian Institution, Washington, D.C., 1999.

Adovasio, J. M., D. R. Pedler, J. Donahue, and R. Stuckenrath. "No Vestige of a Beginning nor Prospect for an End: Two Decades of Debate on Meadowcroft Rockshelter." In *Ice Age People of North America,* edited by R. Bonnichsen and K. L. Turnmire, 416–431. Corvallis: Center for the Study of the First Americans, Oregon State University Press, 1999.

———. "Two Decades of Debate on Meadowcroft Rockshelter." *North American Archaeologist* 19, 4 (1998): 317–341.

Beynon, D. E. "The Geoarchaeology of Meadowcroft Rockshelter." Ph.D. dissertation, Department of Anthropology, University of Pittsburgh, 1981.

Beynon, D., and J. Donahue. "The Geology and Geomorphology of Meadowcroft Rockshelter and the Cross Creek Drainage." In *Meadowcroft: Collected Papers on the Archaeology of Meadowcroft Rockshelter and the Cross Creek Drainage,* edited by R. C. Carlisle and J. M. Adovasio (1984): 31–52. Paper presented at the symposium The Meadowcroft Rockshelter Rolling Thunder Review: Last Act, 47th Annual Meeting of the Society for American Archaeology, Minneapolis, Minnesota, April 14–17, 1982.

Canby, T. Y. "The Search for the First Americans." *National Geographic* 156, 3 (1979): 330–363.

Carlisle, R. C., ed. "Americans Before Columbus: Ice-Age Origins." *Ethnology Monographs,* vol. 12. Pittsburgh: Department of Anthropology, University of Pittsburgh, 1988.

Carlisle, R. C., J. M. Adovasio, J. Donahue, P. Wiegman, and J. E. Guilday. "An Introduction to the Meadowcroft/Cross Creek Archaeological Project: 1973–1982." In *Meadowcroft: Collected Papers on the Archaeology of Meadowcroft Rockshelter and the Cross Creek Drainage,* edited by R. C. Carlisle and J. M. Adovasio (1984): 31–52. Paper presented at the symposium The Meadowcroft Rockshelter Rolling Thunder Review: Last Act, 47th Annual Meeting of the Society for American Archaeology, Minneapolis, Minnesota, April 14–17, 1982.

Carr, K. W. "A Discussion of Recent 'Pre-Clovis' Investigations." *Journal of Middle Atlantic Archaeology* 16 (2000): 133–142.

Carr, K., and J. M. Adovasio. "Ice Age Peoples of Pennsylvania." *Recent Research in Pennsylvania Archaeology* no. 2. Harrisburg, Pa.: Pennsylvania Historic and Museum Commission, 2002.

———. "Paleoindians in Pennsylvania." Paper presented at the 60th Annual Meeting of the Society for Pennsylvania Archaeology, Erie, Pennsylvania, 1989.

———. "Paleoindians in Pennsylvania (Part 1)." Paper presented at the 67th Annual Meeting of the Society for Pennsylvania Archaeology, Fort Ligonier, Pennsylvania, 1996.

Carr, K. W., J. M. Adovasio, and D. R. Pedler. "Paleoindian Populations in Trans-Appalachia: The View from Pennsylvania." Paper presented at the conference Integrating Appalachian Highlands Archaeology, New York State Museum, Albany, New York, 1996.

———. "Paleoindian Populations in Trans Appalachia: The View from Pennsylvania." In *Proceedings of the Conference "Integrating Appalachian Highlands Archaeology."* Knoxville: University of Tennessee Press, 2001.

Cushman, K. A. "Floral Remains from Meadowcroft Rockshelter, Washington County, Southwestern Pennsylvania." In *Meadowcroft: Collected Papers on the Archaeology of Meadowcroft Rockshelter and the Cross Creek Drainage,* edited by R. C. Carlisle and J. M. Adovasio (1984): 207–220. Paper presented at the symposium The Meadowcroft Rockshelter Rolling Thunder Review: Last Act, 47th Annual Meeting of the Society for American Archaeology, Minneapolis, Minnesota, April 14–17, 1982.

Diggs, J. F. "Rolling Back the Clock on First Humans in America." *U.S. News & World Report,* June 7, 1982, 70–71.

Dirkmaat, D. C., J. M. Adovasio, and R. C. Carlisle. "Taphonomic Agents and Paleoecological Reconstructions at Meadowcroft Rockshelter (36wh297), Pennsylvania." Paper presented at the 46th International Congress of Americanists, Amsterdam, Netherlands, 1988.

———. "Taphonomic Agents and Paleoecological Reconstructions at Meadowcroft Rockshelter (36wh297), Pennsylvania." In *Explotación de Recursos Faunísticos en Sistemas Adaptativos Americanos,* edited by J. L. Lanata, 5–14. *Arqueología Contemporánea,* vol. 4, Edición Especial, 1993.

———. "Taphonomy and Paleoecology at Meadowcroft Rockshelter (36wh297)." Paper Presented at the North American Paleontological Society Meeting, Boulder, Colorado, 1986.

Donahue, J., and J. M. Adovasio. "Evolution of Sandstone Rockshelters in Eastern North America; A Geoarchaeological Perspective." In *Archaeological Geology of North America: Centennial Special,* vol. 4, edited by N. P. Lasca and J. Donahue. Boulder, Colo.: Geological Society of America, 1990.

———. "Meadowcroft Rockshelter and the Pleistocene/Holocene Transition in Southwestern Pennsylvania." Paper presented at the Annual Meeting of the Geological Society of America, Indianapolis, Indiana, 1983.

Donahue, J., J. M. Adovasio, J. D. Gunn, and R. Stuckenrath. "Geological Investigations at Meadowcroft Rockshelter." Paper presented at the Annual Meeting of the Geological Society of America, Toronto, Ontario, 1978.

Donahue, J., J. M. Adovasio, and R. Stuckenrath. "Meadowcroft Rockshelter: Geologic Investigations." In *Geology of the Northern Appalachian Coal Field;*

Guidebook, Field Trip No. 2: Ninth International Congress of Carboniferous Stratigraphy and Geology, edited by J. Donahue and H. B. Rollins, E1–E39. Pittsburgh, Pa.: Department of Geology and Planetary Science, University of Pittsburgh, and the Pittsburgh Geological Society, 1979.

Donahue, J., D. E. Beynon, and J. M. Adovasio. "Geological Investigations at Meadowcroft Rockshelter." Paper presented at the 44th Annual Meeting of the Society for American Archaeology, Vancouver, British Columbia, 1979.

———. "Sandstone Rockshelter Development in Temperate Climates." Paper presented at the Annual Meeting of the Geological Society of America, Cincinnati, Ohio, 1981.

Donahue, J., P. L. Storck, J. M. Adovasio, J. D. Gunn, and R. Stuckenrath. "Archaeological Sites: Pittsburgh to Toronto." In *Toronto '78: Field Trips Guidebook,* edited by A. L. Currie and W. O. Mackasey, 65–79. A Joint Meeting of the Geological Society of America, the Geological Association of Canada, and the Mineralogical Association of Canada. Toronto: Geological Association of Canada, 1978.

Dorfman, A. "New Ways to the New World." *Time,* April 17, 2000, 70.

Fitzgibbons, P. T., with J. Herbstritt, W. C. Johnson, and C. Robbins. "Lithic Artifacts from Meadowcroft Rockshelter and the Cross Creek Drainage." In *Meadowcroft: Collected Papers on the Archaeology of Meadowcroft Rockshelter and the Cross Creek Drainage,* edited by R. C. Carlisle and J. M. Adovasio (1984): 91–111. Paper presented at the symposium The Meadowcroft Rockshelter Rolling Thunder Review: Last Act, 47th Annual Meeting of the Society for American Archaeology, Minneapolis, Minnesota, April 14–17, 1982.

Fryman, R. F. "Prehistoric Settlement Patterns in the Cross Creek Drainage." In *Meadowcroft: Collected Papers on the Archaeology of Meadowcroft Rockshelter and the Cross Creek Drainage,* edited by R. C. Carlisle and J. M. Adovasio (1984): 53–68. Paper presented at the symposium The Meadowcroft Rockshelter Rolling Thunder Review: Last Act, 47th Annual Meeting of the Society for American Archaeology, Minneapolis, Minnesota, April 14–17, 1982.

Goldberg, P., and T. L. Arpin. "Micromorphological Analysis of Sediments from Meadowcroft Rockshelter, Pennsylvania: Implications for Radiocarbon Dating." *Journal of Field Archaeology,* 26, 3 (1999): 325–342.

Guilday, J. E., and P. W. Parmalee. "Vertebrate Faunal Remains from Meadowcroft Rockshelter, Washington County, Pennsylvania: Summary and Interpretation." In *Meadowcroft: Collected Papers on the Archaeology of Meadowcroft Rockshelter and the Cross Creek Drainage,* edited by R. C. Carlisle and J. M. Adovasio (1984): 163–174. Paper presented at the symposium The Meadowcroft Rockshelter Rolling Thunder Review: Last Act, 47th Annual Meeting of the Society for American Archaeology, Minneapolis, Minnesota, April 14–17, 1982.

Guilday, J. E., P. W. Parmalee, and R. C. Wilson. "Vertebrate Faunal Remains from Meadowcroft Rockshelter (36WH297), Washington County, Pennsylvania." Unpublished manuscript on file at Mercyhurst Archaeological Institute, 1980.

Herbstritt, J. T. "A Reference for Pennsylvania Radiocarbon Dates." Paper presented at the 59th Annual Meeting of the Society for Pennsylvania Archaeology, 1988.

Johnson, W. C. "Ceramics from Meadowcroft Rockshelter: A Re-Evaluation and Interpretation." In *Meadowcroft: Collected Papers on the Archaeology of Meadowcroft Rockshelter and the Cross Creek Drainage,* edited by R. C. Carlisle and J. M. Adovasio (1984): 142–162. Paper presented at the symposium The Meadowcroft Rockshelter Rolling Thunder Review: Last Act, 47th Annual Meeting of the Society for American Archaeology, Minneapolis, Minnesota, April 14–17, 1982.

Kornberg, W., ed. "The Earliest Known Americans." *Mosaic* 8, 2 (1977): 22–29.

Lemonick, M. D. "Coming to America." *Time,* May 3, 1993, 60–62.

Lord, K. "Invertebrate Faunal Remains from Meadowcroft Rockshelter, Washington County, Southwestern Pennsylvania." In *Meadowcroft: Collected Papers on the Archaeology of Meadowcroft Rockshelter and the Cross Creek Drainage,* edited by R. C. Carlisle and J. M. Adovasio (1984): 186–206. Paper presented at the symposium The Meadowcroft Rockshelter Rolling Thunder Review: Last Act, 47th Annual Meeting of the Society for American Archaeology, Minneapolis, Minnesota, April 14–17, 1982.

May, M. "Gimme Shelter." *Pittsburgh,* January 2000, 46–47.

Nemecek, S. "Who Were the First Americans?" *Scientific American* 283, 3 (2000): 80–87.

Petit, C. W. "Rediscovering America." *U.S. News & World Report,* October 12, 1998, 56–64.

Sciulli, P. W. "Human Remains from Meadowcroft Rockshelter, Washington County, Southwestern Pennsylvania." In *Meadowcroft: Collected Papers on the Archaeology of Meadowcroft Rockshelter and the Cross Creek Drainage,* edited by R. C. Carlisle and J. M. Adovasio (1984): 175–185. Paper presented at the symposium The Meadowcroft Rockshelter Rolling Thunder Review: Last Act, 47th Annual Meeting of the Society for American Archaeology, Minneapolis, Minnesota, April 14–17, 1982.

Skirboll, E. "Analysis of Constant Volume Samples from Meadowcroft Rockshelter, Washington County, Southwestern Pennsylvania." In *Meadowcroft: Collected Papers on the Archaeology of Meadowcroft Rockshelter and the Cross Creek Drainage,* edited by R. C. Carlisle and J. M. Adovasio (1984): 221–240. Paper presented at the symposium The Meadowcroft Rockshelter Rolling Thunder Review: Last Act, 47th Annual Meeting of the Society for American Archaeology, Minneapolis, Minnesota, April 14–17, 1982.

Stile, T. W. "Perishable Artifacts from Meadowcroft Rockshelter, Washington County, Southwestern Pennsylvania." In *Meadowcroft: Collected Papers on the Archaeology of Meadowcroft Rockshelter and the Cross Creek Drainage,* edited by R. C. Carlisle and J. M. Adovasio (1984): 130–141. Paper presented at the symposium The Meadowcroft Rockshelter Rolling Thunder Review: Last Act, 47th Annual Meeting of the Society for American Archaeology, Minneapolis, Minnesota, April 14–17, 1982.

Stuckenrath, R., J. M. Adovasio, J. Donahue, and R. C. Carlisle. "The Stratigraphy, Cultural Features and Chronology at Meadowcroft Rockshelter, Washington County, Southwestern Pennsylvania." In *Meadowcroft: Collected Papers on the Archaeology of Meadowcroft Rockshelter and the Cross Creek Drainage,* edited by R. C. Carlisle and J. M. Adovasio (1984): 69–90. Paper presented at the symposium The Meadowcroft Rockshelter Rolling Thunder Review: Last Act, 47th Annual Meeting of the Society for American Archaeology, Minneapolis, Minnesota, April 14–17, 1982.

Vento, F. J., J. Donahue, and J. M. Adovasio. "Geoarchaeology." In *The Geology of Pennsylvania,* edited by C. H. Shultz, 770–777. Pittsburgh: Pennsylvania Geological Survey, Harrisburg and Pittsburgh Geological Society, 1999.

Vento, F. J., and J. Donahue, with J. Herbstritt. "Lithic Raw Material Utilization at Meadowcroft Rockshelter and in the Cross Creek Drainage." In *Meadowcroft: Collected Papers on the Archaeology of Meadowcroft Rockshelter and the Cross Creek Drainage,* edited by R. C. Carlisle and J. M. Adovasio (1984): 112–129. Paper presented at the symposium The Meadowcroft Rockshelter Rolling Thunder Review: Last Act, 47th Annual Meeting of the Society for American Archaeology, Minneapolis, Minnesota, April 14–17, 1982.

Volman, K. C. "Paleoenvironmental Implications of Botanical Data from Meadowcroft Rockshelter, Pennsylvania." Ph.D. dissertation, Graduate College of Texas A&M University, 1981.

Price, Douglas, 228–30, 286
Priest, Josiah, 18
Principles of Geology (Lyell), 35
proboscideans, 63–64, *64, 65, 65*
pronghorns, 67, 107, 119, 120
Pueblo Indians, 134
Puget Sound, formation of, 54
Putnam, Frederic Ward, 91, 96–97

Q
Quaternary age, 267
Quebrada Jaguay, Peru, 276
Quebrada Tacahuay, Peru, 276

R
race:
   and genetic studies, 242
   monogenism vs. polygenism, 23
   and mound builders, 19, 23, 24, 28
   in World War II era, 23–24
radiocarbon dating, 112–17
   accuracy of, 115–16, 124–25, 130, 142,
      182, 218
   contamination of samples in,
      180–88
   as key to first Americans, 256
   of Meadowcroft samples, xiii–xiv,
      159–61, *160,* 170, 174, 177, 179,
      180–83, 223–24
   use of, xvii, 108, 109, 133
Red Earth, White Lies (Deloria), 124
reindeer, 84, 229
religion:
   and evolution, 29
   and First Amendment, 253
   and legend, 253
   and science, 34, 43, 83, 85, 125, 249
Renaissance, 9
Renwick, James, 21
replicability, 182, 184, 219, 263–72
return rate, 274–75
rhinoceros, woolly, 61, 84, 229
Richardson, Jim, 149
Riley's Switch, New Mexico, 103, 104
Rivanna River, burial mounds near, 15
Roberts, Frank H. H., 102, 147
rockshelters:
   artifacts preserved in, 221, 287
   field archaeology in, 150
   see also caves; *specific sites*
Ross Ice Shelf, Antarctica, 37
Rousseau, Jean-Jacques, 10
Royal Society, London, 85

S
saber-toothed cats, 69–70, 107, 119, 284
Saint-Acheul, France, 73–74, 84
salt, transport of, 213–14
Saltville, Virginia, 267, *267, 268,* 269, *269,*
   271, 272, 279
San Bernardino County Museum, 139
sand dunes, formation of, 52
Sandia Cave, 134–38
Sandia Man, 135–38, 145
San Francisco Bay, formation of, 54
Santa Rosa Island, California, 66
Sauer, Carl, 121
Schöningen tool kits, 76
Schoolcraft, Henry Rowe, 19
Schurr, Theodore, 239
Schwachheim, Carl, 101
Science, 241
science:
   in archaeology, 22, 32, 194
   correlations vs. causation in, 118
   creationist rejection of, 22–23
   funding of, 95, 191
   government influence in, 25, 93, 95
   hypotheses in, 94, 125, 148, 200, 222
   and pseudoscience, 23, 93
   publication in, 95, 227–28
   and religion, 34, 43, 83, 85, 125, 249
   replicability in, 182, 184, 219, 263–72
   social vs. "hard," 111
   specialization in, 108
   see also specific sciences
scimitar cat (*Homotherium*), 69
seasons, changing, 48, 49, 51, 56–57
Seneca Nation, 252–53
serow, 78
sexual dimorphism, 72
Shakespeare, William, 9
shamans, 10
sheep, 78, 120
shell middens, 198
Shoop site, Pennsylvania, 294
shrews, 64
Siberia:
   archaeological study in, 141, 261
   early hominids in, 77, 273, 281, 282, 284
   glacial maximum in, *44*
   migrations from, 17, 67
   molecular genetics in, 240
   woolly mammoths of, 39, 65–66
signatures, of climatic cycles, 49, 184
Simpson, Ruth de Ette, 139, *139*
Sinodont dental pattern, 234

CREDITS

———

Grateful acknowledgment is made to the following for permission to use illustrative material:

Pages xv, 80, 151, 152, 153, 155, 156, 157, 158, 159, 161, 162, 166, 167, 168, 170, 205, 206, 208, 209 (top), 250, 292, and 293: courtesy of J. M. Adovasio; pp. 197 and 198: courtesy of the Division of Anthropology, American Museum of Natural History, New York; p. 202: courtesy of Alan Bryan and Ruth Gruhn; p. 11: courtesy of Cahokia Mounds State Historical Site, Illinois; pp. 122 and 177: courtesy of K. Carr; p. 244: courtesy of James C. Chatters; frontispiece and pp. 26 and 96: courtesy of CORBIS; p. 175: courtesy of K. Cushman, redrafted by J. S. Illingworth; pp. 209 (bottom), 210, 211, 212, 213, and 215: courtesy of T. Dillehay; p. 190: courtesy of Teresa Franco; p. 172: courtesy of P. Goldberg and T. Arpin; pp. 270, 271, and 272: courtesy of A. Goodyear; p. 94: courtesy of The Granger Collection, New York; pp. 263, 264, 265, and 266: courtesy of Mike Johnson; pp. 267, 268, and 269: courtesy of J. McDonald; p. 105: courtesy of J. D. McGee, Brownsville, Texas, via A. T. Boldurian, University of Pittsburgh, Greensburgh; pp. xiv, xvi, and 160 (drafted by D. R. Pedler): courtesy of Mercyhurst Archaeological Institute; pp. 121 and 288: courtesy of *National Geographic;* p. 86: courtesy of the Neanderthal Museum, Mettmann, Germany; p. 8: courtesy of The Newberry Library, Chicago; p. 12: courtesy of the Ohio Historical Society; pp. 287 and 289: courtesy of Jake Page; pp. 60, 62, 63, 64, 65, 66, and 68: courtesy of Bill Parsons; p. 143: courtesy of Dr. Jim Richardson; p. 37: courtesy of Galen Rowell/CORBIS; p. 139: courtesy of the San Bernardino County Museum; p. 91: courtesy of the University of Pennsylvania Museum, Philadelphia; p. 44; courtesy of *Ethnology,* Department of Anthropology, University of Pittsburgh (redrafted by J. S. Illingworth); p. 147: courtesy of the University of Utah Press.

J. M. ADOVASIO, PH.D., is the founder and director of the Mercyhurst Archaeological Institute, generally recognized as the finest small-college-based research and training program in North America. He has achieved international acclaim as the archaeologist in charge of the excavations at Meadowcroft Rockshelter, the earliest indisputably dated archaeological site in North America. He has taught and/or conducted research at the Smithsonian Institution, Youngstown State University, the University of Pittsburgh, the Carnegie Institute, and, at present, Mercyhurst College. He lives near Erie, Pennsylvania.

JAKE PAGE is a former editor of *Natural History* magazine and science editor of *Smithsonian* magazine, as well as founder of the Natural History Press and Smithsonian Books. An essayist and mystery novelist, he is also the author of fifteen popular books on the natural sciences and American Indians. He lives in Corrales, New Mexico.

———

Meadowcroft Rockshelter is still an active research locus on the property of the Meadowcroft Museum of Rural Life, which is operated by the Historical Society of Western Pennsylvania. The site is maintained by the Meadowcroft Museum and the Mercyhurst Archaeological Institute, and may be visited by prior arrangement. Construction is currently under way that should render the site more accessible for visitation in the immediate future. Interested parties are directed to contact the site administrator. The Meadowcroft Museum of Rural Life can be contacted through their website, www.meadowcroftmuseum.org, or by phone at (724) 587-3412.